PAST TENSE

Jean Cocteau

PAST TENSE

 VOLUME II

DIARIES

Annotations by PIERRE CHANEL

Translation by RICHARD HOWARD

HARCOURT BRACE JOVANOVICH, PUBLISHERS

SAN DIEGO   NEW YORK   LONDON

HBJ

Copyright © 1985 by Editions Gallimard
English translation copyright © 1988 by
Harcourt Brace Jovanovich, Inc.

LIBRARY OF CONGRESS CATALOGING-IN-PUBLICATION DATA
(Revised for volume 2)

Cocteau, Jean, 1889–1963.
    Past tense.

    Translation of: Le passé défini.
    "Works by Jean Cocteau" : v. 1, p. 357–362.
    Includes indexes.
    1. Cocteau, Jean, 1889–1963—Diaries.
2. Authors, French—20th century—Diaries.
3. French—Diaries.
I. Title.
PQ2605.015Z473   1987   848'.91203   [B]   86-12060
ISBN 0-15-171289-1 (v. 1)
ISBN 0-15-171291-3 (v. 2)

Designed by Michael Farmer
Printed in the United States of America
First edition
A B C D E

Contents

Note

THE ANNOTATOR is grateful to Louis Évrard for his steadfast assistance. He also wishes to thank Jeanne Gambert de Loche; Francine Weisweiller; Madeleine Wiemer; Marcel Adéma; André Bernard; René Bertrand; Maurice Bessy; Mario Brun; Alberto Calasso; Édouard Dermit; André Fraigneau; Pierre Gaudibert, Curator of the Grenoble Museum; Jean Godebski; James Lord; Jean Marais; Claude Michaud; Bernard de Montgolfier, Chief Curator of the Musée Carnavalet; Pierre Pasquini; and Lucien Scheler, for the information they have graciously furnished.

—PIERRE CHANEL

PAST TENSE

The Diaries:

JANUARY 1, 1953 – DECEMBER 28, 1953

· ·

JANUARY 1 · 1953

At Milly. Francine, Doudou, and I. How peaceful, after a snowstorm on the road. At the house I find the bronze mirror made by Gustave Doré that belonged to the empress of Russia.* I had seen it in Voinquel's film.† Francine tracked it down to a deaf old relative of Doré's who was about to sell it to the Philadelphia museum. It weighs almost two hundred pounds. Cupids holding up draperies around an oval mirror. An object of magnificent horror.

---

*This gilded bronze mirror was one of several examples made by Doré in 1882. Besides the one Cocteau describes, there is the mirror purchased by Maria Fedorovna, tsarina of Alexander III, and one in the Musée de l'Ain, at Bourg-en-Bresse. Since 1942 Cocteau had owned another sculpture by Doré, *Perseus and Andromeda*, a gift from Charles and Marie-Laure de Noailles.

†Raymond Voinquel, born 1912, cameraman of three of Cocteau's films (*La Voix humaine*, 1947; *Ruy Blas*, 1947; *L'Aigle à deux têtes*, 1947), had made with Alexandre Arnoux a series of documentary films on Doré's work, for which Cocteau had written a preface.

I have determined to resist the overwhelming chaos of my affairs: it is probably my own rhythm that is responsible, against which I can do nothing except work and minimize the disaster, with Peyraud's help.

Reread *La Belle au bois dormant*.* Except for the beginning, nothing to use in the film.

Sent the drawing and the text for the anniversary issue of the magazine *Adam* (London). Before coming here, I did a broadcast (in French) for the BBC. I had taken Palmer White with me to revise a translation and perhaps to read it in my place.

Something terrible has returned on velvet paws.

According to the British, Proust was lucky enough to find his translator, without whom Proust would be unknown in the English-speaking world. (Proust and Thomas Mann are always cited as having had good translators.) Raymond Mortimer writes: "All the translations over here are vile. Let me have a look at yours, and I'll tell you which is *the least stupid*."

Edith Sitwell has written Peyraud, recommending a New York agent.

Van Loewen is just like Ci-Mu-Ra. Small pickings: opportunities for fame and millions missed, all to make 100,000 francs. Agents on this level never make contact with reality—with Korda or the Oliviers, for instance.

No doubt because of these agents and these absurd translations, we spend our whole lives *alongside* what might have been.

. . . .

JANUARY 3

I've just read Sartre's article on the World Peace Congress in Vienna (in *Les Lettres françaises*). I was deeply moved by it—Sartre's

___
*By Perrault.

voice is always clearer, straighter than anyone else's. I wonder if I'm entitled to keep out of it—if the vile lies in the press don't compel me to overcome my dislike of public interventions. Maybe I should get involved with what the press disguises, since if there's a disguise, it's because there's a "truth."

France, rich France, who pretends to be poor—who ruins herself out of greed, counting her pennies instead of creating huge cash flows—who finds fabulous amounts for dams on the Rhone which will be demolished in a few years. Her role was not to continue her parsimonious style but to spend her money like water, to fling it out the windows, to circulate her clotting blood by even the absurdest means. Our politicians remind me of those big movie magnates who forget that the film was the basis of the whole affair and who can't think of anything but their wallets. (Directors' fees and deals with the banks.) Stand still as long as possible, get fat, and let the others take in their belts a notch—the agenda of our petty-minded rulers.

. . . .

JANUARY 5

The battle is with men
The battle is with the gods

sings Helen in *La Belle Hélène*, not a bad way of putting it.

Back in Paris this morning with Francine. Doudou is at his sister's wedding in the east. Snow. (Not in the east.) Bad fit of depression. Lunch with López, the American sent by the agency. They all "want what I want"—but they don't. They want what they think I want. What they want, as I might want it. The only way is to reject any money in advance. Deliver the goods. They accept or they refuse . . .

Thinking a lot about Sartre's article. Of course he's right to say that we have no right to intervene in the internal affairs of other countries. But unfortunately, there are no internal affairs any longer: embraces all round at the Vienna congress. But if Stalin's "internal affairs" or Eisenhower's take a different turn, harmony is destroyed. It remains no less true that the conscientious objector stands alone and forms a kind of mass. Possibly that mass influences those who are plotting the great artificial catastrophes.

. . . .

JANUARY 10

The young duke of Kent and his sisters, taken to see a famous illusionist in a London music hall. The number ends with some nudity, and the nanny doesn't know what to do. As they leave she ventures to ask, "How did Your Highness enjoy the performance?" "I'm scared." "Why, Your Highness?" "Mama told me if I looked at naked women I'd turn to stone—and it's starting."

. . . .

JANUARY 11

Today, Sunday, the Americans and Lourau* are supposed to talk to me about the Technicolor film. Nothing is easier than to come to an understanding with these financial bigwigs: they intuit, like diamond merchants, the price and the real worth of ideas. Since neither money nor fame means much to me, but only the need to create a work, they feel in contact with powers which they are not used to in the film world but which are related to their own. "You want a dream ballet in your picture? That's not for me— it's a fashion these days, and I wouldn't count on fashions. You

---

*Georges Lourau (1898–1974), one of the major producers of the French film industry.

want me to do *my* film, so don't force me to make *yours*. You say I never make mistakes, yet you want to persuade me yours are the right ones. If I can't have a free hand, I won't do the film. Millions can't convince me."

Corrected the final proofs of *Appogiatures*.* The book is being transferred from Losfeld to Orengo. A dedication to Parisot† will arrange matters—Orengo fears, since the book was the first in a collection, that he'll be committed to a series.

Last Friday, the Prix Apollinaire, chez Lipp.‡ Usually awarded in utter silence. This year, for some reason, a mob of reporters and photographers.

America has nothing to look forward to but ruin. Now it's Brazil's turn (and Canada's).

This place is becoming more and more of relief committee. Madeleine§ is partially responsible: all you have to do is play with her cats. Two hateful reactions: the ones you help and never hear from again; the ones you help who take root. Larrivet, who had been mugged: I send him to Claoué's to recover and arrange for a lawyer; I recommend him to Plancher so he can sell his little bar on the Île Saint-Louis. Now we can't get him out of the kitchen.

Letter from the Oldenburgisches Stadtstheater, where *Bacchus* is doing as well as in Düsseldorf. The manager writes: "We're taking in more than *Carmen*. In a city which has a strong opera tradition, that means something."

---

*This collection of Cocteau's prose poems, illustrated by Modigliani's portrait of the author and by a drawing by Hans Bellmer, was published by Editions du Rocher (Monaco) on October 31, 1953.

†Henri Parisot (1908–1979), translator (Lewis Carroll, Kafka, etc.), publisher, and editor in the surrealist ambience. With Parisot's collaboration, Cocteau published a selection of his work in the *Poètes d'aujourd'hui* series (Seghers), 1945; *Poésie critique*, 1946; *Oeuvres complètes* (eleven volumes), 1946–1951; *Le Sang d'un poète*, 1948; and *Appogiatures*.

‡Awarded to Armand Lanoux (1913–1983) for his collection of poems *Colporteur*.

§Madeleine Bouret, Cocteau's housekeeper in his Paris apartment in the Palais-Royal.

· ·

JANUARY 18

Impossible to take a single note in Paris. They blow away like dead leaves. Hardly odd that nothing serious can survive in that whirlwind. Everyone has flu. Someone phones from *Elle*: "Do you have flu?" "No." "We'd like to run some photographs of you and do an interview on the flu."

I'm in the habit of keeping things in order, which isn't easy at the heart of chaos. But the machine seems to be running anyway. I'm delighted by the picture of Einstein that Olivier and Jean-Pierre* have given me. He's sticking out his tongue at the photographer, with a childlike and devilish expression. At the world and at himself.

Magnificent letter from James Lord† about *Journal d'un inconnu*. He thinks he'll be able to translate it, and is going to try and find a publisher who will do it together with *La Difficulté d'être*.‡

Lunch with Sartre yesterday at the Grand Véfour: He will write a preface for my monograph.

A pretentious young fool from the École normale de Mérignac writes: "Read my poem, it will do you more good than your nonsense in the *Revue de Paris* (this is the chapter "Des Distances" in *Journal d'un inconnu*). I admire you too much not to warn you against intellectualism. Leave that to others. Etc." The wall of stupidity is the work of young intellectuals. My answer: "I warn you against asininity."

Grasset telephones: "Can you write to Claudel and urge him to vote for me at the académie?" Aside from the fact that I will not

---

*The poet Olivier Larronde and his friend Jean-Pierre Lacloche.

†American novelist and art critic, born 1922.

‡Cocteau's essay *Journal d'un inconnu*, published in January 1953, has some relation to *La Difficulté d'être*, another essay published in 1947. James Lord's undertaking did not bear fruit.

make such an ass of myself, I don't see how a letter from me would persuade Claudel to vote for Grasset.*

Académie. Hugo notes: "Balzac, one vote (mine)."

Wrote the text Mme Cuttoli† asked me to do as a preface for Chaplin's manuscript: "My work on *Limelight*." She ordered the silks for my tapestry in the Biennale.

All the crates from Germany were opened in the presence of an expert.‡ I sorted things out and sent the lot to Nice.

Recorded four sentences in English for the BBC and then said, "You will now understand why I hand the microphone over to a friend"—and Palmer White continued. His first recording on tape isn't clear. He begins over again on a record.

First issue of the magazine *La Parisienne* not at all bad. The *Nouvelle Nouvelle revue française* looks like an old issue dug up from some cellar. House style: *Permanence de Schlumberger*. Several corpses, including Fargue. Mummification.

The longer I live, the truer seems Max Jacob's remark "You must not be known for what you do." Fame is a vague rumor, a solitary name that floats through the air. A few unknown friends are your readers.

Visit from some Israelis. Quick transition from lofty to mundane assistance. I am to help them sell canvases by Picasso and Matisse. Goulding wants to arrange an exhibit and show *Orphée* in Israel. I'll make the trip only if the producers understand that charity is out of the question. Apparently the Picasso exhibit was an extraordinary success.

I've worked out the main lines of *La Belle au bois dormant*. But

---

*At the January 29 session of the Académie française, the poet Fernand Gregh (1873–1960) was elected to the chair of the comte de Chambrun by a vote of 25 to 5 for the publisher Bernard Grasset.

†Marie Cuttoli, a collector and friend of Picasso's, executed tapestries based on the works of contemporary masters.

‡These crates contained the drawings and paintings Cocteau exhibited in Germany in 1952.

the details are demanding. This is why I refuse all contracts and advances. I'll see about it in April.

. . . .

JANUARY 19

Received Mary Hoeck's English translation of *Le Chiffre sept*. It seems quite faithful and strong, insofar as a verse translation can be faithful and strong. A free translation might be less free jand closer to the broken rhythms and the details of the poem.

Saturday, at the Grand Véfour, Maurice Goudeket* talking at the bar with someone wearing a pince-nez. This person spoke my name so loudly that it became impossible for me to ignore them. He wanted to organize a celebration in the Palais-Royal for Colette's eightieth birthday—and wanted me to participate. Maurice and I asked him in whose name he was undertaking such a thing. "I am an organizer of birthday parties."

No such thing as Philadelphia University. So I made a mistake in the dedication (to Einstein) of *Journal d'un inconnu*. I should have put Pennsylvania. I'll add an erratum.

Telegram from Columbia Records (New York), thanking me for the sleeve drawing for *Oedipus Rex* (drawing of the final mask).

I didn't remember that Perrault's version of *La Belle au bois dormant* ended with so many boring stories about ogres. The beginning is all that matters.

. . . .

JANUARY 23

All I can think of is leaving for the Côte d'Azur. I'm getting all my chores out of the way now. Today I did two broadcasts in a

---

*Colette's husband.

row. Interview about *Journal d'un inconnu*—then Colette's birthday for Radio Geneva. Yesterday and the day before, press lists at Grasset's office. Countless visits. Processions of people wanting favors. Dinner last night with Clouzot. He takes me to see his film *The Wages of Fear*. We are alone in the dark theater. Magnificent film. A mystery, how he could bring off this tour de force in France. He didn't want to show the film at the Festival, but he will, because I am presiding. Crucial to have—finally—an important work to show for France, which is busy producing frivolities. After the film, we meet Lourau, and he and I decide that Clouzot will pretend to be still working on his sound mix, to keep the Italian company from releasing the film before the date of the Festival.

Nora Auric telephones that, contrary to all expectation, the revival of *Phèdre** was a success, Toumanova's loss being balanced for by that of Lifar, who made the whole thing so heavy and embarrassing.

Tonight the Opera revives *Antigone.*†

Went to the Théâtre de Babylone to see Beckett's play *En attendant Godot*. This is the representative play of our times. Beside it, Sartre's *Huis clos* seems like a vaudeville. Grim—terrible—hopeless—and the public giggles as soon as suffering gives the characters a tragic clownishness.

Journalism, 1953. *Le Figaro littéraire*, which never tires of denigrating me, telephones for a piece on the theme: "What do you care? You've reached the ceiling, etc." I answered that the ceiling

---

*A "choreographic tragedy" with set and costumes by Cocteau, music by Georges Auric, and choreography by Serge Lifar, first produced at the Opéra de Paris, 1950. During this 1953 revival, the roles created by Tamara Toumanova and Serge Lifar were danced by Lycette Darsonval and Michel Renault.

†A "musical tragedy" in three acts with words by Cocteau, freely adapted from Sophocles, music by Arthur Honegger; first performed in Brussels, 1927, and first performed at the Opéra de Paris under Cocteau's direction, with his set and costumes, 1943.

was like the one in *La Maison du baigneur** . . . I can do without this very nicely.

What's unendurable, since no one in the press is any help, is always having to explain what I do and consequently seeming to talk about myself all the time, since the others talk about me so badly or deliberately say nothing.

. . . .

JANUARY 25

Milly. Slept better than I ever can in town. Wrote the article on Éluard for Marcenac: "My Friend Paul." Answered letters, notably Mary Hoeck's after her visit to Raymond Mortimer, who had told her, "Though better than the rest, your translations aren't good." She's quite vitriolic. "What will our correspondence become, since all that matters to you is your work?" I answer: "I haven't had a letter from Mortimer, but he must be right, for your letter proves that you understand nothing about me or my work."

Drew the cover for Grasset's new edition of *Portraits-Souvenir*. Orengo for lunch tomorrow—Francine is bringing him. We have to explore what might serve as an appendix for the *Oeuvres complètes*.

Orengo lunch. I give him all the papers that might be useful for the *Oeuvres complètes*. Orengo reports that Mauriac (in the forthcoming issue of *La Table ronde*) crudely insults the *Nouvelle NRF*. Was this man created to enter into such nonsensical disputes? If he were a believer, would he compromise himself daily before a supreme tribunal? Does he suppose the confessional is a washbasin? Or that here on earth the Nobel puts him above suspicion?

Everything takes its course—a little higher and a little lower than you suppose.

---

*A play (1864) by Auguste Maquet, one of Dumas père's collaborators, in which the Spaniard Siete-Iglesias, an accomplice in the assassination of Henri IV, is crushed to death by a movable ceiling.

Revival of *La Voix humaine** at the Comédie-Française—with Louise Conte. Saw Louise and Jacques Charon. Suggested all the details for the set. Advised Louise not to shed tears. The actress who weeps keeps others from doing so.

Friday evening I saw Neville's† color film on flamenco. *Le Tout-Paris* very much in evidence, hugging and harrowing. Incredible nobility of these dances amid so much that is ignoble. I should guess that only Spain and China can resist. Especially one dance by a young fellow performed in front of the Escorial. From the period when Italian ballet and flamenco unite. Exquisite in its grace and precision (choreography by a monk). Watching such a performance, one imagines what the elegance of a whole period might have been, of which only the pomp of certain paintings gives us any notion. An automaton with a soul. And those castanets, which must be tiny death's-heads with chattering teeth, executing their roulades. All these dances combine religious ritual and a profound eroticism. The dancers never smile—their faces are actually fixed in expressions of suffering. (In the dance of the young fellow in front of the Escorial—from the sixteenth or seventeenth century—the perfection of the thing managed to make us overlook the notion of human absurdity. Here man invents, and performs something as perfect as the phenomena of nature. No gesture from bullfighting has yet appeared. The young monk, in a robe by Goya, offers a spectacle analogous to those of a flower that blooms, a bird that sings. There is inevitability in his every gesture, in his hands, his legs, his profile.) In the dance at the end of the film, Antonio‡ is splendid, but here a human invention appears: a will to beauty. His dance is that of a great dancer. In the dance in

---

*Cocteau's one-act play was created at the Comédie-Française by Berthe Bovy in 1930, directed by the author and with a set by Christian Bérard.

†The Spanish writer and filmmaker Edgar Neville died in Madrid in 1967.

‡Famous Spanish dancer, born in Seville in 1923. In 1953 he separated from his partner, Rosario, and formed his own dance company.

front of the Escorial, movement and dance are at one with the landscape and the architecture.

. . . .

FEBRUARY 3

In my bed at Santo Sospir. Sick. Very weak. Francine even worse. She has traveled with several degrees of fever but didn't want to stay in Paris another second. Snowstorm until Tournus, where we had dinner and slept. The next morning the bad weather continued until thirty kilometers outside of Valence, where the curtain rose on another scene, with different lighting. After Valence, there was sunshine, and when we reached the sea that afternoon, the wonderful mauve and red colors appeared which people despise because they don't relate to "the aesthetic."

The evening before we left, I thought I would be left alone at last, when Jaujard* telephoned: Would I "organize the Versailles festival"? I stopped in at the ministry to explain that such an undertaking was impossible. I would write a text. Yesterday in Nice I went to Les Ponchettes† and to the city museum to select drawings and examine the condition of the canvases. Pasquini‡ notes how ill I am and says I look terrible. While the drawings are being framed, I'll stay in bed here at the villa and take care of myself. Leaning over the table to select the drawings, I blacked out. This morning I'm feeling better. As though I were recovering from a long and exhausting illness.

The trouble you take, the absurd importance you attach to things

---

*Jacques Jaujard, general director of the Ministry of Arts and Letters.

†A municipal gallery, Quai des États-Unis, inaugurated by an exhibit of paintings, drawings, and a tapestry (*Judith et Holopherne*) by Cocteau, on February 9, 1953.

‡The lawyer Pierre Pasquini, born 1921, served as fine-arts counselor to the mayor of Nice. It was on his initiative and that of Mayor Brun that the Cocteau exhibit was held at the Galerie des Ponchettes. Subsequently a *député* of the Alpes-Maritimes and vice-president of the Assemblée nationale.

on this top spinning out of control—and on which everyone is condemned to death.

Dikes broken in Holland. The sea crushing houses on the English coast as if they were matchboxes. And man persists in imagining himself kind of a solid, privileged, eternal realm.

I've had the five canvases sent from the studio to Nice. Mario Brun* telephoned, his voice very odd. He's just got over an abscess in his throat. Les Ponchettes threatens to become a hospital.

Pasquini has bad news about Matisse. Apparently everyone feels the influence of the storm off Dunkerque. And yet here we find the same flowers, the same life, the same incredible privilege of peace.

Of course I woke up, in my room at Santo Sospir, as if the two months in Paris had been a dream of the night before. I have to make a real effort to picture the missing interval—the edges grow together—and even when I do, I don't believe what I see.

. . . .

FEBRUARY 4

For almost thirty years I've grown accustomed to being covered with secret tributes and public vituperations. There's a rhythm to it, and you learn to adapt . . . In the long run, a kind of moral armor forms, strong enough to withstand the blows and protect your heart, which remains young and brave. People must get upset when you force them to think about certain things. They protect themselves. They protect their comforts. It's logical. That they should protect theirs need not keep us from defending ours. For-tunately, there happen to be any number of solitaries who share our notions of what is uncomfortable and don't just follow the

---

*Reporter on *Nice-Matin*, ultimately director of the paper. His column "Riviera-Gazette" discussed the celebrities visiting the Côte d'Azur.

rules. The way of the world. And until the end of this world, our world, the singular will always and mysteriously win out over the plural, which wins only in appearance, and for the moment.

I was asked during a broadcast what I meant by "outrunning beauty." I made up a poor answer—what I should have said was: "Keeping pace with beauty is creating conventional beauty, pleonasm, postcards. Trailing behind beauty is never being beautiful. Outrunning beauty forces beauty to catch up, compels a strength which seems ugly to become beautiful after the fact."

If I manage to keep body and soul together (which would probably be impossible if it were not for Francine's constant help), it's likely I'll write less and less. I'll concern myself only with putting things in order, collecting my scattered oeuvre. I'll devote myself to drawing and painting.

What could be funnier than the Goncourts' exclamation when they learned that the earth would not last more than a few thousand centuries: "And what will become of our books?" Yet after all, it wasn't so stupid. Unless you write to eat, or to "succeed" in the here and now, you wonder what impels you to exhaust yourself in the void and why you bother to seek distant friends, since you have them here at hand, the kind who read you like an open book without any need of paper and ink. What I would have liked, I don't have: a great human contact, a warmth, a *respectful confidence*. Instead of which, I wear myself out trying to communicate my discomfort to people who protect their comfort with all the strength they can muster. I no longer even believe in a conspiracy of journalists and critics—it's worse than that. They despise me or insult me out of a kind of aggressive sloth—*by contagion*.

I wonder if it's because I'm continually thwarted that I doubt my own works—that I minimize and denigrate them and find only weaknesses in them—or if it's this tendency to criticize and minimize myself which influences others and keeps them from praising me.

Yesterday, at the Musée Masséna,* I was struck by the beauty of my canvases and my tapestry, by the power of my drawings. All of a sudden I realized that there has been a monstrous injustice, one I have got into the habit of regarding as inevitable—and of provoking by a kind of insane modesty which must be a morbid form of pride.

Mechanism: Better nothing than a little.

After writing these words, I think I see more clearly. When I am praised, I run away (I dodge). The only tolerable praise would have to possess a power equal to that of my work. Which is why—because that is impossible—I prefer insults and stupidities.

I am reading (rereading) Hugo's *Souvenirs personnels* (1842–1851).† I knew many of the passages from *Choses vues* and had read them when Jean Hugo‡ and I were going through the Hugo trunks at Fourques.

Struck by Hugo's navigation from chalk to cheese, from lion to lamb: "I am blue with the blues," he says, "and white with the whites, red with the reds. I am blue, white, red." He triumphs by never diminishing himself in any direction, prevailing over all the others, letting them say about him: "He's no politician." A policy stronger than politics.

Young poets no longer read—have never read anything. They read each other. They imitate each other by osmosis. Consequently, all their poems sound alike. (Seghers's little series will soon seem to have been written by just one poet. No spinal column. Scoliosis which will be aggravated until it falls into dust.)

Pasquini says: "I'd like you to become the son of Nice." I answer:

---

*One of the museums of Nice, on the promenade des Anglais. Cocteau was preparing his works there for the exhibit at the Galerie des Ponchettes.

†Collected and edited by Henri Guillemin, Gallimard, 1952.

‡The painter Jean Hugo (1894–1984), great-grandson of Victor Hugo and a close friend of Cocteau, had established his residence in 1929 at the Mas de Fourques, in Lunel.

"You can't choose where you're born. But just as you die any number of times before your death, you are born any number of times after your birth. In Nice, in Villefranche, I was born (at twenty) to any number of things and ideas which rule me still. So in a sense I *am* a son of Nice and of Villefranche. I can say so without exaggeration or absurdity."

. . . .

FEBRUARY 5

Certain kinds of public give off a distorting moral mist. I once saw a so-called elite public spoil and devalue the first Marx Brothers film (*Animal Crackers*) in 1930. I was supposed to introduce the film, but I was requested to discuss it afterward. I had to explain to the audience that this flop was its own fault. And that certain moral exhalations are as subtle as those of the Lake of Geneva, which make the Swiss coast either close or remote or invisible. Nothing stranger than this brilliant film which went dull and *in which the actors seemed to lose their heads and perform poorly.*

Rereading Hugo's *Souvenirs personnels*, I realize that in 1850 he never suspects—not for one second—the coup d'état and the threat of the Second Empire. Instead, he fears a monarchist republic. Louis Bonaparte's remark, which Jérôme quotes to him, at the theatre—*"You'll see"*—should have opened their eyes. (Maybe Jérôme had opened his.)

It reminds me of Colonel Rémy's visit.* He had come to see me at the Palais-Royal so that I could sign a book for him. "France is a monarchist country," he said, "and she has her king within reach." He meant General de Gaulle. The general wanted to avoid the "coup d'état–dictatorship–fascism" style, but he must have

---

*Gilbert Renault (1901–1984), "Rémy" in the Resistance.

dreamed of becoming a monarch in some form or other (first of all, president of the Republic). Malraux telling me: "There's no reason that a Boulanger coup shouldn't succeed." (*"To the Élysée! mon général, to the Élysée!"*: Malraux as Déroulède.)

Here there was no queen of hearts to fear. When the general came to London the second time, London trembled before Palewski as an éminence grise. They were lodged in separate hotels. Palewski protested, and they were put in the same one (the Ritz). That evening one of my friends saw that the little dining room behind the main one was set up with candles and orchids, and she asked the old French maître d'hôtel, "Who's that table for?" And the old man murmured in her ear, "It's for General de Gaulle, who's dining with Countess Palewska." I told Palewski this story, which he didn't seem to enjoy. I found out that in London he passed himself off as a count.

It was this absence of a "Countess Palewska," of a dream countess (the classic dream of an old Parisian maître d'hôtel), which made Malraux say this was one Boulanger who might succeed. But unfortunately the general's greatness was all in his height. One hears he is quite sick now, a megalomaniac surrounded by psychoanalysts at Colombey-les-Deux-Églises. All in all, Lazareff is right to say that any newspaper of any period is like any other. The Hugo period was as mediocre, as sordid as ours.

Académie: Balzac—two votes (Hugo's and Vigny's). Musset—five votes (like Grasset!), which is amazing. One might have imagined Musset was the darling of those idiot schoolboys.

The remark of the minister of the interior at Balzac's funeral, "He was a distinguished man," says volumes about the sense of hierarchy all periods possess. Who dares complain of being invisible when a giant isn't *seen*?

In the confusion of leaving, I've forgotten to tell about saying good-bye to the staff of the magazine *La Parisienne* at François

Michel's.* Sixth floor, rue de Tourville, behind the Invalides, you reach his apartment by an outside fire escape. Any number of lively and extremely agreeable young people, without a touch of "intellectual" manners. Cingria† solemnly strumming the piano. Florence Gould‡ in a black dress looking like Lucrezia Borgia—very drunk. She grabs me: "I'd like to help this magazine." Unfortunately, instead of getting her drunk to do some good, you have to sober her up—which isn't easy. She's always in a kind of cloud, except when it comes to figures. But she's a remarkable old girl.

I was already feeling sick. Parinaud walked me home. We ran into Fraigneau and Saint-Laurent§ walking to get a breath of air. Audiberti shouting at me from the opposite sidewalk, "We never see each other, but I know you're there—and that's a comfort." But what can you believe? Best to live in the shadows, when the sun shines. That's why we escaped, despite our fever, despite the last of the storms in Holland and Dunkerque.

At noon today, Pasquini and Mario will come to the villa to arrange for the session at Les Ponchettes.

Four o'clock. They came. Pasquini turns himself inside out to be helpful. Mario troubled by an arthritic knee. He limps. Necessary to run in all directions. It's tonight that the carnival begins. They brought me the posters, which are fine. They talk about my book. I realize that they have glanced at it, more or less. It takes years to be able to write such a book, and it should take years to read it.

---

*François Michel, born 1916, editor of *La Parisienne* from November 1952 to August 1954.

†Charles-Albert Cingria (1883–1954), born and died in Geneva, published scholarly works on the Middle Ages, as well as medieval music and collections of tales and chronicles (among them, *Florides helvètes*, 1944, and *Bois sec, bois vert*, 1948).

‡Patron of the arts and collector, née Florence Lacaze (1895–1983), in 1923 she married the wealthy American Frank Jay Gould (died 1956), the developer of Juan-les-Pins.

§The writer Jacques Laurent, alias Cecil Saint-Laurent, born 1919, founder of the literary magazine *La Parisienne* in 1952.

I'll hang the show tomorrow. Pasquini is having the gallery heated. Press opening Monday morning at eleven. Tuesday morning at eleven, the mayor's reception.

Salvat* has sent the proof of a new cover for *Portraits-Souvenir* (a drawing).

Montherlant dictates the terms on which Gallimard has to buy his works from Grasset: once a year Gallimard must finance— whether he or someone else publishes it—a book about Montherlant.† Hard to believe.

As a matter of fact, I had written to Gallimard this morning to explain some of my apparent infidelities: the fact that Orengo bought up my books published by Morihien. Books promised to Grasset and to Parisot. No doubt Gallimard will declare he would have given the three million francs to Paul Morihien (who asked seven). Now, aside from the fact that Gallimard would not have agreed to spend any such sum, he would not have got the reduction Orengo obtained, and my books would have remained in some attic.

. . . .

FEBRUARY 6

This is the morning I'm to hang the canvases and the tapestry. Splendid weather. Health not so splendid. I'm coughing less, but I feel as if I were convalescing after a long sickness. As exhausted as after my bout of typhoid.‡

With the regiment, I was the friend of the general and of the troops. Anything but esteemed by the intermediary ranks. The noncoms loathed me. Which is what always happens to me. For instance, in film: the big producers run after me. The critics tear

---

*The painter François Salvat (1894–1974), art director at Éditions Bernard Grasset.

†Not the case.

‡In October 1931, in Toulon.

me to pieces. The public loves me. (The noncoms of the elite cannot endure me.)

Clouzot tells me: You make *Orpheus* or *The Wages of Fear*. But let's call the rest sublime, since we couldn't care less.

Marcel Achard's method: "There aren't any more critics. Since the ones that exist are of no consequence and detestable, only one response is possible: The critic who praises me is admirable, the critic who puts me down is a dolt."

The wreckage of Holland and the English coasts. The storms growing worse. On the first page of *Nice-Matin*, the disaster of Holland and the carnival.

. . . .

FEBRUARY 7

Canvases hung at Les Ponchettes. Everyone very charming and helpful. I'll go Sunday to look over the final arrangements.

Letter from Françoise Gilot, inviting me to Vallauris. She says I should wear plenty of furs, it's so cold in the studio where Picasso painted *War and Peace*.

. . . .

FEBRUARY 8

Sunday. Photograph from Sanford Roth (Hollywood). It shows Sabartés* standing at the far end of the room, like Detective Fix in *Round the World in Eighty Days*. Picasso, wearing a Phileas Fogg cap, is sitting opposite him looking at a photo of me, which is seen upside down at the bottom of the image.

Appointment at Les Ponchettes at three o'clock for the final

---

*The painter Jaime Sabartés (1880–1968), one of Picasso's oldest friends, his biographer, and secretary.

hanging. Would like to visit Matisse, who is not doing well. Colette arrives in Monte Carlo this morning by plane. Somerset Maugham writes that he's leaving for London and returning the eleventh.

No news from Orengo, who was to arrive yesterday with the plates for the *Bal d'Orgel*.*

The style of *Nice-Matin*: my preface to the catalog reprinted so that before turning the page you read, "exhibits on the beach at . . ." and the word "Nice" on the next page. Maître Pasquini's reply to my preface . . .

Mme Guynet† tells me James Lord's letter convinced Cézanne's heirs‡ not to sell his studio to contractors for cheap apartments. They were ashamed. Without fiscal complications, the deal would already be over and done with. But it's a pity we have to rely on Americans to give Aix and the state what concerns France alone. Mme Guynet doesn't even dare write James that the tax people are making difficulties.

If Cézanne's studio is allowed to be torn down, people will call it a scandal. If steps are taken to prevent this, obstacle after obstacle will be raised (despite the ministers, who are entirely in favor of preservation).

Mme Guynet is the former secretary of Georges Salles.§ She is a fighter and does all she can against the environing sloth. She almost always gets what she wants. And it is she who is organizing my show.

Le Bal du comte d'Orgel by Raymond Radiguet, an edition illustrated by Cocteau with thirty-four engravings, March 1953.

†Mme Guynet-Péchadre, director of the Nice museums at the time.

‡Lord reports that Paul Cézanne's son had sold his father's studio shortly before his own death to the poet Marcel Provence, who had kept the premises intact. In 1953 the American Preservation Committee was dealing with the heirs of Provence. The acquisition was made in 1954. The American committee then deeded the studio to the University of Aix, which offered it in 1979 to the city of Aix, which accepted this offer.

§Georges Salles (1889–1966), director of the museums of France, codirector with Malraux of the collection "L'Univers des formes," Gallimard.

. . . .

FEBRUARY 9

Finished hanging the drawings and canvases from three to seven.
Deadly cold in the galleries. Worried about hearing nothing from
Orengo. Since Fauconnet's death, I'm troubled by the carelessness of careful people. I had an appointment (for the costumes
and masks of *Le Boeuf sur le toit*) with Fauconnet in the rue d'An-
jou at ten; by noon, Fauconnet hadn't come, and I said to my
mother, "Fauconnet's dead." "You're mad." "No, if he hasn't
come and hasn't sent word, it's because he's dead." I went to
Fauconnet's place: He had died of a heart attack trying to light
his fire.

Seven o'clock. (Good news from Orengo, who had simply mistaken
the date.) This morning, reporters, newsreels, photographers, radio interviews. After lunch, at three, mayor, prefect, a lot
of ladies and gentlemen who want signed catalogs. Very tired.
Tomorrow morning, at eleven, mayor's reception at the Hôtel
Masséna.

All very good natured—none of the Paris ferocity. Nice gives
you a really warm welcome. Exactly what I had foreseen.

Letter from Édith Piaf, who wants to revive *Le Bel indifférent**
with her husband.† Willemetz can't find a scrap of Bérard's set.
Piaf will ask Nobili to make a new one. She wants to do the piece
in France and in America.

---

*One-act play by Cocteau, created by Piaf and Paul Meurisse in 1940, with a set
by Christian Bérard.
†The singer Jacques Pills (1910–1970).

· ·

FEBRUARY 10

Reception this morning at the Hôtel Masséna.* Very agreeable. Mayor's speech.† My reply. Article by Mario Brun in *Nice-Matin*. Rain.

Letter from Orengo. His copy editor has found more than two hundred typographical errors in Grasset's original edition of *Portraits-Souvenir*.

· ·

FEBRUARY 11

Contrary to supposition, the impressionists who thought they were breaking away from photography invented photography in painting. (Ingres never photographs.)

What was all the stormy and visible boldness of Delacroix beside the incredible *invisible* boldness of Ingres's forms and colors?

The secretary sent by the Uruguay Embassy stayed here four hours. I walked him out. He had left his wife and daughter in the car. I was embarrassed. He said, "Don't apologize, that's how we treat our wives." He said my painting lacks boldness. I asked him what he meant. He didn't have a clue. These idiots don't see that in 1953, boldness consists in not seeming bold. The inner intensity escapes them altogether. Only people who aren't specialists in painting can see my canvases—people who don't have a preconceived notion of "modern painting." In the long run, it's always the dauber who delights people who "know painting."

It takes thirty years to dare paint a canvas. And then another thirty for it to be seen.

------

*Mansion of the Masséna d'Essling family, built in 1900, made into the Musée Masséna.

†Jean Médecin.

Picasso has always insulted habit. People will get in the habit of his insults. Then it's breaking away from this habit of insults which will be an insult.

Answering the radio interviewer's questionnaire impromptu— a mistake. You regret everything you say.

. . . .

FEBRUARY 13

Yesterday I stopped in at Les Ponchettes around six for an appointment with some Italian journalists. There I found the mayor escorting a senator through the show, giving him a lecture in front of each canvas, each drawing.

A. tells me that Mme Chirico sleeps and eats with an enormous bag of jewels beside her, which she collects to finance the anti-Communist revolution (she is a White Russian). She's convinced she will dethrone Stalin and take his place and that Chirico will become the court painter. She's the one who is forcing him to deny his past, to paint what he paints now. Chirico loathes, despises and rejects all modern artists. Only Picasso and I find any mercy in his . . . eyes. The Anchorenas* had already told me that but had not mentioned his wife's astounding delusions.

Telegram from Françoise. Picasso has flu. I'll go next week.

Last night a slight relapse after the dinner with Jean Guérin (who describes the delusions of Nancy Cunard,† covered with bone necklaces and bracelets, who imagines she's something like Stevenson's Mme Menizabad. A queen of the blacks. Her hatred of

---

*Marcello and Hortensia Anchorena, wealthy Argentines who lived for some time in Paris.

†Daughter of Sir Bache Cunard and Lady Emerald Cunard (née Maude Burke). An enthusiast of various avant-garde literary movements. Photographs of her by Man Ray and Cecil Beaton show her indeed "covered" by African ivory bracelets.

Americans. Her very vague communism). Fever again, and an un-bearable weakness in my legs.

This afternoon we visited the little house in Biot, which is turning out nicely. But it was terribly cold.

Overcast morning, rain. I took notes for the text on Versailles and for the Munich monograph.*

External boldness. Now is the time for internal boldness, no showing off (for making boldness invisible).

The golden calf is always made of mud.

The prefect asks, "Are you still painting?" I answer *unthinkingly*, "I have to do Mme Favini's portrait." "Then you're going to Milan?" "Yes, of course." Etc. Mme Favini is beginning to take shape. No doubt I shall be obliged to do Mme Favini's portrait.† Then she will exist. She will own splendid paintings. She will detest Schoen-berg's music. She will have a husband who has made a fortune in shoes. It's quite possible that one of these days Thérèse will say, "Mme Favini telephoned."

. . . .

FEBRUARY 14 · 1953

Visit from Maurice Goudeket. There are old ladies who telephone at eleven at night to ask Colette to endorse checks that everyone else has refused "by mistake." There is J. de Lucinge, who has spent 16,000,000 francs on the tiles in the casino lobby, where people are constantly breaking their necks. There is Maurice de Rothschild, who has brought his chefs with him and lunches at the Hotel Victoria because he's afraid the Hôtel de Paris puts salt in his food. In short, there is Monte Carlo, the same as ever. There is the world which is changing, without Monte Carlo's noticing.

---

*Démarche d'un poète, with seventeen drawings by the author and twenty repro-ductions, Munich, 1953.

†Mme Favini and Her Daughter, 1953. Oil on canvas. Collection Édouard Dermit.

From Jean Genet:

MY JEAN,

This note to tell you that I've read your book and that I was happy with it. It may not have the hardness, the vigor of *La Difficulté d'être*, but the book has a tenderness, even a sense of pity, which make it—especially when one knows you—very seductive. I love your weakness here, but you're wrong to believe in your solitude since you are loved—and often quite intelligently—the world over. I'm writing in haste, and poorly, my dear Jean, because I'm drugged by insomnia. My nerves are all wound up. I just wanted to send you, once again, my great affection, with my gratitude. I embrace you, Jean Genet. Forgive these stupid sentences. Even my hand is tired. But don't imagine I don't love your book. I see that I put what I felt while reading it very poorly; what I mean is that in writing it your hand was flexible but not soft. I love that flexibility. And I'll love you always.

JEAN

René Bertrand* is at Nice. We expect him at Santo Sospir.

. . . .

FEBRUARY 15

Sunday. Reread *Opium*† (apropos of the text of my monograph for Munich). This text will be the last one in which I explain myself, in which I repeat myself. I'm drawing the curtain on this long period. I won't write any more, or only something new.

---

*Philosopher, essayist, Egyptologist, René Bertrand, born 1897, is the dedicatee of *Journal d'un inconnu*. In November 1953 he published *Sagesse et chimères,* with a preface by Cocteau.

†*Opium*, journal of a disintoxication, illustrated with forty drawings and three collages by the author, 1930.

Frightening how many important things I said about the period which have left no trace in people's memories (I myself . . .). Probably we need more perspective. And of course people would have to *read* (reread).

Nice-Matin reports the death of André Brulé.* One more, or one less. The list is growing longer, or shorter. Brulé seemed shellacked, ready to slip into the wings of our drama. His frivolity covered him like an invulnerable armor.

I've added a few lines to *Le Potomak* (after Alfred's ridiculous poem).†

Monograph. Added a few pages on the ethics of sexuality with regard to works of art. You get it up or you don't. All the rest is intellect. (Of course such sexuality cannot be awakened by what the picture represents. That would have no value.)

René Bertrand will visit at four. Thérèse told him on the telephone that I had gone out. "Why did you tell him I had gone out, since I never go out?" "Because Monsieur was sleeping." And she adds, "Some Indochinese empress asked if *The Temptation on the Mountain*‡ was for sale."

In *Match*: "Cocteau has not exhibited his favorite work, *Woman Falling*, because it is painted on the wall of his staircase." Where does such nonsense come from? Each time you ask yourself the same question, with the same amazement.

We've been spared the storms, but we've had a grim February.

---

*André Brulé, born 1883, actor and director, in 1940 had directed two plays by Cocteau: *Les Monstres sacrés*, which he created with Yvonne de Bray, and *Le Bel indifférent*, with Édith Piaf.

†*Le Potomak*, 1913–1914, preceded by a prospectus, 1916, and followed by *Les Eugènes de la guerre*, 1915, with ninety-five drawings by the author, 1919.

‡Cocteau's painting, 1951.

. . . .
FEBRUARY 18

The triad in ancient Greece: Zeus-Poseidon-Pluto (son of Saturn). All the gods tremble before Zeus, save Poseidon and Pluto. They refuse to obey. Are they not sons of Saturn too?

Cement poles are being set up all over the Cape. The old wooden telegraph poles have had their day. They assume the charm of fiacres now. The new cement poles will turn old in their turn, will assume the charm and the absurdity of our gasoline-powered cars.

The kings of Ur lived several centuries; a king must have been what we call a dynasty. Subsequently, kings have aged less well: they rarely reach a hundred years.

I've begun the portrait of Mme Favini and her daughter. Everything comes in triangles and in the curves inscribed within them.

In fact, to read one of my poems (*Le Chiffre sept*, for instance) or to see one of my canvases, it would take a Champollion to discover the secret of the writing. He would teach the others, teach me. I express myself in hieroglyphics.

Added some more pages to the text of the monograph. But I'll never get to the sixty Bruckmann is asking for. I've written him that the rhythm of a text determines its length. Which is quite difficult to understand in Germany. I suggest that he add an article in German or a chapter from *Journal d'un inconnu*: "Painting Without Being a Painter."

Lunch yesterday at Monte Carlo with Colette and Maurice in that dining room of the Hôtel de Paris that looks like Ali Baba's cave. Colette has withdrawn into a kind of naive mist in which she hears only what she wants to hear, thereby escaping our world. At the end of the lunch, Maurice was called to the telephone. It was Denise Mayer (wife of the minister of the interior). She says her husband has signed the nomination of Colette to the rank of grand officer (of the Legion of Honor). She adds, "Break it to her gently." Colette (after Muarice has told her, none too gently): "What officer? Who is Denise Mayer?" When the staff of the dining room greets her, she says to Maurice, "Look, they recognize me from last year."

René Bertrand lives in an icy little house in Nice, at the upper end of the avenue Cyrnos. His wife is ill. As soon as you see him, you realize that the only thing that matters to him is his science, his inner life, of which he never speaks to his wife or to his fellow citizens of Haute-Goulaine.* He never speaks of anything to them but the quality of this year's muscadet. He was looking for some documents in the Nice library, and all he could find there was Bourget, Bordeaux, Marcel Prévost. One evening he described Plato's life, which I knew very little about: Plato as a political adventurer, trying out his governmental system . . . Fruitless in Greece, so he experiments in Syracuse, where he's thrown in prison, sold as a slave; buys himself free for 3,000,000 (drachmas?); returns to Greece and sees that everything is degenerating; tries again in Syracuse, where the tyrant's son is now ruling; imprisoned again. He will die in Greece (having founded his school there), will die *with* that Greece which is collapsing and will never revive, after six centuries of glory. I asked Bertrand how he had learned to read the dead languages. He is self-taught. Drioton helped him a little with hieroglyphics.

Letter from Claude Roy. Valentine Hugo, whom Marie-Laure de Noailles had promised to help with the expenses for her mother's funeral, is told by her—on the telephone!—that she is glad to give money to the living but not to the dead. Hysterical, Valentine telephones Dominique Éluard, who doesn't have a penny and who pays for the funeral. Style of the rich. Style of the poor. I have already given Valentine 100,000 francs. Impossible, alas, to give

---

*René Bertrand was mayor of Haute-Goulaine (Loire-Atlantique).

more. I still owe Jeannot [Jean Marais] a million, and I don't know how I'll reimburse him.

Jeannot telephones: his final performance (*Britannicus*)* a triumph. He had eight solo bows and his dressing room crammed with flowers. Typical of Paris: They sulk when you arrive and celebrate when you leave.

Orengo at Monte Carlo. Will be here this evening with proof covers for the books he's republishing.

. . . .

FEBRUARY 20 · 1953

Royal jelly, subject of biological research: the jelly on which bees feed their queen. It made the gods immortal (ambrosia).

Wrote Bruckmann not to force a framework on me—to wait for the text to assume the shape and dimensions that are suitable.

Saw Orengo. *Le Bal du comte d'Orgel* will come out in March. *Appogiatures* and *La Difficulté d'être* will be done a little later. He is putting *Théâtre de poche* and *Drôle de ménage* back on sale with the new covers.

The director of the Musée Fragonard in Grasse brings me her book on Baudelaire's period. Drawings by Guys and the corresponding photographs. Except for two or three, the photographs of women lack the vitality of the drawings which concentrate on fashion.

Mauriac in a frenzy since his Nobel Prize. In *La Table ronde*, he attacks *La Nouvelle NRF* with a virulence analogous to that of his *Open Letter* to me. Gallimard has been driven half mad himself and telephoned the Publishers' Union to complain about Bourdel (Plon).† He wanted to resign his position in the union. Odd how quickly

---

*At the Comédie-Française, Sunday matinee, February 15.

†Maurice Bourdel, president and director general of Librarie Plon, publishers of *La Table ronde*.

people's indifference to attacks on others vanishes when they are the one attacked. "Mauriac," Gallimard had told me—"what can that matter to you?" *That matters to him.*

I imagine Paulhan will answer.* This war of the periodicals is absurd. Billy, in *Le Figaro littéraire*, asks: "Against whom and for whom is François Mauriac raging?" This in Mauriac's own paper. Since the Nobel, Mauriac turns against everyone who is usurping what he believes to be his position. He told the editorial staff of *La Table ronde*, "We have to find someone to shoot down Malraux."

Montherlant's system: he commissions book after book on his person and on his work. He has just sent all the critics a pamphlet in which a schoolmistress puts *La Ville dont le prince est un enfant* on her reading list and praises it to the skies. An empty and childish play: honor roll and masturbation.

Coincidences? Dinner with Charles de Noailles. Last night, Orengo asked to see *Le Sang d'un poète*. It was projected for him. And this morning comes Charles, who had commissioned me to make the film.

The Valentine–Dominique–Marie-Laure business is settled. I spoke to Charles. He will send the money to Jean Hugo to give to Valentine, so that Mme Tézenas can be reimbursed.†

. . . .

FEBRUARY 21

A young woman writes, "Why are your *Enfants terribles* so rich?" And she claims to know the novel by heart! For these children, only their inner wealth matters, and the world they have made

---

*Jean Paulhan did not reply to François Mauriac's attacks.

†Suzanne Champin, wife of the industrialist Léon Tézenas. Associated with many writers and artists, she also sponsored the "Domaine musical" concerts during the 1950s.

for themselves. I had to show that poverty and wealth have no hold over them.

Some very important Israelis ask what Le Chiffre sept is all about. I wonder how they read the Bible.

I observe everywhere this lack of culture, this forgetting of the old secrets, this inaccuracy in mind and in words.

Sent off to Seghers the proofs of the 100-franc edition of Le Chiffre sept. I've found more mistakes in the deluxe edition. Cut two unnecessary stanzas. Corrected the lines that didn't scan, etc., and added the little note Seghers wanted on the origins of the poem.

Colette's life. One scandal after another. Then everything changes and she becomes an idol. She ends her life of music halls, beauty parlors, old lesbians, in an apotheosis of respectability. Yesterday the papers printed what Denise Mayer's telephone call had told me. She is being awarded the loftiest of recompenses. The kind that is given in extremis. How right she is to face it all in a kind of hibernation, a profound and lucid irony which you can momentarily glimpse in her eyes.

.   .   .   .

SUNDAY · FEBRUARY 22

Dinner last night at Ginette Weill's in Antibes. On the way back, near Nice, Édouard stops at the edge of the highway to let some cars pass. Suddenly we see a cone of sparks facing us on the right, and an empty motorcycle lands in the middle of the road, to our left. The rider must have been thrown between the trees. We can just make out his body. Édouard goes looking for help, and in a second there are people everywhere. We leave when they carry the rider off on a stretcher. At Santo Sospir, Édouard says: "The motorcycle was red—like Picard's (Francine's gardener). Let's hope it's not his!" Legally, we should have stayed until the police got there. But ever since the endless evidence I had to give after Nimier's accident, there's nothing I would rather avoid.

Radio. Telephone call from Radio Monaco: "The dialogue between you and Colette for next Friday won't work. It has to come off tonight. Can you do it alone?" Their car arrives at four. I record, and talk about the Palais-Royal. Afterward the driver of their car tells me: "I think you made a mistake. We don't call it the Palais-Royal, we call it the *Palais Princier*." For all my talk of Colette and the Palais-Royal, he thought I had been talking about the palace of the prince of Monaco.

That morning I had gone to see Colette at the Hôtel de Paris. She was swamped by telegrams and letters of congratulation. Most of the generals very proud to write: "Your colleague. Confraternal homage. Etc."

What the French like is titles, decorations, official honors. A *work* never produces this avalanche of letters.

The electric blender at Ginette's. The results are utterly different from what is done by hand at Francine's. Difference between French cooking and the American variety. Mechanical processes diminish the taste.

Only with the deepest faith can you join a party. To be a Communist without a real belief in the system is to take communion in the Church without a total faith. Sacrilege itself. It seems to me difficult to be a true Communist without being Russian and without being suspect to the Party.

Telegram from Françoise. I'll go Tuesday to Vallauris to see Picasso's *War and Peace*.

The Coccioli affair.* I ran into him yesterday at Orengo's, the latter in the last two days spending a fortune on telephone calls to deal with the most scandalous affairs of the heart as if he were

---

*Carlo Coccioli, Italian novelist born in Leghorn, in 1920; in 1951 published *Le Ciel et la terre*; in 1952, *Fabrizio Lupo* (dedicated to Charles Orengo); and others.

dealing with a broken marriage. Sign of the times. You can parade or publish anything—but you get nabbed for a detail. Genet, for instance, whom the court condemns for the (out-of-print) deluxe edition of *Querelle de Brest*,* though it lets the same book be published in Gallimard's regular edition.

Finished the program cover for the Nice orchestra benefit for Dutch flood victims.

King Baudoin doesn't know his trade. He's like a schoolboy on a spree. He claims he is ill to avoid dealing with the victims of Dutch floods and official ceremonies but plays golf on the Côte d'Azur. He travels between two cops, who look as if they were putting him in a salad shaker. Unlike the queen of England, a model sovereign who knows her business and never makes a mistake. Family, protocol, spiritual distinction: impeccable all round. I don't like professionals who do their job badly. Young Baudoin could just as well abdicate. Why does he need to be king?

Magazines. Everywhere the divorce of Danièle Delorme and Daniel Gélin. Incredible display of intimacies for the public.

Travel into the past would be more curious than into the future. We know where things are going; we no longer know whence they come. We'd like to live a few days with Marco Polo and Genghis Khan's grandson. The Chinese, the Mongols. The invention of paper money in exchange for gold given to the prince. His inconceivable luxury. His hunts. To get from one beater to the next required four days.

Each morning, Prince Kublai (Mongol emperor) ordered the sun to rise. As an old man he assigned this task to a specialist. He knew perfectly well the mechanism of the stars but needed to make his people believe that the sun would not rise without his intervention.

Paper money was a piece of bark bearing the imperial seal. With

---

*This edition is illustrated with twenty-nine drawings by Jean Cocteau.

this bark you could buy gold. Inflation occurred fifty years later.

This prince was curious about the pope. He informed himself about the Catholic religion. But Jesus Christ disturbed him—too great a lord, in his opinion. *Our Lord.* He feared that the use of such terms would diminish his own stature (thirteenth century).

Wintering in Sumatra on his return journey, Marco Polo saw unicorns. Their horn was black. In Europe, they were represented on escutcheons and regarded as fabulous. They obeyed virgins.

On the covers of this week's magazines, the little girl in Clément's film *Jeux interdits* is shown being presented to the queen of England by Odette.

Absurd fashion of publishing one's "journal" in one's lifetime. A fashion launched by Gide. But the Gidean method consists in pretending to tell all in order to conceal all. A journal exists only if you put into it, without reservations, everything that occurs to you. Hugo's interests us much more, as time goes by.

Splendid sunshine. Crocuses out. Tangerines ripening on the trees. Snow in Paris.

I spoke to Francine about Édouard's fears for the red motorcycle. She had thought of it herself, but if it had been Picard, we would have heard this morning.

I plan to redo the whole big canvas of Mme Favini. In this imaginary portrait, there must be a bolder approach. A huge painted caricature exceeding the style of caricature.

S. describes certain Nice families to me—as secret, as private as those of Lyons. A mixture of heroism, irony, and sloth. More Greek than Italian. Homebodies, but giving Nice that atmosphere of charm which is to be found nowhere else on the Côte d'Azur. Insults exchanged by the *niçois* of an incredible violence and diversity. Cannes is a place, Nice is a city.

Visit from Dugardin, here for the performance of Menotti's *Consul* in Nice. He has forced them to hire Marie Powers, whom they no longer wanted at the Opera because she had been booed in *Aïda*. *The Consul* a huge success. *The Medium* a huge success in Paris. The blacks in *Porgy and Bess* a triumph in Paris, after Dugardin brought them from London.

The director of the Opéra de Nice and of Les Arènes de Nîmes is a man of no culture. "I'm only interested in money." He does no worse than the rest. It was from his costume room that the Nice officials borrowed their top hats for the prince of Monaco's funeral. I think I've already mentioned that funeral, where Pagnol wore his academician's uniform and one saw a regular debauch of operetta uniforms with ribbons of every color of the rainbow. Mario Brun and Pasquini told me they were sick with laughing, and that their laughter was contagious, becoming a kind of torture, so that no one had ever seen such a sideshow funeral procession.

It strikes me that this world of honors, decorations, and pictures in the papers is on the whole the real world and ours a kind of family attached to a wreck, drifting no one knows where.

Martine Carol. The papers: "Martine Carol, queen of London." Side by side, the photograph of Queen Elizabeth and of Martine. Apparently the papers base their business on *hope:* You, too, can be here. And household disputes. Magazines live on divorces and overnight successes. The main thing is to find out if journalism and the radio have *definitively* done away with values and if there is nothing left but a chain of false values, without any posthumous correction; *if we aren't dupes of professional honesty* . . . If the world has become *perfectly dishonest.*

Maria Casarès, for instance. A great actress. A great lady. Yet it is a Martine Carol who triumphs. I see in a magazine the story on Jeannot's farewell performance at the Comédie-Française: "This magnificent Britannicus." The journalists don't even know he plays Nero, being ignorant of Racine. The play's title is *Britannicus*, so Jean Marais can only be playing the part of Britannicus.

Were all historical periods vile? Possibly. Only what is noble remains. But I don't believe that our present means of *propagating* the vile existed—of smothering what is noble under immediate laurels. I know of course that Stendhal . . . that Balzac . . . that Baudelaire . . . but actresses live in the moment, and the clamor was made only around the great ones.

Marco Polo was not believed: "the liar of Venice." The priest at his deathbed denied him absolution because he would not admit his memories were lies. The terrible solitude of the poet who *testifies* and who is taken for a *fantasist* resembles this dreadful dialogue. The priest-notary: *"How could Jesus Christ have come down to earth if the earth were round?* That is heresy" (*sic*). And Marco Polo told little enough. It was his description of coal that provoked the greatest ridicule. A black stone that burns and replaces wood. He would never have dared tell about the unicorns of Sumatra. He kept to commercial matters—after all, he was a merchant and continued to be one after the Genoa prison.

In 1936 I astounded the directors of Radio City Music Hall by describing to them the magnificence and the machinery of the theaters of Japan. *They didn't believe me.*

Style of Mme Favini: "We're past all that." "I think he's a bit too subjective." "He's not atonal." "D'Annunzio, really . . ." "I like to keep Favini in his slippers" or "I hear you coming in those big clodhoppers of yours." (Favini got rich in the shoe business.)

Lucia says, "Papa is a B.O.F." "Now, now," her mother says, "leave your father alone." "I've given my daughter splendid toys, and all she wants to do is play with Fly-Tox." "I love factory chimneys and jewels." "My husband has bought some old junk by Picasso." (It's Favini who commissioned the portrait from me. I wonder why.)

The Barebacks were a family of industrialists from Nantes. Mme Favini has kept their accuracy with regard to figures. For instance, she says, "The fisc tried to get the best of us—but we're too smart for them." Very close to Councillor Machiavello, official lawyer of the Communist party. "My wife," Favini says, "is a real modern Gioconda. When she smiles, she terrifies me." Mme Favini: "Leonardo was a dabbler, a fantasist. I loathe fantasists. I stop at Schoenberg." "Paul Valéry entertains me with his childishness." Very misleading, very lofty—very peremptory. "The Palazzo Farnese is a real piece of bric-a-brac, a flea market. I wouldn't live there for five minutes. I made no secret of that with the ambassador." "The pope has a certain chic." "The queen of England is admirable—I wouldn't do such things myself, but you have to admit she does it well." Black and pale green are her colors. She wears nothing but pearls. "You don't catch pearls with vinegar." While posing she tells me about her ancestors: "The Barebacks are municipal magistrates." "I've had my ears done by Claoué. I make no secret of the fact. I think it's absurd to hide such things."

Sometimes she's vicious: "I hear that Colette's been decorated. What's the decorator's name?" Sometimes she simpers: "I'm just a provincial—a poor provincial. Tell me what's happening in Paris. Are they still doing abstract?"

What's wrong with the eyes of this year's carnival committee when they decide that the colors will be purple and turquoise?

. . . .

FEBRUARY 23

Poor André Brulé. He's dead—and he gets three lines. Once the idol of the Parisian public. Jouvet dies. Bad actor. Bad director. National mourning.

. . . .

FEBRUARY 24

Visit from Bebko, with the plans for *La Dame à la licorne*. I've done the sketches and indicated the shape and detail of the masks. Bebko's son wants to drop his mother because of his passion for underwater films. One more workshop going to pieces. And the only one.

The papers print the details of last Saturday's accident. The motorcyclist grazed a taxi full of American sailors on our right. He was thrown against the opposite sidewalk. Twenty-eight years old, and dead.

Lunch in Vallauris. Picasso was in the studio, where I went with Françoise to join him. He opens a locked door and we go into the room where *War and Peace* is kept. The first sensation is of a nave in a church, and apparently everyone who comes in here takes off his hat. I take off mine. The thing is of an incredible youthfulness and violence. A balance between delirium and calm. A marriage between Ingres and Delacroix. No form is realistic, but everything is true, with that internal truth which is the only kind that matters. And when we come out of there, reality seems pale, colorless, stupid, inert, dead.

The fresco which is going to be shown in Rome with a hundred canvases will end up in the Vallauris chapel. The panel will be curved so that the lines meet up above (the curve beginning very low). From right to left, the first panel shows War on his chariot or hearse and on his back a kind of hod filled with skulls. The figure is holding in his left hand a disk covered with microbes and surrounded by flying microbes. His right hand is brandishing a notched and bloody sword. War's steeds are trampling a huge book in flames (library of Alexandria). Above the horses, black silhouettes of warriors wave shadows of weapons. Opposite the horses rises a huge naked figure (Peace) carrying a lance and a shield on which you can make out a woman's face on which Picasso has drawn a dove with outspread wings. On the left panel a nude family is grouped on the grass. A woman is nursing a child and reading. A man is blowing on a pot of soup. Another is engaged in some sort of mysterious research. Farther on, a child is guiding a plow drawn by a white winged horse. Then some women are dancing. A faun is playing the flute, crouching on a seashell. Some sort of swimming or flying child is tipping over at the extreme left. In the air, a child with an owl on its head forms the center of a trapeze of perches, on the ends of which are hung a bowl of birds, a cage of fish, and an hourglass.

The whole thing is painted loosely, thickly, in broad strokes. You can guess at the sketches and corrections. Picasso has left the drips. He says, "You don't tell someone miserable to dry his tears."

He explains what he has done, undone, and redone. He says, "It's still the thieving magpie and the prodigal son—a fable." After lunch at La Galloise, I go back to the studio, and Picasso, after showing me canvases of Françoise and the children, takes me to the Ramié pottery.

He tells me a story to which he attaches the greatest importance and says, "You ought to make something out of it." He had just painted a face on a plate and noticed its resemblance to Huguette, wife of one of the potters. This face had a beard. "Well," he decided, "since it's Huguette, let's get rid of the beard." He takes away the beard and the face stops resembling Huguette. He puts the beard back and Huguette reappears. Worth noting that this young woman is pregnant.

At the pottery he shows me one of his inventions: he draws on the clay with colored chalks and then fires them in the kiln with a slip. The pastel or chalk is fixed and, for the eye, remains pastel and chalk.

I went back to the house to see Françoise. Her excellent canvases. Little girls dancing like mad creatures or monsters in front of groups of musicians. A sleeping woman, which reminds her to ask me for the text I wrote for Emmer's film of Carpaccio's *Legend of Saint Ursula*.

Françoise asks me about the Montparnasse days. "We argued

and fought," I tell her. "It was better than now, when everything is muffled and people are so indifferent, when you can show them anything—when they *know*."

At dinner, Picasso: "I joined the Communist party because I thought I would find a family. And that's what I found, with all the aggravation such things imply. The son who wants to become a lawyer, the son who wants to win the Prix de Rome. Never get yourself into a family like that."

"Besides," Françoise adds, "the Communists only respect people who don't belong to the Party. From members, they insist on the dues they only request from others—from you, for instance."

I ask Picasso what the Communists think of *War and Peace*. "They approve of it," he says. "It's up to me to give them the line."

Picasso gives me a plate he has decorated at the pottery. Mme Ramié gives me a big plate. A ram's head in relief, very fine.

I say to Picasso: "Young people today lack a certain heroism. Strange that no young person has tried to assassinate you." "I got a head start," he answers. This is quite true . . . Next to *War and Peace*, today's painters (I mean the painters of a declared boldness) can only seem weak and absurd.

Picasso: "I don't know what I'm going to do, nor what I'm doing. And if I want to tell Françoise, later on, what I've done, I can't find what to say. Painting is blind man's work."

About Chagall, who is working at the pottery: "I tell him all my secrets, and he thinks I'm trying to mislead him. If I sold them to him, he would believe me."

About Stravinsky (apropos of our quarrel): "He will never understand that between him and you isn't the same as between us."

On *Oedipus Rex*: "You're the one who made the scandal, not Stravinsky. His music gets better and better, more and more beautiful, but he can't make a scandal any more."

A book is being published which will have color reproductions of the whole of *War and Peace*, as well as of the smallest details. Mourlot is in Vallauris. Nothing Picasso invents fails to become immediately "historic."

Only children (exhibit at Muratore's, in Nice) can get this power and this freedom. That Picasso can connect a child's power with a painter's deliberate calculation seems to me a real miracle.

War and Peace is another tremendous insult to one's habits. Especially to the habits of Rome. That's why he's happy it's being shown there.

I say to Picasso, "Your winged horse looks like El Greco's *Cardinal Tavera* [in the Toledo hospital]."

Picasso: "There is no queen bee, there is an ordinary bee the others feed so she will become fatter and more important than the others." He must be right . . . Luckily for England, Queen Elizabeth is a queen, but it's an accident. Yesterday a Japanese woman told me that Kikugoro* was dead (he was Kikugoro IV). Kikugoro V is not his son. If the actor considers his son unqualified to replace him, he adopts a young actor who deserves to do so.

. . . .

WEDNESDAY · FEBRUARY 25

Pasquini's play† is delightful, funny, better than so many others. It's a theme in the air, this healer . . . Picasso was saying: "When all the artists have the same idea, it's not because they influence one another, it's because they're more or less successful at catching what's in the air. It's the proof that the notion is a valid one."

With regard to Mme Favini, Picasso says he spends hours with Sabartés making up such stories . . . It's the best exercise for the

---

*Cocteau had seen this famous Kabuki actor perform in Tokyo in 1936.

†Pierre Pasquini and Henri Mari, *Le Guérisseur*, a comedy first performed in Nice at the Palais de la Méditerranée, February 24, 1953.

imagination. He says, "You can only invent what already exists." Which is why what you invent always ends up being real.

Mme Guynet had told me: "Matisse has taken to his bed because Chagall is showing at Les Ponchettes. Now Chagall is sick because you're showing there." (Stupidity of painters.)

Mme Ramié: "Chagall pretends to seem stupid."

Picasso: "It's difficult to pretend so well."

Mme Ramié would like me to try some ceramics. (I won't.) I say, "I'll come some day." Picasso: "The first day you'll make nothing but junk, the way I did at first. You have to spend a year at the pottery." The potter's assistant tells me, "M. Picasso knows the work as well as any of us now, but he dares what we would never dare imagine or try."

How much you have to understand, how much you have to know for *War and Peace* not to look like the smears of some monstrous child, the Gargantua of painting.

When *Parade* was revived, I was so disgusted by the execution of Picasso's horse that I did it myself, at Laverdet's. The evening of the performance, the art dealers, Paul and Léonce Rosenberg at the head of the line, told Picasso that I had "redone the horse." Picasso, in a rage, dashed into the wings with his entourage. He looked at the horse and fell into my arms. "You're the only one who knows," he said, in front of the stupefied group. I had made the horse exactly according to his drawings.

Yesterday Picasso said to Françoise: "Jean needs only an hour of looking at *War and Peace* to reproduce it faultlessly on the other side of the world. It's an incredible thing." I had once reproduced from memory (I was living at Chanel's, in the Faubourg Saint-Honoré) the big fresco of the *Minotaur*. Picasso had signed it: "Jean did this Picasso." It was this big composition on wrapping paper that Paul Morihien one day cut up into strips for mailing books. (He had found it rolled up in a wardrobe. It was too big for one of my walls in the rue de Montpensier apartment, and he knew nothing, at the time, about the value of painted things.)

Picasso's aesthetic consists in consecrating, in *sanctifying* mistakes. So he can never make a mistake.

This is really the first time Picasso ever talked to me openly about the Communist party. "I had," I say, "the same business with the Catholics. My *Letter to Maritain* was written to create a family for myself. I had to escape."

Marcenac's article in *Les Lettres françaises*: "I distance myself from life, etc." Whereas I penetrate its essence.

. . . .

THURSDAY · FEBRUARY 26

Of course Mario and Pasquini have *asked* me for a few lines on *Le Guérisseur*. Which I produced. Mario is coming for them today. I've written such things often enough for troublemakers—it's only fair I do the same for someone so obliging.

I had told Picasso I was beginning to be annoyed by all the Rosenberg manifestos and declarations I was being asked to sign. "The Rosenbergs are doomed," he says, "and people couldn't care less. Let's do it for ourselves."

Covered the whole Favini canvas. Now it has to be painted.

Mme Favini: "I don't know where my daughter gets her fish-knife profile from . . ."

. . . .

SUNDAY · MARCH 1 · 1953

Health poor. Heart irregular. Fatigue the last eight days. Dr. Ricoux restores me with injections.

No news about *La Voix humaine* (revived Friday by Louise Comte). Odd silence. I had asked them to send a telegram.

Lunch at Bordighera for the show of American painting for which I had to write a catalog piece.

Telephone conversation with Louise Comte. There were disturbances in the house (balcony), as usual. But she doesn't think it was serious—only a few cuts to make in the "hellos." Besides, at the Comédie-Française there are always partisans. Memory of Bovy—sacrosanct. (Telephone call from Jeannot, who was there and describes Comte's success as considerable.)

. . . .

MARCH 2 · 1953

Lunch with the Pinis at Bordighera with Peggy Guggenheim.* Vernissage. Ministers, consuls, old ladies, and old American canvases which I knew. But everything nicely hung, nicely presented, ventilated by Jean Guérin's consideration. His own picture seemed the best one to me, with a serious charm, a deliberate grace. I talk on the radio and take Francine home, exhausted.

England expelled from India for having preferred commerce to wisdom, despite certain acute British intellects which offered to learn. But it was too late. (The Indian answer is admirable.)

France has become a colony, colonized by the uncultured. Her only hope will be to conquer her conquerors the way the Greeks subtly conquered the Romans, the way the Jews always manage to conquer those who massacre them.

At five I went to see Mme Maeterlinck. Impossible to find how to get into the villa.† Francine's chauffeur and I prowl around the platform overlooking the road. We make a stab at the terrace, the pools surrounded by plants. Finally Mme Maeterlinck shows herself

---

*In 1938 Peggy Guggenheim put on a large exhibit of Cocteau's drawings at her London gallery.

†Villa Orlamonde, originally the unfinished Casino Castellamare (1925), between Nice and Villéfranche-sur-Mer, on the basse Corniche.

and explains how we get down to where she is. The villa is enormous—a sort of Egyptian temple. It was the foundation of a casino which Maeterlinck bought and transformed into a place to live. I tell his wife that I have been asked at least eight times to stage *Pelléas*, to do the sets and costumes. Including the Opéra-Comique, to which I recommended Valentine.* And most recently at the Metropolitan and La Scala (which had already asked me to do it last year). For the film, we would have to find a Mélisande. And a Pelléas. Jean Marais would play Golaud.

Mme Maeterlinck lives in these vast halls, these corridors, these vestibules, with a tiny Pekingese and the ghost of Maeterlinck.

On her deserted beach the nudists gather. The villa, overhanging the sea, is exactly opposite the tip of the Cape. It's wedged into architectural fragments which will never be finished—they give it the looks of ruins.

Daisy Fellowes reports that one of the problems at the coronation is that of natural needs. No one can move or withdraw. Various devices have been invented, placed under skirts and in trousers . . .

Mme Maeterlinck: "*Pelléas* has been stolen from Maeterlinck. Sometimes they don't even put his name on the poster."

. . . .

TUESDAY · MARCH 3

Except perhaps in India (?), there is no longer any such thing as a great initiation. The only great initiation is that of finance. In antiquity the governments which do not derive from initiation and from the figure 3 collapse. Only the others flourish—but until the death of the initiated. The figure 2 soon collapses where it stands. The tripod offers the body a solid basis. Napoleon knew this, but

---

*Valentine Hugo designed the sets and costumes for *Pelléas et Mélisande* at the Opéra-Comique in July 1947.

he was doomed by the figure 1, by pride. A disciple of Pythagoras (some still survived, scattered throughout the world) warned him not to attack the Russians. To defend himself without attacking. It was too late. He had fallen prey to the delirium of dictators. He imagined himself freed from the mechanism of numbers.

Today's world is nothing but a preposterous chaos. Positivist science has destroyed the spiritual science, which was invincible and limitless. It was by this spiritual science that the Greeks defeated Xerxes at Delphi, without troops. It was this science which Daniel taught to Nebuchadnezzar. It always rejects a *visible* victory, the immediate result. Scattered, the Jews were invincible. They knew this. They know it no longer and gather together in Palestine. They can build nothing lasting, for all their subtlety. I realized this after my visits from Israelis.

. . . .

WEDNESDAY · MARCH 4

The marquise de Cuevas telephones from her hotel in Los Angeles to her husband at his hotel in Cannes to tell him that she has been ringing for room service for fifteen minutes with no answer. She asks him to telephone the hotel for service.

*L'Aigrette.** A ballet of worldlings who imagine themselves professionals. Success in Cannes, managed by the screaming Cuevas. Mme R. takes a bow on stage. Her huge lover (in Cuevas's box): "I feel just like the duke of Edinburgh."

Marshal Pétain, furious at being told his wife will be authorized to visit him in prison: "Leave me in peace!" The journalists accuse the courts of being heartless.

In Italy a sixteen-year-old student kills his teacher with a revolver

---

*Ballet by Princess Marthe Bibesco, music by Prince George Chavchavadze, choreography by Birger Bartholin, sets and costumes by Rina Rosselli; presented by the Ballets du Marquis de Cuevas at the Cannes Municipal Casino, February 27, 1953.

for giving him a 4 in math. "Did I deserve that 4? I guess so."
(The student fired four shots.) Genet was in Rome. The teacher
gets a national funeral.

In Tunis a doctor beats his wife. She dies. The profession manages
to cover up.

Style of the countless letters I receive: "I know you don't like
to receive letters which require an answer—but mine is different.
Etc."

Olivier Larronde's mother unhinged her son before he was born
by a mixture of misunderstood occult sciences. She believes him
destined for the reconciliation of nations. Olivier's struggle to
escape these fantasies has unhinged him even more. His younger
sister died of the same causes.

Splendid weather. This morning people from American television
are coming.

Every day I manage to add a page to the text for Bruckmann.

Genet phones; he's coming at three.

Pasquini talks about extending the exhibit at Les Ponchettes for
another ten days.

Dictated and sent to Sentein* the preface for the printers' year-
book.

Wrote the Willemetz preface. Dictated the chapter I have to
read for the Sigaux record (chapter of the monograph read by
me—scene from *Bacchus* read by Marais and Vilar—*Un Ami dort*
read by Fresnay).

Dreamed Sunday night that in order to save my friends, I had
to be stabbed in the back of the neck. Later I learned that the
wound would henceforth prevent me from inventing or creating
anything . . .

The Favini portrait almost finished. Mme Favini: "Be sure to

---

*François Sentein, born 1920, a journalist and writer and friend of Jean Cocteau
since 1941.

put in my daughter's freckles. She has to know someday how ugly she was."

The almost unpleasant odor of some yellow flowers growing near the studio. Maurice Bessy* writes that I should be careful never to touch the plant called "rue." It's the color of a salamander, and poisonous.

. . . .

MARCH 5

Stalin is dying. So the papers say. The whole world presents the incredible spectacle of an anxious hive—like the audience last night at a Nice Film Club where I was speaking.

Stalin paralyzed. He will be embalmed. Exhibited. Deified. Disobeyed. Amazing telegram from Eisenhower glorifying the camaraderie of the Russian people.

Charon telephoned: *La Voix humaine* perfect on Wednesday evening. Louise Comte a huge success.

Les Lettres françaises. A periodical supposedly addressed to the people (to the intellectuals among the people). I read it, unable to understand what is being discussed. By dint of trying to combine intelligence and style, the result is a tremendous obscurity.

Stupidity of the press. In *Noir et blanc* an article on the Élysée in which the reporter explains in five columns that the residence of the president of France was originally a brothel. Typical of the articles in which France smears herself with shit.

Saw Jean Genet, who is beginning to write again and tells me about a film project.

Noir et blanc: "Chaplin is as detested in England as in America,

---

*In 1953 journalist and writer Maurice Bessy was the director of the chief entertainment magazines in France. During the Cannes festival he published a daily bulletin, to which Cocteau contributed texts and drawings.

etc." Contagious disease of the age: to cover everything with garbage. Nothing escapes.

Oeuvres complètes. Orengo at work on the project. I am astounded by the number of works accumulated in my life. Since I confronted a problem for each one and struggled to solve it, abandoning my efforts only when I had achieved a result, I had never become aware of the totality. The calculation of each new work made me forget the preceding one. Will we manage, thanks to Bible paper, the tour de force of collecting everything in three volumes? (By eliminating a host of articles and prefaces which in and of themselves would constitute a series of books.) People have imagined I possessed a certain facility. It is precisely my lack of facility which hypnotizes me in my work and screens out all other considerations. Without realizing it, I have drastically *written*.

. . . .

MARCH 6

Stalin dead. The British report he was already dead when Moscow announced his cardiac crisis. The last colossus.

Stalin knew how to laugh, as I fear his successors do not. During a dinner with de Gaulle, he pretended to mistake Palewski for the Polish ambassador. Kissing his generals on the mouth in the Russian fashion, he asked de Gaulle: "Would you like this sort of thing?" Asking Churchill what he thought of this general and Churchill having replied that he felt a physical repulsion for his person, Stalin remarked, "Then find another one."

. . . .

MARCH 7

Malenkov to succeed Stalin, who died Thursday evening, March 5, at midnight.

Prizegiving at the Nice Film Club last night. Spoke a few words.

"If Goethe could have done it, instead of taking a young artist to Rome with him, he would have carried a sixteen-millimeter Kodachrome camera—and on his return he would have shown this amazing magic lantern to Eckermann and to his family."

Yesterday morning Colette and Maurice came to see us. She did not get out of the car, where we joined her for a visit. I find her greatly improved. I told her about the bee film, and she longed to see it. Last night I asked the Film Club to project it for her in her room. This is one of the artisanal privileges of sixteen-millimeter film. Bringing the projector to the house, the way hot water and a bathtub were brought before the invention of plumbing.

Matisse telephones that he went to the exhibit yesterday and that he found the tapestry superb. I'll visit him next Tuesday at the Régina.

I went to greet Chaplin at the airport, where he had flown in from Geneva. He got off with his wife. A man with a gray beard was the first one down the steps, and the broadcaster said: "A bearded man has just appeared. It's not Chaplin. Who can it be?" "Ask Cocteau," the bearded man shouted. "It's Ansermet." Then Charles appeared, whom I was very moved to see again after so many years. We fell into each other's arms amid a storm of flashbulbs.

Inaccurate texts of *Appogiatures* published by *La Table ronde* and *La Parisienne*. I wire Orengo and Parisot to revise the proofs. I had given corrected proofs to Parisot before leaving.

. . . .

MARCH 10

Among the books secretly passed over, the work of Saint-Yves d'Alveydre* (a student of Fabre d'Olivet)—a work republished by

---

*The theosophist Marquis Alexandre de Saint-Yves d'Alveydre (1842–1909) ad-

Jacques Weiss under the title *L'Autorité face au pouvoir*. Needless to say, it is unknown and not to be found. The only important documentation on political figures.

Went this morning to the Villa Mauresque. Raymond Mortimer talked to me about Mary Hoeck's translations . . . He is very severe: her writing is limp. Mortimer has just had a troublesome prostate operation that is being ignored because people are accustomed to laugh off such things, prostate difficulties being the domain of old generals. Somerset Maugham in great form, very lively, with gold rings on his green ascot. He asks me if I don't frequently regret the effort a film costs me. An art form so fragile and so fugitive. I answer that I do, but that everything is fragile and fugitive. What's left of Greece is a foot of the Eiffel Tower and a few statues on the Grand Palais and the Chambre des Députés. Nothing of Pythagoras and Heracleitus.

It sounds as if Green's play* is boring and poorly constructed . . . The funny thing is that Green, who has no sense of theater, should have it in his novels like *Minuit* or *Leviathan*.

Every week I get an idea for a play which would make its author a rich man. But I give it up because an authentic idea for a play must impose itself on you, importune you until you have to write the thing to get rid of it . . . Modern critics see no difference between inevitable plays and the other kind.

Bessy sends me his publication which prints plays and asks for permission to reprint *La Machine infernale*, if Gallimard will grant him the rights. Now *La Machine* is published by Grasset. Bessy's publication is printing Bernstein's *Évangéline*, an embarrassing and vulgar piece of trash: the supposedly "natural" dialogue reveals a

---

vocated "synarchy," i.e., a political organization in which executive powers and the spiritual order would coexist harmoniously. Author of *Mission des souverains*, 1882; *Mission des ouvriers*, 1883; *Mission des Juifs*, 1884; and others.

    Sud, a play in three acts by Julien Green, first produced on March 6, 1953, directed by Jean Mercure. The novelist's first play.

total unawareness of rhythm and of the French language. And the critics never see, for instance, that in my *Parents terribles* I abide by the strictest rigor—that the style of this play is a portrait of the "familiar style," that every syllable counts, and that an actor who changes one word would undo the whole thing.

Incredible persistence of young Michel Haddad (eighteen years old), who wants to make a film of my *Thomas l'imposteur*, against whom I raise—on purpose—a host of obstacles and who manages to overcome them all. *Combat* reports that he himself will play the part. He hasn't dared tell me so. He's only admitted that he's done the scenario, the direction, and the music. I've allowed him to go ahead because I believe it is vile to throw cold water on such enthusiasm and because I'm curious to see how a boy of eighteen imagines the First World War. He wants to shoot it at the Victorine—I've warned him that the Victorine has unfortunately become unusable because of the proximity of the Nice airport.

The mayor of Nice wanted to extend my exhibit, which is profitable for the city. Mme Guynet telephones that this is impossible because of the exhibit of books at the Bibliothèque nationale. The show will close tomorrow at Les Ponchettes.

Voltaire, who started the legend of the Man in the Iron Mask, says of this prisoner (whose face, he declares, *no one ever saw*): "There was sent to the Château de l'Île Sainte-Marguerite, off the coast of Provence, an unknown prisoner, of more than usual height, young, *and of the handsomest and noblest countenance*. This prisoner wore a mask . . . Orders were given that he was to be killed if he removed the mask." The funny thing is that George Mongrédien, who tries to prove in his book that Voltaire's story is ridiculous, collects all the inaccuracies except the one which I've noted and which seems to me the most characteristic of an invention. As for historical truth, I'm always inclined to think Alexandre Dumas is right. You can only invent what's true, and Dumas makes a dead history live.

Sometimes (rarely) before I fall asleep at night, I see, with my eyes closed, after several formations of colored spots with a fringe of other colors, tiny images of figures or objects, initially vague but growing more and more precise. These images are bright colored and extremely detailed. They correspond to nothing in my thoughts, to nothing I might draw or paint. They soon vanish and become vague spots. If I try to provoke these images—I mean if, having seen one appear, I wait for several more to come—they are unlikely to show up.

The papers report that already Stalin's sarcophagus will be displayed in Red Square, beside Lenin's. The pharaonic notion has occurred even to journalism's limited imagination. I had mentioned, in *Maalesh*, the resemblance between the Egypt of the pharaohs and the regime of the USSR. The great idea of our times is to have persuaded the slaves that they are free. But in Egypt they must have managed to convince the slaves that after death they would share in the privileges of divinization.

Prokofiev dead. His timing is bad. Another branch falls off my tree. Diaghilev. *Le Pas d'acier.** Slapping Dukelsky.† Since I hadn't seen Prokofiev again since those days, he remained quite young, red faced, his head shaved. Stravinsky used to say, "He has the stupidity of a Russian policeman." Stalin's death will put Prokofiev's on the fifth page (and a few lines). No doubt it will be mentioned after Stalin's funeral, which will be something extraordinary and

---

*Ballet in two scenes, music by Sergey Prokofiev, choreography by Léonide Massine, constructions and costumes by Georges Yakulov; first performed by the Ballets Russes on June 7, 1927.

†At the premiere of *Pas d'acier*, "a Soviet ballet," Cocteau, following an altercation in the wings, slapped the composer Vladimir Dukelsky (known later as Vernon Duke). In a letter to Boris Kochno, Diaghilev's secretary, Cocteau explained: "It was difficult to endure from Dima (with his top hat, his rose, his Louis XV cane, his tails) slurs on my Parisian frivolity. . . . My judgments were of an aesthetic and moral nature. I blame Massine for having turned something as great as the Russian Revolution into a carnival image accessible to ladies paying 6,000 francs for their box. My attack was not intended for the musician nor for the designer."

which Louis Joxe will be lucky enough to see. Prokofiev's music began the style which rouses interest without emotion. Impossible for such music to provoke a moral erection. Prokofiev had publicly asked to be forgiven for it and had declared, "I won't do it again," because Moscow criticized his music for not following the line. Doubtless not popular enough. French radio plays more of Prokofiev's music than Stravinsky's.

Frank telephoned. He got to Cannes yesterday with his film of *Les Parents terribles*.* After going through customs, he'll probably show it to me at Beaulieu.

Style of Vallauris: Picasso sends me a postcard which reveals his statue of the man carrying a lamb when you lift up a towel covering a bathing beauty's ass. This creature is being attacked by a child dressed as a cowboy and holding two revolvers.

. . . .

MARCH 11

The American radio announces, "The death of a great Russian." There follows the name of Prokofiev.

Flags at half-mast. M. René Mayer, in the Chamber, declares that this is a form of official condolence. Not to lower the flag would therefore be a political action, would express an "opinion." Just so that all the schoolboys are behaving properly.

Frank will show me the film at Beaulieu—Thursday, at five.

On the radio, I am always asked the same question apropos of Chaplin's films: Since you are so sensitive to plastic values in your films, aren't you shocked by their absence in Chaplin's? If I invoke plastic values, it's a matter of instinct, and I do so without being conscious of the fact. Chaplin's values are of a moral and emotional order. It comes to the same thing—he achieves a certain chiar-

---

Intimate Relations, a film by Charles Frank.

oscuro. Besides he is his own plasticity—his walk, his gestures are a dance.

. . . .

FRIDAY · MARCH 13

Mlle Boivin had mixed up all the pages of the monograph and even the original order. Everything had to be redone. This stupid task took over two hours.

Lunch tomorrow with Picasso. Clouzot telephoned from Vence. He'll come here for lunch Monday.

Saw the English version of *Les Parents terribles*. If I hadn't done the French film in '48, the British one would strike me as remarkable. The weaknesses come from the rather insipid *jeune premier* and from the fact that Léo is no longer the dorsal fin of the work: she becomes a nice English old maid. Yvonne is the best Yvonne after de Bray. The discovery is Madeleine. A Swedish girl. First class. Better than all the actresses who have played the part. Perfect to look at *and* to listen to. Frank spoiled the end by being overeager to show that "youth" has the future on its side. I suggest ending the film on Léo's line: "Now everything's where it belongs." I loathe any kind of Exit into the Sunrise—it always counters the dramatic emotion. To my knowledge this is the only faithful remake I have ever seen. Frank came here with the people from customs. Dr. Ricoux and his family were typically French: contrasting my film with Frank's and blind to all his work. (In his presence.) Besides, Frank is wrong to insist on showing the film at the festival. My presidency will make my situation a delicate one.

Apparently *Bacchus* has just had a considerable success in Berlin. But I haven't had any direct word. I heard this from Francine, who got it from Pierre Peyraud.

Jacques Ibert is supposed to come here today to arrange the text and music for the Versailles celebration.

Total stupidity of the magazine *Noir et blanc*; and they dare talk about my book! What will survive of our period: (according to them) Maeterlinck, *Cyrano de Bergerac*, Anouilh's *Antigone* (*sic*).

. . . .

MARCH 15

Lunch at Vallauris with Picasso. I took a big jar of caviar. Françoise brought out a bottle of vodka. Picasso ate a good deal and drank even more. He no longer takes his medicine and drinks no water.

Favini, Mme F.'s relations with Machiavello, the Communist lawyer from Milan. We talked a good deal about this family and about the danger of knowing such people.

Picasso asked me, since I'll be talking in Rome about *War and Peace*, if I would give a lecture when his exhibition opens. We went back to the studio to look at the fresco and various canvases of Françoise and the children. Then to the pottery, where Picasso had me do nine plates—engraved *à la pointe*. He will finish them and show them to me when I get back.

Dinner with Kisling* at the villa. We discussed our memories of Montparnasse. (Modigliani taking one of his drawings to use as toilet paper, just when Kisling had with great difficulty persuaded a buyer to come to the studio. The feuds between the artists. Modigliani's big portrait of me† taken to La Rotonde by Kisling to pay for his drinks. Max saying, "How can you help loving Jesus, since he was willing to play the part of a Père Ubu on earth?"

---

*Moïse Kisling, born in 1891 in Cracow, had met Cocteau in Montparnasse in 1916. He appears with Picasso, Max Jacob, Modigliani, André Salmon, and others in the historic photographs taken in Montparnasse by Cocteau that year. From this period date the portraits of Cocteau by Kisling and of Kisling by Cocteau. Shortly after this dinner, Kisling died in his villa La Baie at Sanary on April 29, 1953.

†This famous portrait of Cocteau (now in the possession of the Pearlman Foundation, New York) was painted by Modigliani in 1916, in Kisling's studio.

Michel Georges-Michel,* whom Kisling had beat up on the terrace
of the Dome. At the police station, Michel Georges-Michel inviting
Kisling to dinner, as well as Apollinaire, who had been his witness.
A friend of Kisling's agreeing to give him 150 francs for Picasso's
Harlequin and for five collages by Picasso and Braque. Someone
awful from the Bourse asking Basler† to buy him all canvases going
for less than 200 francs. Among which were fifteen Modiglianis, a
dozen Utrillos. . . .) Kisling is wearing an American tie, all the
colors of the rainbow. He tells me about his quarrel with Léger
in New York because he had answered a journalist asking him
who was the best American painter that it was Léger. I get a sense
of the terrible bitterness of all the painters against Picasso from
the way Kisling speaks of his "crockery" and from his amazement
that some young painter whose life Picasso has made impossible
hasn't yet killed him. (He does not use the verb in the figurative
sense I give it.)

Before going to Vallauris, I had received a visit from one M.
Mathieu, owner of a big hotel in Nice. He brought me his book,
The Secret of Happiness, and told me: "It's the Bible of our times.
Besides, I'm like Saint Thomas Aquinas—I can save the world.
My wife is an ambassadress of fashion." (He shows me a photograph
of his wife in a bathing suit.) "Here you see her sitting in front
of the poster of a lecture I gave at the Palais de la Méditerranée.
'*I am the secret of happiness*,' she used to say. Paul Reboux has agreed
to write a preface for me. What I prove, I prove as if I were
Descartes. What I prophesy, I prophesy as if I were Pascal. You'll
see, my discovery is that man will be saved by his machines.
He will work less and occupy his leisure in educating himself
and perfecting his character." This astounding imbecile has dis-

---

*Michel Georges-Michel (born in Paris in 1883, died in 1985), chronicler, novelist,
and painter.

†Adolphe Basler, art critic and dealer.

covered the secret of happiness: to regard yourself as a prodigy.

The day before yesterday, while I was waiting for Jacques Ibert, I was told a gentleman and a lady had arrived. I supposed it was the Iberts, but I found myself with strangers. The lady said, "We're here because Mme Favini sent us." It was Solange Morin, sent by Françoise. She had come to ask me for a text for the musicians' homage to Éluard.* I wrote it for her.

Arranged and corrected the five typed copies of the text for the monograph. Sent Orengo the chapter "A New Sexuality" in case La Parisienne asks for a text from me.

Yesterday Picasso talked about opium. "Except for the wheel," he said, "what else has man discovered?" He regrets that we cannot smoke freely and asks if I still smoke. I answer that I do not and that I regret it as much as he does. "Opium," he adds, "inspires kindness. As is proved by the fact that the smoker is not greedy about his privilege. He wants everyone to smoke." Impossible to follow the line less than Picasso—actually he belongs to the Party without being a Communist at all.

Picasso: "People think I'm rich, but they forget the fortune I have to pay in taxes. Even when I give presents, the fisc thinks I'm robbing it."

Cold wind. Picasso says it often freezes on this part of the coast. His son Paulo was living in an icy hotel in Vallauris where the owners would tell him: "When you get up, there's no need for heat: you move about. And at night there's no need for heat: you go to bed."

The police chief of Vallauris is always with Picasso. Picasso asks him what people think of a police chief who is inseparable from a Communist. The police chief couldn't care less. Picasso suspects

---

*Concert given April 15, 1953, at the Maison de la Pensée Française, avenue Matignon, Paris, consisting of poems by Éluard set to music by Claude Arrieu, Georges Auric, Elsa Barraine, Robert Caby, Henri Cliquet-Pleyel, Louis Durey, Francis Poulenc, and Henri Sauguet.

him of secretly writing detective novels. He takes him along to
the bullfights at Nîmes.

Picasso tells Mme Ramié: "You can give seventy plates to Cocteau; he'll do them for you one after the next." He and I are the
only ones who have that kind of faculty for work.

I mention the invasion of visitors and journalists. Picasso answers:
"We can't complain about a full house. Sometimes I send them
over to see Prévert. But that doesn't interest them. They tell me
he's not 'international.' "

Someone will be sure to say that Picasso's creative impulse is
of a diabolic order. But the devil cannot create, he can only destroy.
And of course someone will be sure to say that Picasso's creation
is a destruction. Perhaps, but there cannot be creation without
destruction, without destruction of what is. That Picasso disturbs
painters, that he crushes them, that this huge glutton devours
them, is perfectly true. If they dream of his death, they are wrong;
his works will be even more active than his person. But his death
would be a catastrophe. Such a genius will not come again.

Worked for Versailles. I'd like to finish the text with two stanzas
in verse. I've already written about a hundred, but I'll only keep
two of them. When I tell Picasso about this, he says that he has
several notebooks full of preparations for *War and Peace*. They'll be
published in the book.

Picasso. He has established as a kind of dogma that everything
"well made" betrays a will to aestheticism, a lack of spiritual
elegance. So that he smears a face over a host of well-made faces.
This "ill-made" quality so characteristic of him, and which results
from a thousand investigations, deceives the young, who do not
suspect the rhythm of his work. So that he misleads those who
like to smear anyway and discredits in advance those capable of
contradicting him, who will be taken for aesthetes. He is a terrible
warrior, knowing every trick in the book, agile as a matador.
Matisse cannot say five words without mentioning his name. He

is the nightmare and the idol of painters. Unique situation. Besides, the money involved with his person makes it impossible to carry out his destruction. He rules, against painters, against politics, against everything.

. . . .

MARCH 17

Matisse. He still has that baby face, those pink cheeks emphasized by the white beard, just like Saint-Pol Roux. His body rather shapeless in the wheelchair. You can guess at a sort of armature under the sweaters. His granddaughter (Pierre Matisse's daughter) is here from America: Twenty years old. A redhead. Charming, and very American in the way she dresses. A white blouse, pointed breasts, black leather belt, gypsy skirt. She says that in America no one dares open his mouth—immediately suspect. Police very active. Everyone under observation. Matisse shows me a huge wall decoration in cutouts which he is finishing for a garden in America. Sun. Head in the center. Flowers. He works the way Renoir used to sculpt, from his wheelchair with a long stick. He cuts up the colored paper himself and indicates where the pieces should be pinned.

Picasso's (defensive) critical spirit dissolves as soon as you work alongside him. He then becomes quite fraternal. Each time I finished a plate, he would take it away to Mme Ramié, exclaiming, "He hasn't missed once." He also enjoyed showing indirectly that Chagall "missed" frequently.

Last night read the translation of Goncharov's *Oblomov* that Dimitri Markevich sent me. A strange book. In Dostoyevsky the Russian confusion is admirable. Here its edges fray out, and it diminishes the strength and relief of Oblomov's character, which might be a "type."

Matisse had telephoned—"Your tapestry is splendid." Picasso

has nothing to say. I think this success was intolerable to him. He spoke most of the drawings of Francine and the portrait of Mme Favini, which he prefers to all the rest.

Russia has the best scientists, especially the best biologists. Five doubles of Stalin were under observation to discover the leader's possible reactions. Nowhere more than in Russia does man seek to hold himself responsible, [and nowhere does he] react more violently against irresponsibility. The world's only chance is that the foreseeable proves to be unforeseeable, and things always turn out differently from what was feared. There exist vast secret powers. A rhythm of nature which cunningly opposes the correctives we try to impose upon it.

.   .   .   .

MARCH 19

Turin.

Yesterday, leaving Sospel, we had an automobile accident which might have been very serious. Attempting to avoid a military jeep which had turned in front of us without warning, Fernand must have thrown the car against the cliff and a telegraph pole. The Bentley is wrecked, but we had only the shock of the collision: Francine's left cheek was scratched, Édouard's forehead—Fernand and I were unhurt. Police, lawyer, photographers for the insurance. Telephoned from a hotel to Toso (the garage at Saint-Jean) to send a big car with maps and a chauffeur with a passport. At five the car arrives. We change vehicles. Fernand stays with the wreck. The second time that he cannot follow us to Italy. The first time he had taken along an old passport which showed him with a beard. We had to leave him there in the mountains, like an admiral sinking with his ship. Yesterday poor Fernand had tears in his eyes. The mountains full of snow. Reached Turin around nine o'clock.

Visit this morning from Mlle Antonetto. Very gracious and quite

understanding. She gives me our program with a certain appre-
hension. Lunches, journalists, radio, and television. Francis Poulenc
appears in the lobby. He played last night before a public of very
chilly old ladies. Arthur Rubinstein had sworn he would never
play again for such a public. All of which alarmed me, for my
text* is rather severe. But it seems that the lecture public is much
more mixed, younger and more agreeable. More accessible.

Five o'clock. Lunched at the house of the president of Fiat and
of the association. Apparently he wanted to arrange a sort of
Annales† in Turin. His lecturers would then go on to Milan, Genoa,
Rome. This is why, he tells me, the association has widened its
circle to include these cities. At five-thirty he calls for me at the
hotel for the press conference. To spare me others like it, they
have brought the journalists from Milan, Genoa, Rome.

Nothing intimidates me and embarrasses me more than such
sessions, where, in the last analysis, the journalists are quite as
intimidated and embarrassed as I am. And what is there to say?
They form a notion of us, a false notion, which is convenient for
them and which they abide by. To destroy this notion would compel
them to do more work. I shall try to speak as little as possible.

Rome centralizes more and more. Milan centralizes to the det-
riment of Turin. In the old days, Italian cities were autonomous—
like the cities of Germany. Turin, Milan, Genoa were countries.
Rome's growing importance relegates them to provincial status.
They suffer from this condition and try to preserve some shred of
their old autonomy.

What do people know about me in Italy? Some films, some
books, for French is widely read, so that the Italians wonder why
translations are made. But my name has outstripped my work, and

---

*Apparently taken from *Démarche d'un poete*, an unpublished monograph.

†Organ of the "Université des Annales" founded by Yvonne Sarcey, *Les Annales-
Conferencia*, suspended in 1940, revived since 1946. As the title suggests, this was an organization of lectures as well as a periodical.

the latter is too numerous to catch up. Everything I'll say tomorrow will be so much Chinese for the people listening to me. I dread it. It's true that I prefer anything to answering falsely to what is expected of my person. I prefer to disappoint and to remain true.

Press conference—very friendly and simple. Except for two lady journalists who wanted to see me alone and who asked me questions of detail impossible to answer, I spoke to groups, and readily.

Television in the evening. Not too bad. Always difficult to answer succinctly the questions the lady asks. You see yourself on a tiny screen placed between the cameras.

. . . .

MARCH 20

Lunch today with Igor Markevich.

Traveling, you wonder if that intolerable Paris isn't the only capital not a provincial city. My talk is at six. Tomorrow Genoa by car. Genoa–Milan by car. Milan–Rome by plane if possible. Poulenc tells me "everyone is in Rome." Which must mean the several individuals I avoid meeting in Paris.

When I ask Markevich why he has given up his own compositions to conduct those of others, he tells me that he tried out *Le Paradis perdu**** and that there was nothing wrong with it now, that the score had *hardened*, had actually gained strength. He had been disappointed by the reception his works had met and had turned his back on them to become an orchestra conductor. He believes his works have labored in the darkness and that he will now, gradually, start performing them. I should certainly like to hear our cantata again. I had written the words to music already com-

---

*Oratorio by Markevich, 1934–1935. In 1934, while staying with Markevich at Corsier-sur-Vevey, Cocteau had collaborated with him on the text of this work.

posed. This method gave a certain mystery and strangeness to the piece.

One scarcely conceives of a foreigner coming to speak to a French public in his own language. Yet that is what happens almost everywhere in the world where the French speak their own language in public and are understood.

The press is full of the affair of Picasso's portrait of Stalin.* I had lunch with Picasso the day this portrait was published in *Les Lettres françaises*. He discussed it with a smile and a certain anxiety. The portrait, executed in five minutes, certainly had something of a caricature about it—something satirical. To say that the portrait is not sufficiently realistic is inaccurate. It is one of the first bad drawings Picasso ever did. Aragon must have asked him to send it too quickly. And after all, Picasso did not know Stalin. The affair is therefore an excuse to do damage to Aragon and his "intellectualism." Moscow must have issued severe orders against the French Communist party's intellectual and opportunistic tendencies. I'm glad to be in Italy and to avoid this nonsense in which Mauriac finds an opportunity to play his part. Some say, "The portrait isn't realistic enough." Others: "This is what comes of forcing Picasso to do a realistic portrait." Both are absurd. Picasso is capable of anything, as he has proved countless times. But I was astonished by the freedom he was allowed. First blow: Aragon. Second blow: Picasso, very likely. Éluard is no longer here to defend him.

Evening. All done. Wonderful theater, all gold inside, and packed. I read without reading. Extremely warm and attentive audience. A thousand times better to be hard to follow than to treat a foreign audience as if they were children. The mistake made by Jules Romains and Maurice Garçon. Nothing is more wounding to a foreign audience. This audience is grateful to believe it can follow

---

*This charcoal portrait was published on March 12. On March 18 a dispatch from the Central Committee of the Party categorically disapproved of the work.

you, even if it does so with difficulty. I was to speak for an hour. I spoke for an hour and twenty minutes. In the other cities I shall make some cuts. After the session went to the reception at the center. The French consul was lavish with his thanks.

. . . .

MARCH 21

Reached Genoa by highway. We had brought Mlle Antonetto with us. I am to speak at five-thirty. I cut the passages which extended the text. It's not stage fright I have—but a special uneasiness comes over me whenever I have to speak in public.

Three A.M. Nightmare. The Doge's Palace. There were too many people for the little theater. Freezing. The microphone hisses. Doors open. I realize no one can hear me, and I skip pages. The audience really very kind. We go for a drink at the center. Dinner that evening at the Marquise Doria's. We stay till two in the morning because the atmosphere is charming. Back again for lunch before leaving for Milan.

I spoke fifteen minutes too long. Cuts for Milan and Rome.

. . . .

MONDAY · MARCH 23

Lunch at the Dorias. Leave at five, in the car. Milan by eight. Grand Hotel. Dinner at Giannino—where I am given a book published by the restaurant.

Wealth and avarice of the Genoese. The shipowners have huge fortunes and give nothing for the construction of a concert hall. Concerts are given in the ducal palace where I spoke, and where the acoustics are wretched.

We are received in Milan by the giant Visconti.* I see his belly. Édouard his chest. Francine his legs.

At the Dorias, someone says: "Unfortunately, Catholicism has neglected Christianity and left it in the hands of the Communists, who have made what they wanted out of it. So that it prevails nowhere."

Stendhal would have liked the Palazzo Doria. Here anything can be discussed with an incredible freedom.

We were talking about great actresses without theaters. Luisa Casati,† the Morosini (in Venice, women in the marketplace would say to her, "God be thanked for making you so lovely"). I ask if such women are ever seen nowadays among young Italians. Doria says not, that what is prized today is a "good mother" style—the style of Queen Elizabeth.

In my text I say: "Poets are jails. Works are the convicts who escape." Doria tells me that one society lady understood me to be an escaped con.

Others had decided I must be a Communist because I admire Picasso.

The Genoese high court is renowned for its terrible severity toward any form of licentiousness, however slight, and hands down its judgments beneath a vast fresco of naked women.

The Dorias have kept only the top floor and rent out the rest of the palace. Their terrace overlooks the garden and the silver tide of the roofs of Genoa. An amazing carapace of slates and flat houses on which the corner windows are painted in trompe-l'oeil.

The lawyer tells me: "The Genoese shipowners have a surprising ability to conceal their fortunes. Even what they admit exceeds

---

*Ferdinando Visconti.

†Luisa Amman, heiress of a great industrial fortune of Viennese origin, wife of the marquis Camillo Casati and a companion of D'Annunzio. The extravagance of her behavior, costumes, and residences was celebrated. She died in London during the 1950s.

the wealth of all the other cities of Italy. When they suffer a loss at sea, the captain is always held responsible."

In Milan the traffic is so complicated that we take a taxi to return to the hotel. The police dog sitting beside the driver lies down as soon as he catches sight of a policeman, drivers not being permitted to take their dogs.

Four o'clock. Reception at noon at the Centre Français, where Simone de Beauvoir's sister is the directress. Simone's voice and face. Incomparably graceful reception. Everyone speaking impeccable French. Lunch alone. Rest until six.

Five o'clock. Filmed at the hotel bar.

. . . .

TUESDAY · MARCH 24

Yesterday it went off just right. Vast and magnificent new theater underground. In fact, it is the first new theater which surprises me by its luxury. Packed. My voice carries. The cuts kept me from getting tired. I spoke for exactly an hour. The success has a meaning. The young dancer from the Latin American ballet company listening in the wings says, "I wish I could dance the way you talk." I could see from Francine's face and Édouard's that everything was going well. That evening we dined with the giant. We're taking the plane for Rome at two—I'm speaking at six.

"Which side is Cocteau on?" a journalist asks Rognoni, who answers: "No side. He's an independent anarchist."

Filling the house in Milan and taking several bows is, apparently, a tour de force in a city where Geraldy's *Toi et moi* is the only popular French work. True, it's not the same public who comes. The success of *Toi et moi* nonetheless remains a rather pathetic proof of the lack of understanding of our works. I'm sure Simone's sister has done a good deal to change this situation. She and her husband, a teacher who is a former student of Sartre's . . .

. . . .

WEDNESDAY · MARCH 25

We get to Rome by plane at four-thirty. I'm to speak at six. Still the same uneasiness—it must be the same feeling as when they come to your cell to take you to the scaffold. Once on stage I leap right in. But beforehand I can't manage to convince myself that there's nothing to it.

A good audience, perhaps more sensitive but perhaps more superficial as well. The photographers get up on the stage and blind me. The audience yells at them. Letters: "We don't want to have anything to do with that audience—come to ours. Etc." But it seems to me that people who despise this audience would do better to come and hear me. "I didn't go to *Orphée* because the wretched Malaparte was there introducing you. Etc." Now it is just those people we need in the audience. Reception. Fatigue. Flight. Calm dinner at Apuleius in Ostia, which gives us two "Etruscan" vases. I fall into bed. Besides, the "lecturer's" chair was too low and I had to read standing, hampered by the ridiculous microphones, which distort your voice and never help at all. But on the whole, a very good final session.

How quickly you create ghosts out of what you no longer see in front of you—you fool yourself in this strange farce of time. For me, Francesca Bertini was a lovely ghost of the silent screen. And yesterday I hear she is living in the hotel and would like to see me. I go into a vast salon like the set of one of her old films. An orchestra is playing off key, like those in the hotels of my youth. Francesca gets up from a table where she was writing me a letter. Absolutely not the same person. But whether she's had surgery or whether she keeps her looks by the determination and will of women of her generation, she doesn't look old at all. She tells me that she's acted *La Dame aux camélias* in Spain and in Spanish three hundred times and that she's going to be in a film of *Moll*

Flanders. I ask her if she'll make it in England, which seems to me indispensable. She shrugs a shoulder covered with pink daisies: "They don't understand anything nowadays. They want me to shoot their *Moll Flanders* in modern times and in Rome. It's my dream to play the queen in *L'Aigle à deux têtes* or any other role in one of your plays. (I immediately think of Jocasta.) I answer that for the moment I have no stage projects. She must be much younger than I had imagined. You always add years to the lives of famous actresses who begin very young.

In Rome, Count R. shows me a picture of Vesuvius by a "modern" Italian painter. He says, "I can't go any farther." I tell him that the journey wouldn't be very tiring.

During these four performances in four very different cities, I came to realize the value, the necessity of studying the audience for a proper presentation of one's words. Despite a real knowledge of the French language in all four audiences, it was indispensable to help speech along by gesture and to find a slow rhythm which gives the illusion of being rapid. Little by little I cut all the paragraphs where the writing was too concise to cross the footlights. The Rome public seemed to understand the nuances better, because it didn't venture as deeply into the whole. I think the audiences in Turin and Milan were more attentive, less distracted by Rome's busy frivolity. I wonder what will happen to the Picasso exhibition—if it will provoke anger or astonishment.

The Russian story is inconceivable. The triumph of bourgeois art, of the platitude of the Salon des beaux-arts in a revolutionary country which entertains all the affectations of bourgeois painting, bourgeois literature. Russian communism should annex the left of every kind and country to itself. It admits only the vilest right. Picasso a Communist, "Comrade Picasso" is the most amazing anachronism of all. It actually happens (in Italy, for instance) that one is thought a Communist because one admires Picasso, who represents precisely what communism condemns.

And those idiots on the right, who should take advantage of the situation to exalt the left in art. But the Church and communism are just alike in their hatred of genius.

Moravia is on the Index. Yesterday he told me: "My books are on the Index but not the films made from them, because they've already undergone a diminishing transformation."

Picasso's paradoxical strength—although a Communist, he's managed to have his Roman exhibit held under the auspices of the Italian government.

Idealist naïveté of French communism. Like the French lady who had slept with Wilhelm II and refused to take money. "What can I do for you?" She flings herself at his feet: "Sire! Give us back Alsace-Lorraine."

· ·

THURSDAY · MARCH 26

I've done twelve plates for the Grand-Véfour. And prepared a dozen more with colored backgrounds. Oliver wanted seven. I'll advise him to publish two services of twelve.

A visit from Chanel, with Déon. She tells me about Green's play Sud. Anouk Aimée doesn't look like a jeune fille but an old maid schoolteacher. Jean Mercure didn't leave the young actors free enough, when all they had in their favor was the instinctive charm of their clumsiness.

A letter from Green yesterday: "I cut a good deal and added a few little explanatory sentences." Julien is a man of interiors and solitude. Not a man of the theater, of crowds. This business of the stage seems like a dream to him. When Chanel asked him, on the first night, if he were afraid, he answered: "Afraid? No. Why?"

The garden when we return is filled with flowers. After the plates for the Véfour, I'll get onto the Versailles business. I dealt with Ibert in Rome. He wasn't too sure of what I would do;

he must be used to very specific outlines. No, this kind of thing requires a certain amount of luck, a synchronism *of the last minute.*

Letter from Parinaud: "*La Parisienne* is being surrounded by a kind of conspiracy of silence." Of course it is. Silence is the great weapon of noise.

Mme Favini. I sent Picasso this telegram from Milan: *Demanding apologies and explanation from Cocteau for my portrait. Counting on your testimony. Léonor Favini.*

Remarkable that in the preposterous affair of the Stalin portrait, no one ever attacks Picasso: they attack Aragon. Letters from concierges. Outraged letter from Fougeron, a social realist who reveals all his rancor against a great painter nothing will ever enslave.

This business of Stalin's portrait would be funny if it weren't tragic. The portrait isn't criticized for being a bad drawing by Picasso. It is criticized for not being realistic, whereas it is the height of realism but, alas, a failure—which is quite natural, since Picasso didn't know Stalin and was obliged to make the drawing in five minutes. Total misunderstanding, over which the world press licks its chops.

Picasso's answer to the journalists: "You don't insult someone who sends a funeral wreath just because the wreath is ugly."

I was forgetting to say, because those who will someday read these lines won't know what I'm talking about, that *Les Lettres françaises* published a page of "outraged" letters from all the Communist cells in France. "What was needed was to show the genius, the kindness, the fatherly warmth, the humor, the nobility, etc., of our Stalin." ("We know the attachment of Comrade Picasso to the workers . . . etc.") The affair of the Stalin portrait is too symbolic of our period for me to pass it over in silence. The public raised to the rank of critic. This has never been seen before.

· ·

SATURDAY · MARCH 28

Finished the twenty-four plates for the Véfour. I'll wait for them to dry before reworking them in detail. Preparing the preface for Venice.

Dufy dead. The funeral was in Nice while we were in Italy. Telegram from Parinaud for *Arts*. Sent him the article this morning. "Raoul Dufy's work is a great inimitable signature . . . etc." Another man from our crew who's fallen into the sea.

Lunch at Monte Carlo with Chanel and the Mille brothers.*

At four o'clock, visit from the organizers of the Versailles festival.

Picasso told me that Aragon had a slight stroke in Moscow, with some loss of memory. The campaign against him continues. I am afraid all this exhaustion will be dangerous for his health.

Telegram from Seghers. The commercial edition of *Le Chiffre sept* appears Wednesday.

· ·

SUNDAY · MARCH 29

Carole arrives.

For Picasso, everything always turns into fame. The Communists dare not attack him. The world of *Le Figaro* exalts him against the Communists. *Paris-Match* is full of color photographs of his family and his works.

Visit from Pierre Larivet, whom I had sent to Claoué to have his face put back together. In the same state as all the young people whose letters come every day. What is to be done? Advice is

---

*Hervé Mille, born 1909, journalist, editor of the magazines *Paris-Match, Marie-Claire*, and others; Gérard Mille, 1911–1963, decorator.

useless. If I recommend a young man, it is immediately assumed that I am trying to unload him on someone else.

In Anouilh's ballet *Le Loup*,* Roland Petit has copied the teeth and fur out of *La Belle et la bête*. No one notices where he gets his inspiration.

The *Bacchus* episode with the Church. The Communists came to my defense. The portrait of Stalin episode with the Communists. The Catholic circles come to Picasso's defense.

Chanel luncheon yesterday. The Mille brothers now realize the danger of a theater gala (Green). Even the best-disposed people understand things only when they suffer the consequences themselves.

Received the organizers of the Versailles festivities. I offer to record my text in Nice, to record Ibert's music separately, and to come up and mix the tape later. The lighting of Versailles will cost 40,000,000 francs. The whole thing will cost from 60,000,000 to 70,000,000 [francs]. I don't see how they can make this up by what they take in. Tickets will cost 200 francs. They count on ten thousand spectators for each session. Under Louis XIV the fountains could function only ten minutes at a stretch. The mechanism has remained the same, so they can function only during my text. The loudspeakers will be hidden behind the Latona basin and up in the trees.

I've prepared the Versailles text. Two stanzas form a balance at the beginning and the end. Between the stanzas sentences will be spoken, like columns. The loudspeakers, the darkness, the park enforce a certain (slightly funereal) pomp. The converse of the "autumnal" genre.

No one dares state in public what he says to me in letters and

---

*Ballet in three scenes by Jean Anouilh and Georges Neveux, music by Henri Dutilleux, choreography by Roland Petit, sets and costumes by Jean Carzou; first performed in Paris on March 17, 1953, with Roland Petit in the role of the Wolf.

dedications. From all over the world I receive the evidences of a love which remains a secret. No doubt this is a kind of occult power, a style of fame that is inevitable. My style.

Incredible number of ignorant, illiterate people who are driven by the craving to write and who ask me for help.

.   .   .   .

APRIL 1 · 1953

Lunch at Vallauris with Picasso and his daughter Maria-Concepción (Maya). She is eighteen, and her profile looks like those I used to draw of her father in Naples in 1917 (as Picasso reminds me). We talk about the affair of the (Stalin) portrait. When I say, "They're going to kill Aragon," Françoise tells me that Elsa has written her, "This portrait is a homicide by carelessness." *Aragon is unable to write at all.*

We go to the pottery to see my plates. Georges Salles, whose portrait Picasso is going to do, joins us there. Mme Cuttoli was in the shop. Copenhagen and Stockholm have asked her to persuade me to come in November. The woman who is working on my tapestry has broken her arm, which is delaying the work. But she is unwilling to entrust it to her assistants. My plates are very simple, and Picasso has left them white. I give one to Mme Ramié, one to Françoise, one to Maya. And bring the others to Francine. On the bottoms Mme Ramié has left the mark "After Picasso." I tell Paulo, "Your father always finds a way to come out on top, even when he is underneath."

.   .   .   .

APRIL 3

Disturbing letters from Rosen. By making stupid economies, they're going to ruin the ballet.

For the last four days, I've been working hard on the big canvas: *Birth of Pegasus*. Linear organization of an extreme complexity. I was able to manage it all this morning. I dare not begin to paint. I know what I must do—but I wonder if I am able to do it. It's been a year now that I've been dreaming of this picture. How I'd like to bring off this characteristic version of the "literary picture"!

Telephone from the secretary of the Cannes festival. Dinner Sunday in Cannes with Favre Le Bret. Meeting of the jury at four. The *Orphée II* is docked near the Virginie Hériot monument.

. . . . .

APRIL 5

I am sent a magazine in which young Haddad says he plans to become the French Orson Welles and other self-advertising stupidities. I have had to write him a letter that will be unpleasant to receive. Moreover, in the same paper he has been so indiscreet as to publish in facsimile the letter I had written to André Bernheim* to do him a favor. He had introduced himself to me as a worker. The sauce is curdling. I never dare throw cold water on enthusiasm, and this is the result. Nothing more difficult than to help young people.

Cannes. First jury meeting, which elects me president. We are shown the Disney film *Peter Pan*. Delighted by its grace and surprising technical achievement. Spaak says: "I am amazed by your enthusiasm. It bores me to tears. I have other games to play." Now it is precisely because this film is quite far from my own preoccupations that it delights me. I too have other games to play, and I regret it. Traffic between Nice and Cannes intolerable. Too many cars on narrow roads. From Antibes to Juan-les-Pins, bumper to bumper.

---

*Parisian impresario, owner of the Théâtre de la Madeleine.

I hadn't understood that Cannes required my presence from tonight. I'll go Tuesday to see the film and will put up Wednesday at the hotel until the *Orphée II* is ready. I didn't think I was expected at Cannes until the twelfth.

I'll take notes on each film seen in order to read them to the jury before the vote.

A newspaper has repeated that I found Clouzot's film splendid. Whence the ill humor of the Americans, who claimed we had made up our minds in advance. Favre Le Bret has had to go to Hollywood to persuade them to take part in the festival.

Finished the main work of *The Birth of Pegasus*. I've rubbed in the paint dry, which gives the picture the style of fresco.

. . . .

APRIL 8

After the Cuttoli lunch I'll go to Cannes to see a film and put up at the Carlton until the *Orphée II* is inhabitable. Next Monday probably. The festival is over on the twenty-ninth. I'll reserve tickets for Munich (May 2). Bebko made a mistake, sending a carnival head to Munich instead of the little unicorn masks.* We'll probably have to repaint and recut everything.

Cannes. Odd jury. Chauvet has to explain the films (which he has difficulty understanding) to Spaak, who doesn't understand them at all. Yesterday, as we were leaving the American film, Maurois was arriving to give a lecture in the rather chilly big hall, escorted by about fifty people who constituted his skimpy audience. Visit from Maurice. Colette is returning to Paris the day after tomorrow. She didn't even know that Michel de Bry had asked me in her name for a drawing for the cover of the record of *L'Enfant et les sortilèges*. Nor did de Bry even thank me for sending

---

*For Cocteau's ballet *La Dame à la licorne*.

him the thing. Nor has Sigaux ever mentioned the recording I made for him in Nice. Contemporary manners. Colette says, "When they've fired their shot, you never see them again." Oliver telephones, asking for his plates. Édouard will photograph them in color tonight. We'll pack them tomorrow. In my absence I've asked Édouard to paint the crab sketched in at the extreme lower right of *Pegasus*.

Dinner here last night with Chanel, who wants to rent Jeannot's houseboat so as not to spend the sunny days in the rue Cambon.

If I were the only judge of the festival, I would give the prize for best actor to Walt Disney for Captain Hook. We have to award a grand prize and six others of our choice, which isn't hard to do. If I create a prize for magic, a prize for dance, etc., and if we have to have two for actors, there's no room for direction, music, shorts . . . I'll suggest giving prizes for interpreters outside the cinematographic prizes. Impossible to create a prize for dialogue, because of the foreign languages. The more films I see before the festival, the freer I'll be afterward. I'll show Francine and Édouard only the films that are really worthwhile.

I'd like to leave the yacht as little as possible to avoid contact with the critics and the personalities I don't enjoy—and the journalists, to whom the rules forbid us to give our opinion.

I'm still trying to figure out the meaning of the myth of *The Birth of Pegasus*. Poetry born from the Gorgon's severed head. I won't show Perseus's face. Impossible to "represent" the face of the hero who takes part in this mystery.

Endless Austrian film.* (And of the nationalistic variety.) After which I spent a horrible fifteen minutes, which proves how right I am to be living elsewhere. The radio had me questioned by three children between ten and thirteen—a boy and two girls. These wretched kids talk about everything under the sun, and stupidly

---

*April 1, 2000, a film by Wolfgang Liebeneiner.

besides! They don't even understand the words they use. They judge. They ask our qualifications to judge. They imagine that there's something called a "modern period." This modern period, according to them, should exclude poetry, definitively dead and outdated. This must be the fault of their schools and their teachers, who have dried them up prematurely. *I was trembling with disgust.* And I thank heaven for preserving my childhood. These kids have lost theirs. They are worthy of the ladies and gentlemen in the Carlton bar.

. . . .

APRIL 9

No question about it, I belong on the side of the accused, not of the judges. Edgar G. Robinson said to me last night, "I've always played thieves and criminals, and now I'm a judge." We went to have a drink together after the Brazilian film*—which is, in my opinion and in his, "a little too pretty." It lacks what keeps the French from understanding *Les Enfants terribles.* Photographic beauty, skillful composition, picturesque faces and costumes—everything keeps you from believing in the drama.

Those children yesterday: I understand why a boy shoots his teacher for giving him a low grade. The blame goes to the teachers who create monsters. Where did those three monsters come from yesterday? Probably from a school where they are taught nothing at all.

Some questions asked by the three children: "Why should you judge? It's up to the public to judge." "Why does Picasso exhibit his pictures, since no one understands anything about them? He should keep them for himself." "Surrealism is ridiculous. You see what you see." "Your film *Orphée* made me think of Virgil. Full

---

O Cangaceiro, a film by Victor de Lima Barreto.

of old stuff." "Why do they always make old stories? It's not modern." Etc. And the blame also goes to those who allow children to speak in public. I'm beginning to understand why children used to be forbidden to speak at the dinner table.

Spaak. They made an exception by taking a Belgian. He's against everything and understands nothing about the Japanese film, which I haven't seen yet but which is apparently first rate. They tell me he spent his time making jokes about gnocchi because one of the characters was called Ioki. I'm beginning to be embarrassed about accepting this presidency.

Those three children. I'm beginning to wonder if they weren't prompted to say what they did. They may have mirrored the stupidity of the grown-ups who are using them.

Yet I have noticed in Carole a certain tendency to be incredulous. But she has Francine to oppose that tendency. And on the other hand, she is very sensitive to works that grown-ups dislike.

I'm happy to have chosen my son. And where did he come from? From a displaced family of Yugoslav peasants who live in the eastern minefields. In Bouligny, tyrannized by crass stupidity. Neither his father nor his mother know how to write. But the mother knows all the sagas by heart and can sing them. Édouard lived like a little savage. His brothers and sisters aren't the least bit like him. A boy of his sort is as rare as a great artist. I've never given him a single piece of advice. I've asked *him* for advice. He divines everything. A perfect soul. Last night, after that wretched radio interview, I telephoned him just to hear his voice. I was demoralized, disgusted. The spectacle of King Farouk in the bar didn't help matters.

Maybe if children were taught biology they would understand that we are surrounded by mysteries. In what they are taught, there is no room for the magic of reality, i.e., for the problems our slightest action provokes, the terrible riddle of living on this dangerous globe and imagining ourselves to be safe here. Those wretched children yesterday were quite happy to live on the surface and imagine they were beginning a new era in which "no one can put anything over on you." The film of *Peter Pan* was the height of absurdity for them.

Another grotesque situation. I am wrested from the "children's radio" by that "Josephine"* who publishes with Seghers and who appears all over the place. She takes my hand and stares at me in silence. "Now I believe in the gods—they exist, they appear. I see you. How beautiful you are!" Luckily she had to catch a train. I escaped, hid in my room sick to my stomach. Ready to give up my soul. Exactly, to *give up* my soul.

Graham Greene's film *The Heart of the Matter*. It's all starting over again, just the way it was in the days of Hervieu and Lavedan. Adulteries and priests. Priests in the morning and priests at night. And God with every imaginable sauce.

(This morning Hitchcock's *I Confess* was at least told by a *storyteller*, a great director. Another priest story.)

Cannes: Farouk and La Môme Moineau.† La Môme Moineau like a bad joke. And a huge little boy crammed into a naval officer's uniform and wearing a carnival mask: Farouk is an insult to women, to men, to monarchy, to democracy. La Môme Moineau is an insult to the sun, to flowers, to decent people, to the Côte d'Azur.

---

*Author, under this pseudonym, of *L'Antipoète* (Seghers), 1953.

†Lucienne Dhotelle (1908–1968), a Parisian street singer discovered by the couturier Paul Poiret. The director of the Olympia music hall, Paul Franck, put her on stage under the name La Môme Moineau. In the early 1930s she married Felicio Benitez Rexach, the richest entrepreneur of Santo Domingo, whom she had met on tour in New York. Every year she stayed in Cannes at her Villa Bagatelle, while her yacht lay at anchor in the harbor.

. . . .

APRIL 10

Now I know from experience how a jury proceeds and rejects an accidental beauty if someone is not there to influence them and to shake them up.

Seeing very bad films makes you sick. You come out diminished and ashamed.

. . . .

APRIL 11

What am I doing in this festival? I wonder. It's certainly not where I belong. And why have all these people who have always pulled my films apart chosen me for their president? The same rhythm continues. Prestige without understanding. Powers which function in spite of everything, in the margins of what provokes them.

Gradually we are getting to know one another. For instance, Spaak, who played so dumb, is turning out to be quite astute, and if a certain imaginative quality escapes him, it's because it isn't powerful enough to persuade him. He was revolted by the grotesque sentimentality of Dréville's *Hélène Boucher*, by the vulgarity of the dialogue, whereas Lang, whom I had supposed cleverer than that, fell for it hook, line, and sinker.

I dread tonight's session. We're being shown Clouzot's *Wages of Fear*, which is a thousand miles above all the others in the race. But aside from the fact that my colleagues don't seem to have much taste for strength and balance, there are some of us who are upset by my desire to award this film the prize. They will take the opposite tack systematically (Lang).

The short-film judges are younger and subtler. They tell me they've seen a British sketch and a Japanese animation film of the first rank. Disney's famous *Seabirds* struck them, despite everyone's admiration, as a conventional mechanism.

Naturally several members of our jury prefer *Snow White* to *Peter Pan*. Dwarves and mushrooms—much more to their taste.

The sad thing is to quarrel with different countries for no valid reason. A real Austrian cannot approve the Austrian farce, but the Austrians at the festival are counting on it and give a huge party where we will be embarrassed, our minds being made up—unanimously. Embarrassment about England too, which overlooks its best films (like the Italians) and sends us a grim bore, which is surprising from Graham Greene after films like *Brighton* and *The Fallen Idol*. From what Somerset Maugham told me the evening before I came here, this film reflects the home life of the Greenes. Self-torment and confession. Don't forget that he's one of Mauriac's translators.

Splendid weather. Went to see the *Orphée II* yesterday—still at sixes and sevens. The workmen will be through on Monday. I'll go into hiding on the yacht if the Carlton wears me out.

The consequence of this festival is that I realize, inevitably, how rarely any authentic beauty shows itself except to very few persons, not one of whom lives in Cannes. How ignorant people are of boldness and the secrets of beauty. How utterly the cinema is in the hands of idiots who have no contact whatever with the salient points of the period. What constitutes the prestige of *Greed*, of *Sang d'un poète*, of *l'Age d'or*, of *Les Enfants terribles,* of *Orphée* is a dead letter for them and remains so. They like films that are polished up, glowing Technicolor, superficial problems, lovable actors.

The failure of *La Belle et la Bête* and of *Orphée* in Cannes was inevitable. At the last festival J.-J. Gautier's article in *Le Figaro* on Menotti's *Medium* summed up that ignorant state of mind. The day before yesterday, I slipped a copy of *Le Chiffre sept* into Gance's pocket, because Gance, with all his enormous faults, is truly sensitive to greatness. The poem overwhelmed him. I was sure it would. I would be ashamed to have the others read it.

Spaak had brought his limited edition of *Les Enfants terribles* for me to sign.

The day before yesterday, the whole Communist party was out to meet Maurice Thorez at the station. But he had been taken off on the way and continued by car to avoid the crowd. Which the Party didn't know about. An American journalist who looked like Thorez was carried off, embraced, borne in triumph. A Chaplin gag.

Festival gossip. One Cannes journalist has spread the news that I locked myself up with Favre to see the films and that I refused to let our colleagues into the projection room.

Difficulty with seats. We should always have the same seats. I chose mine, a seventeen at the edge of a balcony tier. But if I don't come to films I've already seen, someone will say my seat was empty, even if I give it to someone who wants to see the film (which I shall not do, since I'll only miss the mediocre films). Which will mean that these films are condemned in advance.

Ran into Alexandre Alexandre last night. We pretended not to see each other. What will I do when I run into Claude Mauriac or J.-J. Gautier, for instance?—it being my duty not to make the atmosphere unbreathable.

Tonight we saw *The Wages of Fear*, hiding Clouzot in the projectionist's booth and then in my hotel room. The film produced a considerable effect. In order not to seem to be conspiring, we went back downstairs through the kitchen. And the Clouzots could get to their car without being seen. Clouzot says, "They hate us— but they take it."

Tati. *Monsieur Hulot's Holiday.* In 1935 Chaplin told me that after finishing a film he *shook the tree.* "I made everything not solidly attached to the branches fall." Poor Tati picks up the overripe fruit from that tree and sets it out in rows. He has no presence.

Except for some funny gags, which tend to fizzle out, the only thing that works is the accuracy of the dialogue and the cross-conversations (like those in the theater box of *Le Sang d'un poète*). But that was thirty years ago.

. . . .

APRIL 12

A Swedish lesson in morality.* A natural child. A denatured father. A family at fault. It all comes out all right. Zero.

Clemenceau.† The spell of old prints in film. They come alive. Remarkable documents. A film in which Clemenceau speaks in person through the voice of mediocre actors. Everything which would be of interest is missed. Incredible nerve of the government, which imposes on us, for an international festival, a film speaking only of *boches* and the German hordes. I asked Erlanger‡ to find out who wanted to have this film shown and why we were compelled to take these extracinematic detours.

. . . .

APRIL 13

Cinema. Paulvé tells Bessy, "Cocteau should pay me a salary: I've made him famous." The headline has already appeared in one newspaper: "Gide was read by the elite, Michele Morgan offered him glory." And in another (same size type): "Martine Carol doesn't agree with Victor Hugo."

---

*A film by Arne Mattson, *Pour les ardentes amours de ma jeunesse.*

†*La Vie passionée de Clemenceau*, a film by Gilbert Prouteau, text and images by Jacques Le Bailly.

‡The historian Philippe Erlanger, born 1903, director of the Service des échanges artistiques at the Ministry of Foreign Affairs, founder of the Cannes festival.

I've been asked to do a big panel for the festival hall. I'll go paint it either this morning or after the five o'clock film.

Still no answer about the text for Versailles. I had warned them that it wouldn't be what they expect. Yesterday Philippe Erlanger lectured me on the reign of Louis XIV, Saint-Simon's mistakes, the result of picking up any anecdote he was told, the king's calculations, whose entire purpose was to smother the glory of the princes in his entourage, particularly of Monsieur. The latter's military successes made Louis ill. He wanted to be the only one to shine and stopped at nothing to extinguish the bright lights around him. If he had realized that Racine would triumph with his plays and not as *his* historian, no doubt he would have invoked his censorship. Molière was his circus, and to him he handed over his Christians—i.e., doctors, Turks, provincial nobility. People laughed because the king laughed, but out of the wrong side of their mouths. Monstrous egoism. He would say, "A monarch must be attached to no one."

Committees, commissions, prerogatives, paperwork. When I say, "We need merely refuse," people look at me as if I knew nothing, as if I were expressing a lunatic's opinion.

Édouard's parents move into the little house in Biot tomorrow. Such things happen only in the novels of the comtesse de Ségur. It took a Francine and an Édouard for them to happen in this day and age.

Last night, coming home from the film and as I was passing a crowded restaurant, the diners gave me a round of applause. In France you never know what to expect. Heads or tails.

Answer to Erlanger, who telephoned to find out who had thought up *Clemenceau*: "The ministers." "And why was that?" "It's none of your business to psychoanalyze our feelings."

Orson Welles and I remark how seriously all these people take a festival. If they saw it the way we do, we wouldn't have to worry about provoking such resentments, such *hatred*.

. . . .

APRIL 14

Surprised by the intelligence governing the film *La Provinciale** (from Moravia's book). The whole film is rather Maupassant, even Proust. But the skill of the narrative, the economy of dialogue and gestures saves everything. Every second has power without the help of "finds"—except for the actual fabric of the film, consisting of flashbacks done with real mastery. The big Roman woman is an unforgettable type. (Film impossible to see again.)

Francine has fever and stayed in bed on the Cape. We are afraid she has caught her daughter's measles.

I plan to suggest this morning an ideal prize, taking into account everything I've heard everyone else say. I'll ask for a discussion on this basis. Erlanger suggests a Cocteau Prize, to be given to America, which has come off rather badly.

. . . .

APRIL 15

"The dance begins."† Sun and clouds. Not hot at all. I brought my letter and my model for the voting system to be mimeographed. They'll be passed out tomorrow. Spoke on the radio, which is not easy, since we've been told to keep our mouths shut.

Lunch with [Charles] Frank, who doesn't realize that his film of *Les Parents terribles* has been put outside the competition as a special favor and [who] wants a prize for his young actress. After lunch Picasso telephones, asking for seats for the Ramiés. Photographs on the *Orphée II*, back from its trial run. In short, one thing after another, a habit I've got out of.

---

*A film by Mario Soldati.
†In 1953 the Cannes festival took place from April 15 to April 29.

Dréville speaking about his pathetic film: "You can't look at it without an audience in the house. When the house is full, there's a lot of laughing." And a lot, unfortunately, when it's empty.

Complaints of the filmmakers whose films are shown in the afternoon. I said on the radio that we weren't concerned with the program. Any program would run the risk of indicating preferences. It is Favre Le Bret who is in charge of that; he hasn't seen the films.

Nothing would be more unpleasant than to attend the parties given by one country or another, once we had made up our minds against the film shown by that country.

Actually, since I've never been particularly well treated by festivals, there's no reason for me to be so concerned.

· ·

APRIL 16

Last night a good opening. Clouzot's film was like a battering ram which knocks down the wall and opens a breech for the sessions. Tremendous impression. Picasso didn't have his seats—I gave him mine, and Erlanger gave his to Françoise. After the film, supper at Les Ambassadeurs. Very fancy, very boring. I leave before the end with Arletty, who was seated next to me. She'd like to revive *L'École des veuves.** I shook hands with both J.-J. Gautier and Claude Mauriac. It was clear they were wondering what I would do. No feuds during the festival.

I looked at the women attending last night—some very beautiful. It is the first time in ages that there is *no fashion*. Impossible to say, "The style of 1953." Each woman and each couturier do what they want. The same is true of hairstyles. In a period of deindi-

---

*A play in one act that Cocteau had written for Arletty, after the tale "The Matron of Ephesus" by Petronius. First performed in 1936 under the author's direction in a set by Marcel Khill (supervised by Christian Bérard).

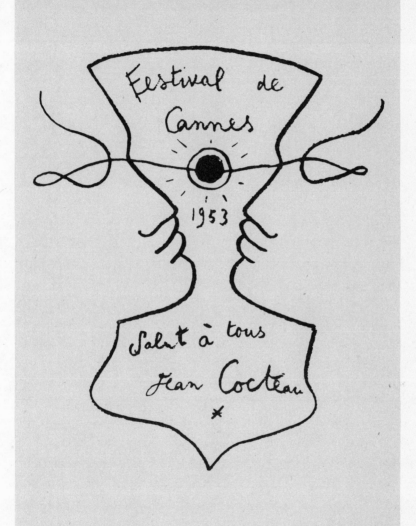

vidualization, this spectacle offers a show of individualism without strength—an individualism of weakness, of disorder, of inelegance.

. . . .

APRIL 17

The English film of *Les Parents terribles* produced a very poor impression. A literal photograph of the play which was a *painting* in the direct manner, whereas my film was a *painting* of the play. The Swedish girl charming.* The other actors talk as fast as they can, to assume a French manner. The Michel† is wooden, and the sinuous Léo‡ becomes a stiff old maid. Those who knew the play and the French film found the thing hard to take. Others were caught up by the action. The actress who plays Yvonne§ reminds me of Dermoz.¶ She's interesting, a little too theatrical, which was avoided by splendid Yvonne de Bray in my own film.**

Evening. Outrageous bad manners of the public. People come in after the film has begun. People talking, getting up and down, leaving before the end. I asked Flaud to request the public to be on time and show some respect for the participating countries.

An American trick: The *Herald Tribune* publishes an article accusing *The Wages of Fear* of being a Communist film and insulting to America. This was neither the American delegation's attitude nor Edgar G. Robinson's. I can see that Robinson is afraid of something—which is natural. Myself, I shall never admit that extracinematic considerations can influence our votes.

Reception for the Swedish Madeleine. She continues to be

---

*Elsy Albin.
†Russell Enoch.
‡Ruth Dunning.
§Marian Spencer.
¶Germaine Dermoz created the role of Yvonne on stage in 1938.
**Cast of the film *Les Parents terribles*, 1948: Yvonne de Bray (Yvonne), Gabrielle Dorziat (Léo), Marcel André (Georges), Jean Marais (Michel), Josette Day (Madeleine).

charming. I managed to spill my glass full of Cinzano onto her dress.

This morning I saw the documentary Technicolor film on the trip to Brazil (Italy).* Unforgettable images of a calf eaten alive by piranhas (which leave only the carcass) and of one huge snake swallowing another.

Evening. *The Great Buddha.*† My announcement was read during the intermission—but it couldn't be very effective tonight, and the film provoked exhaustion and escape. This afternoon I was visited by the Japanese producer who understands exactly what doesn't work. He offers me a coproduction in which I would direct everything. I told him that maybe later on I would think of a silent film with commentary (something like the performances at the theater in Kōbe) by choruses and narrators.

There comes a moment of exhaustion when we can't look at any more films. A kind of sleep like that of children who don't hear the bedtime story any longer but only the murmur of their mother's voice. I followed and failed to follow. Painful.

.   .   .   .

APRIL 18

The other day, Robinson was trying so hard to understand the French subtitles that he didn't realize the film was in English.

Last night stopped in at the Brummel. Farouk sitting in the entrance. He's there every night—he seems to like doors, vestibules. Maybe because he's never yet had to wait on someone else.

Back to the Cape. Will return for the American reception.

Clouzot lunched with the American delegation. Things are work-

---

Green Magic, a film by Gian Gaspare Napolitano.
†A Japanese film by Teinosuke Kinugasa.

ing out. They thought O'Brien's "shit to you" was an insult, not knowing it was our French formula for good luck. (Actually, it's the choice of Yves Montand, which makes the film suspect in their eyes.)

Since we were serious enough to see the films first for ourselves, people are saying that the prizes were awarded in advance. Nothing less true. Except for one or two films, I haven't a clue which will win a majority of votes.

Evening. Strange period. Make a moral film—everyone thinks it's stupid; make an immoral film, everyone thinks it's cruel. Disney's *Seabirds* acclaimed by the audience. The jury for short films loathes it. They say, "It's the Folies-Bergère."

. . . .

SUNDAY · APRIL 19 · 1953

Sunday at Santo Sospir. Back to Cannes, seven o'clock. I'm taken up to Disney in the bar. Spaak had read my text, and Disney had it in his pocket with the medal of the Legion of Honor. Robinson very annoyed by the American offensive. I'm sorry about it, but I won't be colonized for the time being. For the time being, France is still free.

Tonight the Belgian film,* full of splendid images (not enjoyed by the audience) and *The White Reindeer*,† a piece of clumsiness which reminds me of the film clubs of twenty years ago . . . O incomprehensible, absurd, blind, and deaf public. People talked about the *Reindeer* music as if it were a wonder. Pretentious and hateful. Then at the bar the Finns come over to shake my hand. I had to speak German and took advantage of how badly I speak it to avoid discussing their work.

---

*Bongolo, a film by André Cauvin.
†A Finnish film by Erik Blomberg.

· ·

MONDAY · APRIL 20

A bad Mexican film (*Las tres perfectas casadas*).* In the afternoon,
Dréville's film *Hélène Boucher*. Better audience than in the evening.
Dréville had hired a claque which didn't quite know where to
applaud. They applauded a hitch in the projector. Success. Flowers.
Embraces. A crowd at the exit. Vulgarity always pleases.

Tonight the ordeal of the Austrian film and the Austrian reception.

· ·

TUESDAY AND WEDNESDAY · APRIL 21 AND 22

Too tired to write. Film after film. None of them wakes up anyone.
Children of Hiroshima.† I was dreading the American reaction, but
the Americans approved. The Federation of Film Authors make
me honorary president. I read a text full of deliberate mistakes in
which I give examples of scandals from the cinema world. This
text, published and broadcast, will provoke outrage. Saw Descaves‡
who will restore Bovy's cuts in *La Voix humaine*. Last night, *Lili*.§
It takes place, it seems, in a window of the Galeries Printemps.
Splendid close-ups of Leslie Caron and Mel Ferrer. Nothing stranger
than this Côte d'Azur seen in Technicolor by the Americans. Absurd
festival in which I will make myself play my absurd part to the
very end.

---

*A film by Roberto Cavaldon.
†A Japanese film by Kaneto Shindo.
‡Pierre Descaves, new administrator general of the Comédie-Française.
§American musical comedy by Charles Walters.

· ·

APRIL 23

Surprise of the festival: the short film *Crin blanc*.* The only film
which makes the trip and all our fatigue worthwhile. The Spanish
film *Bienvenue, Mr. Marshall*† remains charming. Each time America
is made fun of, the audience applauds. With the same rudeness, the
audience interrupted *Crin blanc* with violent applause for the picturesque moments, which kept us from seeing and hearing the rest.

That night, at midnight, Spanish party at the Martinez. Flamenco
dancer—she whirls, slides, falls, rages: splendid. Animal and plant.
To bed at four in the morning. And this morning the Ricoux girl's
wedding at Beaulieu. Three-quarters of an hour late. The Ricoux
cat had torn the bride's veil to shreds. Back to Cannes for the
battle of flowers, with the mayor and Robinson. Old fiacres, military
marches, flowers which, by the fourth time the fiacres come round,
make the Croisette look like a cemetery. Exhausted, back to the
hotel with Robinson.

In Tati's films, the gags provoke the situations. In Chaplin's, the
situations provoke the gags. (He should be given the Prix de la
Critique.)

· ·

APRIL 27

Too stupefied to write.

Nothing further from my mind than a festival. I've always been
shot down by juries. My only prizes in France were by plebiscite,
or exceptional prizes—a Prix de la Critique, a Prix Delluc.‡ Embarrassed to be a judge. I wouldn't want to make others suffer

---

*A film by Albert Lamorisse.
†A film by Luis García Berlanga.
‡For *La Belle et la Bête*, in 1946.

my fate, and the number of films, the obligation to choose compel me to take this attitude. Besides, a jury president doesn't have any more of a vote than the others, and if they tend toward my choice, it's only natural that I should tend toward theirs. In short, the exhaustion of a festival necessarily leads to an atmosphere of embarrassment and uneasiness and bad humor. I deplore it. I wish festivals didn't hand out prizes and were just a place for exchange and encounter. To preside over the Cannes jury is an experience I won't repeat. I've been as serious about it as I possibly could— never missed a session and salved as many wounded feelings as I could. My colleagues and I went to the films as an audience, not as a tribunal. We never assumed a style of silence, of reserve, of mystery. We can therefore accept all the grievances with a clear conscience. I nonetheless regret having to pronounce (and ratify) the verdicts.

. . . .

MAY 1

Finished. Jeannot came with me to rest for a couple of days at Saint-Jean. Francine and Édouard are coming back tonight. On the whole, the festival was a success. The last evening, at Les Ambassadeurs, the whole room tossed me the daisies from their tables. I said on the microphone that I hoped to see the festival assume its true meaning: a meeting of minds and hearts. After me, Robinson and Gary Cooper spoke. Yesterday the hotel presented me with an additional bill for 50,000 francs. Which is how France rewards the services it asks of you.

I had agreed to the presidency in order to obtain prizes for Clouzot and Charles Vanel. To do so I had to drop ballast. For example, with regard to the Mexican film *La Red,** which I loathe.

---

*A film by Emilio Fernandez.

And we had to reward Japan for *Children of Hiroshima*. The De Sica story. Mme De Filippo* having declared that any secondary prize would be an insult to Éduardo, we didn't cite *Stazione termini*. Whereupon Mme De Filippo had the Italians castigate us and kept to her room.

From my contacts with the serious filmmakers, it is clear that the cinema costs too much. The page on which we express ourselves comes down to an almost irrecoverable hundred million francs, if the film isn't made with a commercial goal. Which explains why the best films of the festival are the shorts. The young people find them a lighter vehicle and a less expensive one, with the chances for television showings. I persist in believing that the standard length of our films is wrong. Too long to correspond to a play, too short to correspond to a novel. The short film is always sacrificed in the programs.

The case of Buñuel. His film *El* horrified me, as if a friend were dying before my eyes. But the "specialists found a way to see it as a paraphrase of *L'Age d'or*, using the system of our Saint-Germain-des-Prés young people: "It's deliberate." Whereby everything you're blamed for is a triumph. Buñuel is going academic: it's deliberate. Tati is going amateur: it's deliberate. Everything turns upside down. Real work is despised as an attack on sloth, and only what reflects the height of modern aestheticism is accepted, considered from an antiaesthetic angle. These young people do not realize that the "badly done" of a Picasso is the result of countless preparations and "well-done" figures which he covers up—he removes the structure and leaves only the scaffolding, but the scaffolding was built on the structure, and the phantom power of the structure remains present underneath.

---

*Tina De Filippo, actress and the sister of Italian dramatist, actor, and director Eduardo De Filippo. She accompanied Vittorio De Sica to this Cannes festival.

. . . .

MUNICH · MAY 9

Work in the theater* hasn't left me a free minute to visit the castles of Ludwig II, buildings which ruined Bavaria and whose visitors' fees are now financing the country.

I've had to order fabrics and redo all the costumes and the entire set. The workers were afraid to cut the material—they thought it was too fine to cut. The whole thing is very odd and a little Chinese. I've made up the dancers in white and reconstructed the heraldic lion and the knight's mount from scratch. Little Veronika is amazing, as the unicorn. A real actress. Her death is very moving. Rosen, about whom I knew nothing at all, has invented choreography of great nobility.

I don't know what people will think tonight, but the musicians in full dress on a little grandstand in the set have disconcerted some young people who don't even know that this is a German tradition—that of Reinhardt, Kurt Weill, Piscator. Youth here has been completely cut off by the war, as in France, where young people think the venerable methods of Barrault and Vilar are news.

Last night Dior's gowns at the Bayerischer Hof. Contrast between the mannequins and the tables. At one table was a stout, red-faced lady with a vast hat bristling with white feathers and more of these around her neck. The mannequins, circulating as if they were looking at no one and swirling in another world, had seen the room very clearly and told me about it afterward.

I was in the middle, at the top of some steps, at the minister's

---

La Dame à la licorne, ballet, set and costumes by Jean Cocteau, music by Jacques Chailley, choreography by Heinz Rosen, with Veronika Mlakar (the Unicorn), Boris Trailine (the Knight), Geneviève Lespagnol (the Lady); first performed in Munich, May 9, 1953.

table, between two little princesses who were half asleep and dazed by this parade of gowns.

Tonight the mannequins will attend the performance. Radio people, photographers, cameramen, journalists, one after the next, wearing me out. Cannes all over again. Saw Gründgens chez Desch— he has been in a doctor's care in Switzerland. He looks fine, his eyes brighter.

Bacchus has been put on in Berlin, with cuts, an old cardinal, and an absurd production all round.

Here, in a cabaret, someone is doing *Le Bel indifferent*. I haven't had time to go, and I don't imagine I'm missing much. And there's always a new actress doing *La Voix humaine* somewhere.

. . . .

MAY 10

La Dame à la licorne turned out to be a triumph. Everyone embracing, Veronika cheered. I take many bows, and there are more cheers.

Two dinners with the consul, one at the consulate. Back at five in the morning.

The French do not realize that Europe is reappearing in Germany. When they say les boches, they have said it all. They cling to the old bitterness about Alsace-Lorraine and do not even suspect that Bavaria has lost as many citizens as France (proportionally) because of nazism. How many Bavarians died in the camps—how many mothers have had their sons beheaded!

Munich is a capital of the arts. The bombs cannot destroy this *Stimmung*. Yesterday I visited the ruins of the opera, where the ravens nest up at the top, and on the ground there are pools of stagnant water. Deep pools. Of this whole vast theater there remains only an unreal arch, a half circle of what were once the boxes, a cast-iron carcass, some twisted cables dangling like death's own braids. Yet this strange ruin preserves within it a continuity of song and cheers, those cheers which do not come from the hands but from the heart. The cheers which rewarded us last night for all our work.

A triumph like last night's seems like the sort of thing you can hope for only once in a lifetime. Each time I do a film or a play in Germany, this is what happens. The plasticity of the German soul is something feminine. It marries the strength offered to it. To reject this marriage is a crime and a piece of stupidity into which our politicians inevitably fall.

. . . .

MAY 14

Milly. Paris confounds me. Impossible to move. Cars too big for the streets. Saw Piaf in *Le Bel indifférent.** She makes a tragicomedy out of the little play. An audience of foreigners. I can stay in my seat without a soul recognizing me.

Le Bal du comte d'Orgel almost completed. A book of impeccable luxury. The new *Difficulté d'être* already on sale. An article by Mauriac in *La Table ronde.* He notes bitterly that his own review publishes an article (moreover a remarkable one, he says) by Michel Déon on *Le Journal d'un inconnu* in which I abuse him. He tosses me flowers and thorns. He cites letters from Morocco in which he is called an old fool. The Nobel Prize seems to have turned his head.

Horrified by the number of letters to answer.

Paris sleeps and snores very loud.

Luxury dead. There is nothing but spiritual luxury which counts any more. And money is its enemy. High cost of seats. Impossible

---

*Édith Piaf and Jacques Pills had revived *Le Bel indifférent* at the Marigny theater in April 1953, directed by Raymond Rouleau with a curtain and set by Lila de Nobili. Piaf recorded the play on this occasion.

to put on anything for the only public worthy of it. In Munich, where life isn't expensive, the theater is a ceremony, a church open to all. Enthusiasm results from a mixture of publics. At the Marigny, for instance, there are two publics. That of the expensive seats and that of the gallery. After paying 1,000 francs for a seat, the audience believes it owes the artists nothing more.

Wrote the article for *Arts* on *La Dame à la licorne*. Also the article for Serge Lido* on dance. Did the drawing for the exhibit of child artists. Now there remains the terrible chore of letters to answer.

In Munich Margaret Rosen was annoyed because the dancers did not get invited to the ministerial dinner. "This consul is a lunatic. Disgusting. (And whispering in my ear) Sapotage . . ." As a matter of fact, consuls don't make anything easier. Terrified of responsibilities and of losing their job. Their work consists of keeping files on everyone. I must have mine: "Met Leni Riefenstahl in his hotel room." Mme Riefenstahl came to ask me to intervene with Marais for her film *Red Devils* (final version of *Penthesilea*). "Where will I find four hundred white horses? Skis and snow will be simpler."

Saw Paul Morand and his wife yesterday; they've rented an apartment in my street, no. 28. They live between Tangier and Switzerland.

Talked with Morand about that kind of "*journal intime*" which is published in the writer's lifetime: "Reread *Andromaque*. Lunched with Mme So-and-so." A journal has to be published posthumously.

Disputes among Kisling's sons began the very night he died. Whether or not to sell the house. "The car is mine." "No, mine." Poor Renée in all this wrangling . . . In Montparnasse she was like a wild horse. And became a model mama. But her secret preference is for the son who reminds her of her own youth.

---

*Serge Lido, 1907–1984, a dance photographer.

Problem of correspondence: What will I do with the letters that accumulate during our cruise and while we are in Spain?

For an agreed-upon amount of dollars, the next Nobel will go to Léger.* Morand says, "Dynamite is the least dangerous thing Nobel ever invented."

. . . .

SATURDAY · MAY 15

Splendid sun in the garden. I won't see the fragrant peonies they gave me in Barbizon; they bloom later than the red ones. I walk with Annam in a racket of birds.

Visit last night from François Michel. Parinaud had given "remarks" he had "collected chez Cocteau" to *La Parisienne*. These remarks amazed Michel, who shows them to me. Astounding to realize that the people you talk to hear nothing, understand something entirely different from what you say, attribute their style to you, and fill the gaps between the four or five notes they have scribbled (inaccurately) with nonsense. I advise Michel to use passages from *Entretiens autour du cinématographe.*† Fraigneau has lost his mother. She had fallen asleep near an open gas line. Now she's dead. He's just back in Paris—she lived in Nîmes.

Unable to sleep last night, I tried to arrange my books for the *Oeuvres complètes.* Alarmed by their number and by the difficulty of any classification which would permit publishing them in three volumes on anything but Bible paper.

This morning, books I forgot leap into my mind. Besides, Variot (Plon) has found a host of articles and prefaces at the Bibliothèque nationale. I'll take advantage of this to correct and cut and give

---

*The diplomat Alexis Léger, a poet who wrote under the name Saint-John Perse (1887–1973). He was awarded the Nobel Prize in 1960.

†Interviews made with André Fraigneau, first published in 1951.

the whole thing a tone which any really *complete* works wouldn't have. What the "work" should be: that's the work. It seems to me quite justifiable to correct yourself down to the last minute and, for instance, instead of the two versions of *La Machine à écrire*,* to publish the first,† the one I regret not having put on.

Mauriac on *Le Journal d'un inconnu* mixes his praise with vinegar: "He even manages to think. Very strong stuff." No doubt this great thinker has decided I never *thought* in my life. Most likely to think differently from Mauriac signifies that one doesn't think at all, or that one *thinks badly*, as they say.

It is true that I've always *thought* in a sense which is not theirs and which escapes them. What can a Mauriac make of the *Essai de critique indirecte*, of *Opium*, of *Le Secret professional*, of so many works in which good and evil, God and the devil have no part? "I sin, therefore I think."

Madeleine is going crazy over her cats. She separates them, one to a floor. The grandmother, the mothers, the sons and daughters all fight when they are together. Each one wants to live on Madeleine's shoulder. Before the male kittens were born, they got along splendidly. Madeleine suddenly finds herself baffled by the complications of a Dostoyevsky family.

Milly: peace. Annam is a huge and adorable puppy. The cats ignore him and live like egoistic savages. We never see them. Sometimes they vanish for days.

Munich is already far away. Cannes still farther. The trouble you take over snowmen which melt as soon as your back is turned . . .

And letters . . . letters! Everyone wants you to read him, to praise him, to write a preface for him, to influence his publishers. Every-

---

*Cocteau's play in three acts, first performed in 1941, directed by Raymond Rouleau, with sets by Jean Marais.

†First performed at the Comédie-Française on March 21, 1956, directed by Jean Meyer, sets by Suzanne Lalique.

one wants you to make his films, to place his plays. Everyone imagines that fate is against him and that luck is always on your side.

The older I grow, the more I realize that fame (what is called fame) is the consequence of an architectural and geometrical phenomenon hidden under the apparent disorders of nature. It is not our works which get us anywhere. It's a harmony of energies which escape our individual ethic, invisible to everyone. Everyone experiences them, though they oppose them and are utterly unaware of them. This is how a name is formed and becomes powerful outside works that are almost always misunderstood and poorly read. I would have been abandoned long since if my works had to function by themselves. It is true that works also release energies which exceed in effectiveness any knowledge of them people might have.

In his next book René Bertrand should apply the geometric laws all forms obey to these secret forms of the mind, explaining why certain works *function* despite the misunderstanding they encounter, a misunderstanding which, against every expectation, assures their permanence. Hence, what matters is neither pleasing nor displeasing, nor being talked about nor being passed over in silence. What matters is never to make a single faux pas in your internal progress. What matters is to make yourself invisible, distracting the heedless world by superficial exercises of a high visibility. (Larousse. Cocteau, Jean. French writer, born Maisons-Lafitte 1889. His *fantasy* is expressed in poems, plays, films. *Sic.*)

. . . .

MAY 17

Letter from the minister: "I award you the Grand Prix des Présidents des Festivals de Cannes." Why I accepted this presidency: (1) I wanted Clouzot's film to win the Grand Prix. Otherwise he would never have had it. Any other president would have been scared of the Americans. (2) I wanted to prove that my solitude is not a system. That I am perfectly able to make contact with what I avoid. That I knew how to work the cape. And in the end the bull has thrown flowers to the torero.

I gave up opium after 1940 (after the exodus), because opium, which is *the converse of vulgarity*, risks bringing you into contact with *the height of vulgarity*: the police.

Nouveau Larousse. Raymond Radiguet simply forgotten. I pointed out this scandal to Hollier-Larousse. Rimbaud the "poet-fantasist" has been corrected. Now I'm the one who has inherited the "fantasy."

. . . .

MAY 24

Milly. Arriving from Paris. Who could write in that Palais-Royal where cats, visitors, correspondence overwhelm every minute, every inch? And everything accompanied, inextricably, by the telephone.

Green's play *Sud.* Very beautiful. Some people fail to understand it because they refuse to do so, others because they understand nothing anyway, neither *Sud* nor *Andromaque* nor *Hamlet* nor even Molière, and for whom the behavior of Green's women seems inexplicable. And if you can't understand it, Green's play seems very boring. "What's it all about?" Understood (and every line is perfectly clear), it seems quite short. Several centuries of cuckoldry have put the audience on a branch line whose derailment has left them stupefied. It will be said that the lieutenant's infatuation for young C. is rather sudden. Immediacy is precisely the definition of infatuation. And the theater demands these foreshortenings. Everyone says the play is poorly acted. I was so happy to hear real French spoken on the stage that I didn't even notice.

In the period when the play takes place, it was impossible to display feelings that were never mentioned. But the lines of the daughter and the father prove to us that they know.

A timid man, Green has an authentic heroism at his desk, alone with paper and ink. This heroism explodes over the footlights. It even functions against Catholicism, in favor of Christ.

Went to thank the artists. First of all the young actor who plays Ian (Pierre Vaneck). First rate.

The Rosens were in despair over my article in *Arts*: I didn't talk enough about them. At the Palais de Chaillot, people made sure to tell them I found Rosen's choreography disappointing. Parisian manners. Wrote an open letter to Rosen in which I cover him with the praises he deserves.

People want you to do their work for them and never realize you have your own: The minister of the PTT visits and asks for a film on the telephone. Haddad never gets off the phone, overwhelms me with his project. Versailles must be saved, the children of the artists of Pont-aux-Dames, charity balls, cocktails in honor of X and Z, fifty vernissages. I tear them all up. I went only to the Picasso show, rue d'Astorg, where his genius is a consolation. Splendid brown, pink, and blue landscape. The washhouse near Françoise's studio.

The bronze baboon. Her head made of two children's cars on top of each other. Her tail out of a stove iron. Metaphors. Picasso excels in making something surprise you by becoming something else. I am to speak of his work on the twenty-seventh in Rome. I'm not preparing anything—I'll try to invent, to improvise on the spot. I used to manage such things wonderfully. Now I'm afraid, and it's to conquer such fear that I force myself not to take notes.

The heat. Paris and oversize cars. The policeman: "It's not the cars that are too big, it's the streets that are too narrow." Paris a city of trees. If it weren't for this stream of cars, you would like to walk—to stroll. The day before yesterday I wanted to sit down on the café-terrace near the Carlton. A photographer appeared to take a photograph. A fellow asked me for an article on Django Reinhardt. Ladies asked me for autographs. Etc.

Vercors showed me his film on Leonardo. But Leonardo's work doesn't respond to shorts. And he should have shown the bird in the dress, the same model changing sex, the things in the wings. You feel no need to see *Saint John* and the Gioconda if the indiscretion of a camera doesn't add something to them.

Vercors the victim of a dreadful accident. An oven exploding and the fire that followed have hurt his foot and ruined his work. Picasso had told me that his reproduction methods were extraordinary.

Visited Plon yesterday to establish, with Variot, the basis of three volumes of the *Oeuvres complètes*. Since I never keep anything, the documentation and the dates make the job a difficult one. I plan to put into the first volume novels, travel writing, and plays under the title *Poésie romanesque et dramatique*. In the second volume, poems and the first critical pieces under the title *Poésie et poésie critique*. In the last volume, the rest of the critical pieces and the prefaces or articles. Review this arrangement with Orengo at Saint-Jean.

Gallimard writes to complain of my infidelities with other publishers. "You belong here more than at Plon." Maybe I do, but would he have paid several million francs to take the books from Morihien? His dream is to have everything . . . Friendly blackmail from Grasset. He is making up his mind to publish Dubourg's essay on my plays and films. But he adds, "We must make this publication coincide with a major work from you." I've given him *Journal d'un inconnu*. And already he's insisting on another book.

Nico's delightful entertainment at La Rose Rouge.* Yves Robert has the talent of establishing in a tiny frame those improvisations

---

*Nico Papatakis, director of the Parisian cabaret La Rose Rouge, in the rue de Rennes.

Bérard and Sauguet used to manage so well by dressing up in whatever they could find. *Around the World in Eighty Days* very ingenious, very funny. I miss the shipwreck. "Twenty thousand in banknotes, Captain, if we get to Liverpool before tonight!" All they needed was two strips of waves, a swaying mast with Passepartout and Phileas clinging to it, a black background, and the lights of Liverpool on a model.

Color film made by eleven children from one to five years old. A wonder. Like living canvases by Bonnard.

Excellent underwater scenes made with a sort of ballet of hands in red and white gloves.

The performance begins with a wretched creature singing the eternal complaints of Prévert and sub-Prévert.

Béranger must have been the Prévert of the Hugo period. He was regarded as a poet.

So often have the Japanese touched and kissed a page I wrote for them that they are asking me to do another one.

. . . .

MAY 25

Nijinsky's journal. I had always imagined that Nijinsky's scowling silence concealed hatred for the milieu of the Ballets Russes. His journal is like what Chaplin's would be if he were overcome, in Switzerland, by some form of madness. For Nijinsky is not mad. He is the victim of a rather childish mysticism, a humanitarianism which divinizes him. He is God. He will save the world. He will have "pity on the hearts of men." He suffers from Diaghilev's coldheartedness, and Stravinsky's—that's what disgusts him. Marriage has upset him. He was doomed to solitude—a marriage to himself. The quite terrible journal poorly documents this because of his idée fixe: the terror of being shut up, being put in a lunatic asylum. He had told me the story of his posing for Rodin in an

entirely different way. Diaghilev, who had obtained an article from
Rodin on the *Faun*, after the Calmette scandal (*Le Figaro*, even
then!), asked Rodin to make a statue of Nijinsky. Rodin shut himself
up in the Hôtel Biron studio with his model. Diaghilev was waiting
out on the terrace, near Rilke's old room. In the first session, when
Rodin was drawing, Nijinsky was amazed to hear the sound of
snoring. He was posing with his back to Rodin. He turned around.
Rodin was asleep, collapsed in an armchair and his beard. The
next day, the same pose—more strange noises. Nijinsky turns
around. Rodin, fly open, is masturbating. The statue stopped there.
Diaghilev laughed a lot over this episode. Nijinsky loathed hearing
him tell it. He no longer tolerated sexual "disorders." He was
already on his way toward that idealism which even his wife's
adoration violated. He offered to burn down the Bourse. To dance
for nothing. To reconcile all mankind. He ran away from his rooms
in Saint-Moritz. The chapter where he tries to find lodgings and
escapes into the mountains is admirable. Like certain pages by
Charles-Albert Cingria. It's likely that this idealism of his (which
one recognizes in Einstein and in Chaplin) idealized his dancing,
projected certain energies, unconsciously affected even the least
generous souls. Everything he planned, brooded over, concealed,
must have functioned unbeknown to him and provoked his triumphs.
Such a case of madness is confined. Hitler's overwhelms the world.
The journal is signed: God and Nijinsky.

Nijinsky was furious that his wife ate meat. He himself ate
nothing but vegetables. He believed that meat impels human beings
toward sexuality. He gave himself to Diaghilev as a means of
carrying out his mission. A sort of sacrifice *à la russe*. His wife's
physical desires disgusted him.

Off to sea soon! Sooner! My soul is awry. But I'm going to have
to leave this wonderful garden again, and the iris, and the peonies,
and everything that grows and that falls—the cherries are just
beginning. What you miss on the Côte d'Azur is this extraordinary

disorder in order, these masses of foliage, this jungle between the orchard and the rabbit hutches, Annam panting and sniffing at every hole. And the inimitable scent of roses.

. . . .

MAY 27

Rome. Grand Hotel. The New York plane three hours late. Lunch at Orly. Reached the Rome airport at six. Senator Reale met us. (And the inevitable photographer.) Reale put a car at our disposal. But it was impossible to find the driver. Which allowed us to take an old fiacre—I love the fiacres of Rome. You make a kind of direct contact with the city. After dinner I go to bed. I have to be at the Picasso exhibit by eleven. I speak at six, in the same theater as last time. The show is apparently too noisy for anyone to talk there. Picasso hasn't come to Rome. They don't know much of his work here. This matador needs toreros and picadors to wear out the bull—i.e., Cocteau. And the bull is the public. Tzara and an Italian painter have already wielded the red cape. I have brought no notes. I shall improvise. I'll try to do what I used to do. A letter from Maurice Sandoz,* who lives in Rome, reminds me of what that was. I haven't seen him since Switzerland in 1914.

Last night ran into Kenneth Anger.† He's making a sixteen-millimeter film here.‡ He's finally got the capital for it and is shooting by moonlight with a single character in costume, multiplied in the gardens.

Splendid folly of the fountains of Rome. Giants and monsters

---

*Swiss writer, author of texts illustrated by Dali, memoirs about Diaghilev and Nijinsky, and others.

†American avant-garde filmmaker, born in Hollywood in 1930. Creator of *Fireworks*, 1947; in 1951 he filmed Cocteau's mimodrama *Le Jeune Homme et la mort*, with Jean Babilée and Nathalie Philippart.

‡*Waterworks*, shot at Tivoli in the gardens of the Villa d'Este.

spitting water in all directions. The facades of the buildings arranged like stage sets. Banners for elections. Considerable Communist material alongside the very modest posters for the Christian Democrats. I asked Reale if the exhibit has provoked any political demonstrations. He says no, because of the personalities from every party sponsoring it.

Tiresome always to seem involved with political matters. You can't talk about anyone or anything without seeming to take sides. In our Montparnasse days, the one party was the party of the arts. We were divided, we judged one another, condemned one another, but in a realm where politics played no part whatever.

The committee announces that I will be speaking about "Picasso and his Friends." Most likely I'll be talking about something else. I prefer not thinking about it. If I do, I'll try to remember, and get confused. Diving into the void may be better: you swim in order not to drown. I have to swim for an hour.

I swam for an hour. Everyone pleased except me. They taped this improvisation, which I regret. It will be clear that I lost my footing several times. The show is magnificent. The canvases are free, set on laths which stand away from the walls and allow you to turn them in several directions. A young architect has given the whole affair the look of a quite simple unreality. Everything that is not painting remains invisible. He has stretched white canvas between the ceiling windows and the rooms, which produces a very powerful yet gentle light. The panels of War and Peace are shown side by side and not face to face. Ramps lead from one room to the next. A lot of people, a lot of priests. One lady asked me what one of the canvases would cost. The same lady was then at grips with one of the guards, who was explaining a portrait of Françoise to her. He hid Françoise's chignon with his cap and said: "What do you see? A profile." Then he hid the profile and said, "Don't you see another profile?" It was Françoise's chignon. For a Latin, one must *understand*. Solve a riddle. It seems to me that very few people took much pleasure in seeing a man distort the world for his own purposes and compel forms to follow him into his own inferno.

What disconcerted me was that title, "Picasso and His Friends." As a result, I passed over Max Jacob, because I was following my own line, and each time I thought of the poster, I stumbled and was afraid of mixing things up. At the moment of telling about Max, I saw Édouard signaling to me in the wings. I had talked for an hour. So I stopped short. Then everyone assured me they were expecting me to talk another twenty minutes. My only fear is that the text will be taken off the tape and my blanks will be attributed to unforgivable oversights.

. . . .

MAY 29

Letters, letters, letters. I answered them all morning. I want to be free to paint—to finish *The Birth of Pegasus*. Francine arrives tomorrow.

As soon as I have a moment's peace on the Cape, a phone call from the Italian Embassy to say that the mayor of Ventimiglia is dedicating their flower festival to me next Sunday. If I refuse to go, it will be a wretched return for the honor being paid. All these things I try to avoid are what suggest I like to make a show of myself, when all I care about is my solitude.

From Julien Green's letter in answer to my compliments: "By the joy your letter has given me, I measure my desolation if you hadn't cared for *Sud*. You're right to imagine that I put a good deal of myself into this first stage venture. I knew that you would understand me, and I hoped that my tragedy (for that is what it is) would please you. . . . I thank you for your words and send you my warmest embrace, Julien."

. . . .

MAY 30

Finished *Pegasus*. Beauty makes us lose our head. Poetry is born of
this decapitation.

. . . .

SUNDAY · MAY 31

I had forgotten young Haddad's visit to Milly along with his producer. The affair turns into a farce. M. Damilou says, "It's understood that it's you who will actually be making the film." I reply
that such a thing is out of the question, that if I were to make
the film, I would make it myself, alone. Haddad had led me to
believe that he would handle everything and that the producer
was in agreement.

Rain. Bad luck for the Ventimiglia battle of flowers.

Reconsider the painting. For Perseus, I had adapted a costume
by Bramante. Too elegant. Too deliberate.

Received Bruckmann's proofs. Difficulty of a French text in
Germany: a mistake in every line. Instead of the *Groupe des Six*,
they print *Groupe des Sioux*.

The amazing thing about the Picasso exhibit in Rome is that
everything is formed into knots and waves. There's always a period
of waves, of grace, between the knots in which the painter's true
personality is expressed.

. . . .

JUNE 1

Telegrams from Willemetz, Jeannot, Clairjois, Lulu, after signing
the contract for Les Bouffes.

I do so much in my dreams that I wake up exhausted. How

often I'd like to write down what happens in them the way one might write down what happens in real life. Only all the specific singularity evaporates in the morning. I'd have to have the will to write between dreams.

Last night I fell back to sleep and didn't dream the precise sequence of my dream—I dreamed it approximately. The same people but in different circumstances.

If our verticals plunge into the imagination's pool, they cease to be vertical. The water of the imagination distorts them.

Yesterday, worked on *Pegasus* from nine to five in the morning. Took out the draperies and the surfaces that were too "pretty" for the subject. The picture must be baroque but without baroque details. I wish I had treated the subject on a larger scale. I would have had it made into a tapestry at Aubusson, where I guess the Bouret workshop is finishing up the second version of *Judith and Holofernes.*

In the proofs Bruckmann has sent, the German typographers have made errors in almost every word—some are actually incomprehensible. Wrote Dr. H. to entrust the work to other typographers. We'll never get done at this rate.

Preparations for the trip to Spain. We hope to be in Granada on the twenty-second for the dancing in the Alhambra.

The trouble with a public improvisation like the one on Picasso is that afterward you keep correcting yourself with an amazing recollection of the mistakes you made. It's no help now, and it fills up your mind, keeping you from thinking about anything else. I'd be curious to hear the tape. Curious and disconcerted.

Ran into Jacques Chardonne at Grasset's: "I didn't want to see you again. You've become a myth. You're here and not here. Very strange." I try to explain to him how little I have to do with the myth, that it's being created in spite of me. Chardonne imagines that I travel all over the place, that I'm never still. Grasset assures him I never leave the Cape. Most likely Cannes and Munich are enough to give the illusion of perpetual movement. You don't see the people move who move all the time. You don't see people go out who go out all the time. Move a little. Go out one evening. People notice. You then pass for someone who engages in obsessive activity.

Prepared the poems Ponti wants for the Biennale.

Franz Kafka, until his death, seemed to be eighteen years old. A girl he mentions in his diary thought he was sixteen. He says: "I struggle. No one knows it." Max Brod must have been the only one to follow the drama. Another method of protection against the invisible.

Strictly speaking, there's no such thing as abstract painting, since all painting represents either an idea of the painter or the painter himself. As for Picasso, he's never claimed to do an abstract picture. He ferociously pursues resemblance and always achieves it, so that the object or the figure at the origin of his work often loses all relief and strength compared to the representation. Sometimes, when I left the shed where Picasso had just painted *War and Peace*, nature looked weak and confused to me.

He represents a danger for young painters because he closes all the doors he opens. Trying to follow him means bumping into them. He also represents a hope, because he proves that individualism isn't doomed and that art rebels against a termite ideal.

. . . .

JUNE 2

From nine this morning to six this evening, we haven't turned off the broadcast of the coronation of Queen Elizabeth. The radio seemed to come out of the night of time. It must have been an incredible spectacle to see—but it was fabulous to hear. It was related to those great bards, those troubadours who recount and embellish. The difference, in our day and age, is that in each house,

the troubadour-reporter doesn't invent and doesn't try to embellish. He observes and holds his microphone toward the music, the
bells, the tides of the crowd. The ceremony in Westminster inspires
respect. Impossible not to be moved, excited, amazed by such a
belief in the temporal and in the eternal, by that gold talon thrust
so deep into our poor earthly globe, by that solid unreality, by
rites as strange and inevitable as those of the hive. I don't think
anything analogous can happen anywhere else. Perhaps this is the
last time that the world will see such a thing. It began with pages,
fairy-tale servants, scarlet cavalcades. It ended with jet squadrons
in the sky. And all these centuries whirled around a pumpkin
transformed into a coach, in which sat a charming young woman.
She carries the orb, the scepter and wears the crown through a
shouting crowd which had been waiting for her since the night
before, in rain and cold. Great Britain might have said, "Hard
times force us to make the coronation an intimate affair, to marry
the queen to her people without pomp." On the contrary, Great
Britain has set off her fireworks, has expended the greatest luxury
imaginable, has given an example of excess of which the modern
world seems ashamed—a shame which leads to gloom and despair.

The exhausted, hoarse reporters who relayed the procession
from one to the next, from end to end of London; the military
processions over three kilometers long, the carriages, the princes'
coaches and the royal coach, all this without a moment's hitch,
with the precision of figures on old clock towers; the crowd clinging
to everything and anything, like swarms of bees, obedient down
to the minute when, the queen appearing at the window of Buckingham Palace, it rushed forward and broke the barricades. And
it was sufficient to fly over London in a plane for this enormous
machine of luxury to vanish, for the city to seem empty and dead,
just as the auditory spectacle vanished during the brief period when
our electricity was out.

The queen was anointed, the queen was sealed in the armor of her ancestors, the queen saw kneeling before her the duke of Edinburgh, the archbishops, the dukes and peers. The queen was changed into a symbol. The queen will no longer be the same woman tonight. Power of a ceremony. A ceremony, in all its forms, spares humanity its fear of being nothing.

After such a day, you wonder if England isn't strongest of all. In order to defeat England, you would have to sink the island itself, and everyone on it would die standing up, like an old admiral. No one in England tonight is thinking, "Earth is a filthy trick." As our present mediocrity tends to make us believe.

Politeness—enthusiasm—precision in the theater—respect for words—all forms of ceremony which we lack. Abroad, the slightest effort in this direction is rewarded. As each trip I make proves to me. But still our diplomats would have to help us a little. At the Cannes festival I realized what could be done with a little precision, a little frankness, a little courtesy. England may be stupid. So is France. But I prefer a respectful stupidity to an insolent one.

Received the record of *Oedipus Rex* sent to Villefranche (?) by Columbia. On the cover my drawing of Oedipus's mask and photographs by Sanford Roth.

And tonight Queen Elizabeth will think, like Joan of Arc after Reims, "the evening of a fine day." Great sadness of all festivities. The duke and duchess of Windsor watching the coronation in front of a little television set, cups and saucers visible in the picture. Intoxication of the crowds. Hangover. Realism of England. Ruinous spectacle. Deals with Communist China.

. . . .

JUNE 4

I was thinking about that letter from an Englishwoman last month: "Our order conceals a disorder. Your disorder conceals an order." I wonder. Mendès-France's speech is a truism. France is committing suicide. Politics and literature come down to the same thing with us. Blind and shabby. As long as we don't follow the directives of one man, we fall into the error of those who consult many doctors and mix several diets. Durupt tells me that that's how Kisling died. But alas, unless there's a disastrous takeover, incompatible with our style, what member of the government will allow any head to be higher than his own? French vanity. Nothing to do with British pride.

Wednesday I'll leave France, happy to be at sea. Our France of 1953 is like a little "literary" cafe, filled with smoke, pretentiousness, and stupidity.

In 1930 I invented, in *Le Sang d'un poète*, the hubbub which supplants texts. I mixed several recordings of my own voice in order to obtain the frivolous hum of the worldly theater boxes in the snow. In 1953 Tati is glorified for this discovery in his film *Monsieur Hulot's Holiday.*

Wretched imitations of *Appogiatures* by some poet in the latest issue of *La Parisienne.* Our intellectuals are beginning to see things only when they are at the bottom of the ladder, when they are corrupt and vulgar. No sense of the new, of the invisibility of the new. Moreover, their lack of memory allows what is invisible no opportunity to become visible eventually. Nobility, boldness, style fall between two stools, unless some young archaeologist discovers them. My one effort must be to prepare the *Oeuvres complètes.*

Yesterday I had the barber cut my hair very short so as no longer to resemble the man my photographs advertise. No longer resemble in any way, shape, or form, physically or morally, the image that the world creates of us.

(Genoa) The marquis Doria's unforgettable stare at my Legion of Honor. Why do you wear that? his eyes said. I no longer do.

Cold as March.

JUNE 5 · 1953

Storm. Eleven waterspouts—you could see them like long dark strips between the clouds and the sea. Suitcases. (Mendès-France refused investiture, as expected.) Perhaps France, more shameless than other countries, exhibits a disorder which the others conceal.

Went to Biot. Édouard's charming family. Their hearts show in their faces. Accustomed to hard times. Difficulty of adapting to comfort. His mother's frankness—"Even in paradise, I'd have to get used to it." She misses Anna.*

The bad weather is making complications for our trip. The yacht was to leave Saint-Jean last night. Francine has asked for a delay until this afternoon, if Paul thinks this is possible. It is raining, but the wind has changed. Blowing from the east. It is possible that the weather will improve after the rain. Depending on the weather, we'll leave as planned or else give up on the festivities in Granada and not leave until July first, after Carole's birthday.

What makes me advise Francine not to put off our trip is the sort of void formed by such postponements. You're no longer here and you're still here. Your work suffers. You languish, waiting for the new date. Paul comes this morning to say whether he will leave or stay.

I'm already in a void. The ink resists. I dare not begin a new canvas. Yesterday Édouard photographed *Mme Favini*, *The Birth of Pegasus*, and the little picture of the garden (for Bruckmann). I wonder—with a certain anxiety—if I have come to the end of my reel. Am I painting only to plug up this void which keeps me from writing, from planning any serious work?

Reread the last poems, the ones I intended for the Biennale. They reflect this void I suffer from. The essentials are missing. I'm

------

*One of Édouard Dermit's sisters.

suppressing them. Better the void than a decline. Keep still and wait for that state of hypnosis where nothing exists except what one is making.

I console myself by saying that I've already had this sensation before, this feeling of being incapable of serious work. Each time I would think, "This is it; it's here for good." But alas, from certain signs it seems to me that the threat is more serious this time, that my darkness is emptying out, no longer tormenting me to begin again. No longer leaving me in some form or other. It leaves me *free*.

Picasso's luck. He is like those "men-mothers" Nietzsche speaks of. An uninterrupted childbirth saves them from the critical spirit. Nothing paralyzes them in their work.

Power of organized manual work. Picasso relaxes at the kiln. He never lets his flame die down. His motor turns. He needs very little to start up again.

I let my motor go cold. Painting is my one safeguard. But I don't paint enough. I should sculpt. Struggle with something that resists. Never remain inactive.

My famous "intelligence" has never functioned. All I could count on was the waves coming from . . . where? Intelligence is of no help to me, except with regard to the control of the forces which escape me. Without these waves I am a victim of *stupidity*—a stupidity which is, in fact, amazed by the intelligence of magazine articles, by that formidable intellectual authority of the mediocre.

Begin my life over again? No, this drama requires a last act. You always wonder if this last act is taking place now. And a good play rarely ends well. It is the perspective of that denouement which gives you a sort of fear.

Seen from outside. Riviera workers. I was telling Pasquini that I watch them (building the house next door) and that they seem so happy. Pasquini then tells me about the real lives of several of these men who are paid so poorly. One has committed suicide;

another kills his wife or his child to avoid poverty. The sun deceives us and disguises all that.

Have seen Paul. Meteorologist pessimistic. We'll wait till Monday to decide whether we leave or postpone the trip.

Telegram from Reale. They're sending the Picasso text Tuesday for me to correct.

French politics is covering itself with absurdity and tries to save face with the celebration of Versailles. It would be better to let Versailles fall to ruin and reconstruct the house of France, which is no longer able to stand on its own.

. . . .

SUNDAY · JUNE 7

Rain. It is more than likely we'll postpone our trip. Especially since Lily Baudon telephones that we could move up the little party for Carole's birthday—which would leave Francine free on July 1.

Portrait of the mason's assistant in a paper cap. For his eyes— very big, naive, and cloudy—I've used marbles that Ginette Weill brought me. I embedded them in the panel before painting.

Fragments of the Versailles text in *Paris-Match*. No news of the celebration. It is possible that the rain and cold will cause a cancellation. My own text has false rhymes in it—I had not expected the words to be published. Maurois's text very weak.

A color film? I hesitate. A play? It would have to come of its own accord. I'll keep to this journal. Read and reread Kafka's. After the writer's death, reading his journal is like receiving a long letter.

Portraits-Souvenir. I correct the proofs of the new edition, for which I've drawn a cover. Will I ever regain that energy?

Little Prince Charles asks a gentleman of Buckingham Palace, "Where are you going?" "To see the queen." "Who's the queen?" "Your Mother." "Ah!"

He had fallen off his chair during the coronation ceremony. The photograph has been published of his disappearance from the box, the Queen Mother and Princess Margaret looking for him. He will hear about this fall for a long time. In other ages it would be made into an omen. In the countless documents of the magazines, two surprising things: The royal banquet precisely where Charles I heard his death sentence. The Windsors letting themselves be photographed at the house of an American woman, watching the coronation on a wretched little television set.

My ear saw it all. No document is a surprise to me.

The queen dreamed of winning the derby. So much for her dreams. It was a Jew, Victor Sassoon, who won. The queen knighted Sassoon's jockey. I traveled in the next cabin to Victor Sassoon on the China Sea. His black pajamas, his pockets full of precious stones, his icy eye behind a monocle. He limps. You could hear him limp from my cabin. Chaplin would listen to his cane in the corridor and say, *"Treasure Island!"*

The coronation coach. As if Charles I had been brought to London by Cromwell in a limousine.

Europe clings to her past (Versailles). Russia and the Orient cling to the future. Both are mistaken—for neither past nor future exists.

Odd telegram from Barcelona: "Alberto Puig will be at airport. Watch out for a sort of wicked dwarf who might be there. Neville." This dwarf makes up my mind for me. Put off the trip till July 1. Wretched weather.

Coronations have always taken place in the costumes of their period. Napoleon was the first to invent a coronation in masquerade. The crowd laughed when the coaches passed, because the imperial procession was disguised and painted in broad daylight (memoirs of a man in the street). Elizabeth's coronation is a magnificent avowal of the discrepancy which exists between our period and true pomp.

The great Elizabeth entered Westminster on horseback. This signified: I shall show you. And show them she did. Today it matters little whether the queen "thinks." The queen is not questioned. She does not even question herself. She would refuse, with hauteur, to answer herself.

Last year, I dined at the Anchorenas with the Windsors. After dinner the duke had lost his cigarette holder. We were all of us down on all fours. "He loses everything," the duchess murmured, "and I'm always the one who finds it for him again." I was thinking: "Not his crown." In front of that television set, the duke and duchess look as if they were at the police station identifying lost objects.

· ·

JUNE 8

Description of the picture *Birth of Pegasus.*

The whole is mat, quite bright, as if painted in fresco. In the center, Perseus, faceless, nude, and striped with white ribbons which hold his cape, in the style of a figure by Bramante. In his right hand he holds his sword with a black and yellow handle, in his left, his white shield, on which is perceived the sketch of a face, half human and half animal. The head (without features) stands out against a storm cloud. To the right, above, one of Medusa's sisters escapes, in silhouette against pink sand and a mauve sunset (the sun itself orange). Of the other sister we see only one leg, running. At the far right, down below, is a crab, almost touching the hand of the dead Medusa, whose arm (under Perseus) leads to the far left, where her decapitated body retains the tension of a spasm. The folds of her gown are turned back over her body, up to her left hand clinging to one of them, near the head bristling with snakes. From the blood she is bathed in escapes a white vapor which becomes, at the far left toward the top, the horse Pegasus flying away on huge wings, in an iridescent cloud. Perseus is brownish mauve with pale blue reflections. Medusa is green with russet patches.

Poetically speaking, I have worked so much on this canvas that it seems to me impossible it should fail to release a certain power. I had conceived of its mechanism in Greece (Delphi). I didn't dare begin work on it until much later.

To create expressive forms is to bring into the world objects which live a life of their own, which are no longer under our command. The life of a completed picture possesses a silent activity that is very disturbing. Do such pictures want to be seen or to remain in the dark? One realizes that this is their affair and that they will behave as they choose.

Picasso is sensitive to the portrait of Mme Favini because this canvas is something like the mechanism of his. My other canvases proceed from a mechanism of my own (from a syntax of my own) which tends to make them invisible, like my writing, too rapid and too precise for the sloth of modern minds.

Man seems unable to live without a totem, because without such a totem he would require a sublime intelligence, the kind Voltaire believed himself capable of. To be an unbeliever is possible only if unbelief is based on the certainty of an insoluble enigma transcending that of God's existence.

The totem idea of God creating the world is absurd because it implies a beginning, which makes no sense in the realm of eternity. That our world should begin and end, i.e., that this fragment of an atom should change its chemical figuration in the course of a sort of continuous explosion—that is conceivable. But that our wretched little world should be privileged, created *with love,* punished, moreover—that is inconceivable. This dogma of original sin is born of our grotesque pride and our need to be exceptional. Something like the magic knitting needle in Andersen's fairy tale.

Without the notion of sin, of punishment, of immanent justice, nature's apparent chaos and injustice are inadmissible. Man must explain and account for everything. He has had to construct this fable.

. . . .

JUNE 9

Self-hypnosis and the deceit of events which the present moment sets before us must never fool us as to what matters. Radiguet's fiftieth birthday—that is the typical event of our world right now. No one is even aware of it. Total silence.

Sartre, so generous, so interested in everything, is a perfect figure to serve as an excuse for an empty-headed generation of youth (which hasn't even read him).

. . . .

JUNE 11

Spoke yesterday in Nice—forty-five minutes on the radio with Poulenc, about the Groupe des Six, about Satie, Stravinsky, Schoenberg, and the present tendencies of music. Great freedom in what was said. Odd document.

One always has the craving to believe one is "passing through a crisis." What crisis? There are nothing but crises. Without a crisis there would be nothing.

Poulenc spoke of Stravinsky being influenced by Satie—he told how he himself had been influenced by Stravinsky's works, the ones influenced by Satie. I told about Stravinsky at Mont-Boron— becoming more Catholic than the Pope and the primary adversary of *Sacre du printemps*. He reorchestrated *Sacre* while we were working on *Oedipus Rex*. Poulenc contrasts Stravinsky's "white" works to his "motley" ones. I remark that Schoenberg means to the young today what Satie meant to us. Satie and Schoenberg, in opposite directions, scour music clean.

Bad weather everywhere. Tornadoes in America. Floods in Spain. Torrential rain in Berlin. Hot spell in Moscow. On the Côte d'Azur, what they call "the devil beating his wife."

I've been asked to do the poster for Vence—like the one Matisse made for Nice. Chagall's character discussed. I say, "He belongs to the race of students who hide what they're writing behind a dictionary."

Did the poster for Vence.

Received the Picasso improvisation and Reale's letter. Just as I thought. (Reale will come Saturday or Sunday.)

In Great Britain the conscientious objector is free to say what he wants in public, but everyone shuts him up in the pub. In France the conscientious objector is thrown in jail and everyone is entitled to say whatever he likes in the bistro.

Poulenc here for lunch. He's starting to work on an opera for La Scala, *Dialogue des Carmélites* (Bernanos).

Redid the blue background for the Vence poster. It wasn't "hard" enough for a poster. (Worked with my left hand since I can't do anything with my right.)

If I think, I think badly. Better not to think. Acknowledge the void. Wait. Colette is right, I am a poor idler. Forcing myself to do nothing is a real torture.

Even the preface to the *Guide to Greece* seems like an insurmountable mountain.

There are moments when my stupidity alarms me.

Poor Désormière.* He's being re-educated. He hears, he thinks,

---

*The orchestra conductor Roger Désormière (1898–1963), stricken with hemiplegia in 1952.

he expresses himself by gestures. He can no longer speak a single word.

Poulenc and I listened to the recording of *Oedipus Rex*. The last work suspended between *Les Noces* and a frenzied classicism. Stravinsky carried this classicism to the point of putting a verse of Boileau as an epigraph on his score of *Orphée*. At Mont-Boron his whole oeuvre became suspect to him. He wasn't yet its enemy.

Apparently Hindemith is deliberately desiccating himself, and in the same direction as Stravinsky. They become professors after having been such splendid bad boys. America may have something to do with it.

Schoenberg was a professor too. But he had the advantage of the young not knowing about him yet, so that they received the shock long after it should have occurred. It comes as an antidote to Stravinsky, who gains nothing from having wanted to be his own antidote.

What is called my intelligence is nothing but my capacity to pay attention and a morbid horror of inexactitude.

. . . .

JUNE 12

I must reach some decisions about opposing the malaise that's paralyzing me. But it's increasingly important to consider Picasso as an exceptional and quasi-monstrous case: he has become *the visible*. Do everything in order not to fear *invisibility*.

Tried a poem on Picasso from the same group as the Góngora sonnet on Greco. Began with "Les yeux tristes en bas vers le rire des bouches." I'll send it to Ponti for the Biennale.

Find first, seek afterward. Valéry *finds by dint of seeking*.

. . . .

JUNE 13 · 1953

Just read in the papers that Marcel Herrand died. Heurtebise—
Romeo—the Pitoëffs—Fauconnet—*Le Dit des jeux du monde*—*Les
Mamelles de Tirésias*—the dust of memory.*

No man has ever made himself greater by diminishing another
man.

Shakespeare's dates. A play a year, written and acted. The splendor comes from the fact that there is no concern with splendor,
only theater. The Globe troupe had to have one play after another.

Visit at eight from Reale and some Italian friends. We will all
have lunch with Picasso tomorrow at Vallauris.

. . . .

JUNE 14 · 1953

Evening. Dinner at Juan-les-Pins with Françoise, Paulo, Reale, Luciano Emmer, and the other Italians whom Françoise calls "bicycle
thieves." Earlier, at La Galloise, Emmer had shown us his project
for the big color film on Picasso, for which he wants me to write
(and speak) the texts.

Picasso is going through a crisis but doesn't show it. I see him
borne on the fetishist fear and admiration he inspires the world
over. Being the most negative and destructive mind, ever ready to
find everything absurd, futile, useless, it is indispensable that he
resist his inclination by a continual labor. His almost empty studio
(since everything which had filled it is now in Rome) is an incredible
bric-a-brac of the objects he collects, which are waiting to change

---

*Cocteau evokes Marcel Herrand's roles: Heurtebise in his *Orphée* (1926), with
Georges and Ludmilla Pitoëff; Romeo in his *Roméo et Juliette* (1924); and roles in Honegger's
Le Dit des jeux du monde, costumes by Buy Pierre Fauconnet (1918), and in Apollinaire's *Les
Mamelles de Tirésias* (1917).

their signification into something else, to assume whatever he imposes upon them. Pots, toy cars, broken bicycles, useless tools and ironware heaped up in the corners and hanging on the walls. All of which, if he wants it to, will turn into a little girl skipping rope, a pregnant nanny goat, centaurs, and satyrs. And everywhere are perched the doves he whips off, striped owls made up as old women in carnival masks, sketches of shapeless furniture, profiles of Françoise and portraits of Paloma and Claude. Emmer was a little dazed by this alarming flea market from which he will have to choose, to organize . . .

Reale, returning to Milan by car, drove me back to Santo Sospir. Emmer was taking the plane at Nice.

Last effort throughout the world to save the Rosenbergs, by no means proved guilty. They're to be electrocuted the seventeenth. This is the fourteenth. I was reminded of Talleyrand's remark to Napoleon after the death of the duke d'Enghien: "Worse than a crime, Sire, it is a mistake." The American insistence—they're afraid of seeming *weak*. By reprieving this couple, America would win favor in the world's eyes, and it would cost her nothing. Even if the R.'s were guilty, what could they do in jail? Giving in to the Communists—that is what Washington cannot admit, forgetting that thousands of people who are not Communists are intervening to keep this execution from happening. The moment you intervene, you're a Communist. It's that simple and that absurd.

Gregh received at the academy* after thirty-five failures and an exemplary patience. Ridiculous speeches. Léautaud walking up to the quai de Conti, wanting to come in to hear an acceptance speech by Gregh *"that old clown."* Turned away because of his filthy smock, his slippers, his shopping net. So that poor Gregh, mocked by the reporters, sees on page one not his own portrait but the

---

*Fernand Gregh was received at the Académie française by Jules Romains, on June 4, 1953. See note at entry of January 18.

grimaces of Léautaud, unexpected star and very grand in this charade. Mauriac's remark quoted: "Gregh has written a lot of bad verses. But we've forgotten them: that's our excuse." And another: "Our only amusement consists in keeping out of the academy the men who deserve to be in it." Exact quote.

Yesterday went to see Delannoy shoot his outdoor scenes at the Victorine, with Fresnay. Lunched with Delannoy, Pierre, and Yvonne.* They're coming to Santo Sospir for dinner tonight. Rain. I can imagine the expressions of the Berchols, who must be getting stiff necks from consulting the heavens.

I mention to a reporter that there's a great exhibit of Greco in Bordeaux, and he answers, "I didn't know she was a painter too." It reminds me of the duke de Gramont telling me, "Verlaine . . . You mean that lady who used to paint on fans?"†

Newsreel of the coronation. To be fair, nothing that might have been ridiculous turned out that way. By acknowledging an obligation to resort to ceremonial costumes, England defies the degrading mediocrity that rules the world over. In this spectacle, I find an incredible daring of an entire people risking absurdity and avoiding it by dint of belief in everything our times teach us no longer to credit. An act of collective dementia against our present indifference. A grand-style provocation. I know that such a spectacle disguises many weaknesses, failures to acknowledge authentic values, bad taste concealed under a scarlet cloak. Nonetheless, the whole world feels, before this spectacle, a nostalgia for vanished pomp. Here is advertising in its noblest form. The queen once again teaches niggardliness a lesson. And France's ship of state, bursting with hidden wealth, can take an example from this lion

---

*Yvonne Printemps, Pierre Fresnay's wife.

†A confusion with Madeleine Lemaire (1845–1928), painter of flowers and illustrator of Proust's first book, *Les Plaisirs et les jours.*

and this unicorn, both penniless. Money thrown out the windows that comes back in through the door.

The only roles properly played: the people and the ecclesiastics.

Fiftieth version of my *Sacre*. You drive yourself mad with a text and no one will understand a single word.

.   .   .   .

JUNE 17

At dinner last night, Pierre Fresnay inexhaustible in his memories of our youth and of the shows we used to put on at the Dietzes'.* Yvonne the proverbial type of the stage wife: "A woman has to play a part, otherwise her man will eat her up, etc."

The weather still bad. Clearing toward evening. Rain this morning. Sea calm. We leave for Spain on the first.

Sent off my *Sacre*. Did the preface for the *Guide to Greece* (sent). Lunch Saturday at Vallauris.

Informed Mame Guynet of my desire to show the *Judith* tapestry and the drawings for it either in Turin or Milan. James Lord is in Paris with the Cézannes for the Aix exhibition. Will wait for Orengo to photograph the canvases.

Someone always asks if I have a secret (the secret of my strength). Someone always asks such questions, with the insistence of a Delilah. *Yes, I have a secret.* But if I told it, if I wrote it, even in this journal, it would cease being a secret, and I should lose my strength.

Reale has brought me a carved and painted Sicilian axletree. *"The Battle of Ponte Ammiraglia—inspirata dal quadro del pittore Renato Guttuso."* On the left: "Lo stemma di Bagheria." On the right: "La

---

*Pierre Fresnay was related to Hermann Dietz, whose private school Cocteau attended in 1906–1907.

Trinacria—stemma della Cicilia." In the style of our fairground shooting galleries. Splendid bright colors.

I wonder if this painful vacuum I'm drifting in isn't a *turning point*. So the latest poems suggest. Unless they're a struggle, a rage against the vacuum.

Disgusting vulgarity of the voices on French radio. Of all languages, French is the one that falls most readily into vulgarity.

. . . .

JUNE 20

Television requests a commentary on the film *Lumière* (life of the Lumière family).

. . . .

SUNDAY · JUNE 21

Lunch yesterday at Juan-les-Pins with the Picassos, the Braques, Yves Montand, and Simone. Back to Vallauris afterward with the Braques.

Leaving the restaurant Picasso asked me, "Do you always do what you intended to do?" I answered, "That's the question I keep asking myself."

Braque visits Gris, looks at a canvas he doesn't much like. To cover an awkward moment he says, "Down there, in that corner, there's something that looks odd." Gris looks through his sketches. "Yes, I see it now," Gris says, "I made a mistake." "Be careful," Braque says, "if you make a mistake, you might put three bowls in an apple."

Picasso (when Françoise quoted a remark by some painter—Marcoussis?): "Gris is the accountant of cubism"), answers severely that Gris constitutes an example of noble privations—of austerity.

I tell Picasso, "You sign your canvas first and then you paint the picture to honor your signature."

Gave Françoise the Rome text.

My latest poems. Written for translators. A poet's language is always translated. Might as well go all the way into the chiaroscuro. "Homage to Góngora," twelve stanzas.

The slow-motion sequences of the film on Matisse show us what finicky hesitations, what long study his line comes from.* He seems to dash it off without a thought, but the flowers photographed by the same method prove the deep thought that colors them. Matisse: courage and elegance. Never, in the middle of his room in the Régina, in a bed of raw silk, pink and calm, never have we heard him complain. Not one shred of life has been lost. If he can't paint, he cuts up paper and pins the shapes. He remains the example of the painter that Renoir used to personify. Picasso says they've been giving Matisse shots for his heart which are ruining his eyes.

Clouzot thinks he's a painter. So he's told Braque. I tell Françoise, "He must have begun by painting a bottle and a napkin." That's always what happens when you think you're a painter.

Write a play? I'm the last to know. I'm writing poems.

Is it that they know nothing, or do they *want* to know nothing? The latter, alas—that's how it looks to me. Then where are the ears going? Do the ears have walls?

A fencing studio, Françoise said, that's the best way to describe Jarry.

Braque said: "A lot of the cubists started out as caricaturists. They tried to make us forget it by the narrowness and severity of an Aristotelian discipline." (Which was a kind of prologue to Picasso's panegyric of Gris.) Gris had started in the comic paper *L'Assiette au beurre*.

---

*Henri Matisse, 1945–1946, a film by François Campeaux.

I ask Braque what became of the painters in [the] Rosenbergs' cellar (not the Sing Sing ones: Léonce and Paul): Metzinger, Herbin, Gleizes, etc. I had never heard a word about them. And Braque tells me they are working, selling, writing manifestos.

I report my amazement in discovering that every student in the School of Fine Arts in Istanbul was doing Lhote, in spite of the van Goghs, Matisses, and Picassos tacked up on the walls. It's true that Lhote used to teach in Istanbul.

In 1912 cubism was much more in favor with the theoreticians than Picasso or Braque. In Anatole France's *Revolt of the Angels* a "modern" young man speaking of Delacroix declares, "I prefer Gleizes and Metzinger."

My first contacts with "modern" painters were Gleizes and Lhote.* I had to meet Picasso to have my eyes opened.

The ban placed on certain painters does not keep them from working or from selling. But it drives them permanently out of the histories of painting. These bans are occult, ferocious, and correspond to a certain line, which an artist is ruined for neglecting. Which is why Picasso is right when he vaunts Gris's attitude. It saved him from that quarantine in which Kisling, for instance, will remain. At first glance, such bans seem an injustice—but ultimately they correspond to the course of a stream which implacably ferries subversive works into the Louvre and keeps agreeable ones out. I mean agreeable works which *seem* subversive. Surrealism has observed this savage classification. Woe to those who become déclassé by mistaking a certain family lineage (a certain family look, even outrageousness). What seems strange is that the Prix de Rome and the French Academy in Rome still enjoy a certain prestige, since their misguided path is so obvious, even on the commercial level.

---

*Albert Gleizes (1881–1953) and André Lhote (1885–1962) met Cocteau around 1915. They illustrated the last number of *Le Mot* (no. 20, July 1, 1915), a periodical founded and edited by Paul Iribe and Jean Cocteau.

Yet one must not forget that all the great daubs of the Salon—a Chabas, a Detaille, a Didier-Pouget, a Bail, all the cardinals at dinner and the chimney sweeps in the snow, the heather-covered hills and the servant girls polishing brass basins, the patriotic allegories and all the rest—fill countless unknown salons and that very few people own a van Gogh, a Cézanne, a Renoir. The daubs do not disappear, as one might think. All the "Riviera painters" sell very high and very well. At the Magasin du Louvre there's a painting section where the *Arabs at the Well* and *Sheep at Twilight* never discourage a countless clientele. The model is of more interest to these customers than painting itself, and this is true even among people who know their onions. I said to Braque yesterday, "You're the first one not to have fooled the public." Apelles had fooled even the birds! It is this substitution of pure interpretation for "subject" which leads collectors nowadays to be wary of any representational canvas. Buying the impressionists, they are buying stock options, bonds, names. Which is how the shrewd ones will miss the boat and scorn the young, whose role will be to turn the smoke the other way. These young painters will remain as invisible to them as van Gogh, Cézanne, and Renoir were in the rue Laffitte galleries, when the Rothschilds laughed at them all. And it is natural that these young painters should get the worst of it, like the others. If they do, it will prove that they are new. To displease by pleasing will be their inferno. Likely that these Monday painters will be treated as Sunday painters, naive painters. Each has his turn.

The notion of difficulty, of boldness parading boldness has become so powerful, so deeply anchored in men's minds that Radiguet's work (and R. had the revolutionary notion of contradicting an active disorder) still suffers from it, while Rimbaud, who owed it to his period to contradict a passive order, happens to correspond exactly to the modern credo. Henceforth nothing will be more difficult, more ungrateful, more tedious to impose than calm. The young must realize this—that their role is a thousand times more difficult to perform than a tendency in the opposite direction. Perhaps, after my death, if this journal is published, the thing will have occurred. I wonder. Surface excesses have spoiled eyes which recognize a fashion by its costumes and never consult the work's own gaze. Yet it is by the *gaze* that we recognize new beauty, whatever its costume.

Certain values are changed only by depending on them while demolishing them. Rimbaud judges Baudelaire severely, but he *classes* him. Baudelaire demolishes Ingres to the advantage of Delacroix, but he does not make him déclassé: he locates him. Picasso demolishes impressionism while buying Vuillards. He adores Corot, whom fools have no use for. At a splendid Fabiani show, the idiots of the intelligentsia walked right past one of Corot's magnificent Italian women, supposing that it was an old canvas put there by mistake. Intellectual snobbery has replaced snobbery itself, which followed the example of kings by consulting specialists in outrage for fear of committing a howler.

Jeannot telephones that he has signed for *Monte-Cristo*.* I urged him to do so. Unless he does certain roles like those of my own films, I prefer to see him enjoy himself in a piece of foolishness rather than to wear himself out on boring scripts or pulling on straitjackets like *Nez de cuir*.†

In the film he had played Benzi's father, because he thinks he looks so much older than he is. Now the film, which is a good one, calculated to please,‡ isn't doing well because the jeune fille public refuses to see Jeannot in a father's role. Nothing more unexpected than the reactions of this audience which we know so little about. I was worried that this anonymous public, so preferable to the aesthetes, would turn away from Jeannot, yet he

---

*A film by Robert Vernay, who had already created a *Comte de Monte-Cristo* (1942).

†A film by Yves Allégret, 1951, based on the novel by Jean de La Varende.

‡*L'Appel du destin*, a film by Georges Lacombe, 1952.

had a real triumph the other evening at the Cinéma Kermesse. Whatever he may say about it, an actor needs that absurd warmth. Simone Signoret told me, "Even if he makes a mistake or does a poor film, his passion saves him." Now the same public was incredibly hard on Alain Cuny. This is because Cuny, whose physique perfectly corresponds to everything this little world approves, has no radiance and no ease, that ease which modern youth parades in its way of dressing, its way of moving. These young people resent his failure to correspond to what they expect of him. On the other hand, Jeannot's "beauty," which alienates them from him, seems contradicted by an inner beauty which they identify with an indifference to intellectual style, an indifference which is—oddly enough—characteristic of the *intellectual style of our times.* That famous "nothing" demanded of artists who know "everything" and must not show it under any pretext. I note these random thoughts because they may some day illuminate our complex times. The success of my film *Les Parents terribles* was achieved, in this milieu, by a limitless admiration for the two old ladies ("*It would be nice to be old soon,*" said Juliette Greco, when she came out of the theater) and for the disorder, the abandon in which Jeannot was inimitable. The same for Marcel André—his scarecrow gestures, his grimaces, his look of letting everything go. I was amazed that this milieu showed as much favor to Dorziat as to de Bray. It was because the disdain attached to the old values—beauty, grace, youth, makeup—was overwhelmed by those grotesque faces. Nothing else is respected nowadays. Jeannot, in *Les Parents terribles,* achieved a grotesque face by his fear of profiting from a good physique.

All this was brought home to me by a young actress who uses no makeup, no hairstyle, and who does stupid roles: not only does Simone Signoret delight this young audience, but she pleases foreigners who are susceptible to these fashions without being aware of it. I noticed this at the Cannes festival.

Orson Welles benefits from this craze for grand-scale grotes-querie in which he excels and which this young audience prizes far above a success I am often made to pay dearly for, on the excuse that it falls into aestheticism.

The British, in the remake of *Les Parents terribles*, missed the boat by supposing that only a French audience could understand a relaxation of style. They replaced it by a fake propriety without understanding that my relaxation was the pinnacle of propriety and that this propriety-in-relaxation was nothing but life itself. That intense life which stage and screen demand, whatever one's nationality. Frank's Aunt Léo became a good sport and Michel a poor victim of Oxford's respectable chill. Only the girl is superior to the actresses who have done the role for me. A Swede who reveals her soul without fear of being found shocking.

I might add that onto relaxation and grotesquerie is grafted the cult of the domestic virtues, bourgeois morality (as among the surrealists): to marry, to have children.

In Italy a fashionable young woman affects to be bored with everything. She calls herself "magnolia." Pale, hair down, sitting on the steps of the Piazza di Spagna, they reinvent the style of Dietrich in 1934, especially on the records where she deliberately sings off key, laments which herald the teary pessimism of a Prévert. Piaf perfected the genre by doing away with Marlene's physical beauty. The radio corrects the balance by turning out a lot of little 1900-style songs, very hearty.

Don't forget the letter Heinrich Mann wrote me before *The Blue Angel* was made: "Sternberg insists on using a plump creature from the cafés; her name is Marlene Dietrich." (*Sic.*)

And Hébertot's remark when I told Edwige she was taking too many pills: "You're forgetting that Edwige is a plump brunette." Edwige managed to be a thin blond, but she fell into disfavor because she's a "camellia," not a "magnolia." A suspect morbidity. Heroic struggle that betrays a certain optimism. She was rejected as a young lady. She will be rejected as an old lady. She is not a "magnolia." Besides, she is not sexy. (For you can be sexy and still be a "magnolia.") These young ladies, out of boredom, sleep with boys bored to sleep with them.

In short, and to be done with our absurdities, the fabrication of Saint-Germain-des-Prés must have the look of a supreme disgust with all fabrication. A naturalness without the shadow of the natural. Artifice made to look normal. Insolence and indolence. All this comes out of Sartre, who didn't suspect the monsters he was bringing into the world.

It would be curious to make a study of the Incroyables, the Merveilleuses, the Zazous, the Existentialists, and their ancestors. Including Alcibiadism, Dandyism, etc. The amazing hairstyles with sideburns of the male Zazous. The females like Thomas Diafoirus (Molière) for the hair and a little Breton cross around the neck. The tiny beard and the tight jeans of the male existentialist. His checked shirt. His loafers. The careful slovenliness of the existentialist female, her hair hanging down to her shoulders in long, limp locks. The black turtleneck. The vast scorn of everything that doesn't belong to this race. The racism of fashion. The exaggeration of our youthful fashions among the British or the Americans. The Zazou jacket came from the Harlem blacks. The communism à l'américaine from existentialism. The cellars. The cellar clubs. The books and magazines carried under the arm. Accessories. No one ever reads. In *Orphée* I made them a hive as if for the bees (place Stalingrad). After the last day of shooting, they stayed there. They had gotten into the habit of my artificial hive. The beginning of *Orphée* is scrupulously accurate. The realm of Roger Blin, stammering actor, anti-intellectual intellectual, charming sloven. In *Orphée* I couldn't give the role of the leader of the pack to anyone else. He was the only one who could say, "Quite remarkable, I admit" the way André Breton would say it. In the outdoor shots (Orpheus's house), Alain had brought me a busful of extras he wanted to dress up as existentialists. They looked like a village wedding, and I wasted a whole day. The next day the bus brought me the whole terrace of the Café de Flore. Everything became rich and true and gave me no trouble at all; the work went of its own accord.

Reread Chamfort. Almost every page could be written this morning. A journalist would make his fortune by publishing them and then admitting the deception afterward.

. . . .

JUNE 24

At the fleet celebration for the coronation, the British took the Russian sailors to Karl Marx's grave. A fine thing.

Translation of poems. Obscurity translated: something always remains. Excessive clarity translated: nothing remains.

America—her contempt and our debts. England—turning toward Moscow. Germany—our incapacity to win her over. Falling among three stools.

The Rock of Monaco: a tiny, exquisite city out of Stendhal. Remote from everything. People who never come down from it. Orengo lives there . . .

In Paris a society like mine confines itself to keeping books for thieves. The harder I work, the closer I come to ruin. The state robs me blind. It is only natural I should try to protect myself against the state by every legal means. Pagnol carries this method to extremes. He is threatened but protected by Monacan legislation.

Orengo brings the first copy of *Le Bal du comte d'Orgel* to Santo Sospir.

Francine is staying in Paris until we leave (July 1). Took her to the Nice airport this morning.

Did the eight drawings for the special edition of *Le Bal* (walnut stain).

The printers and engravers of *Le Bal* are so delighted with their work that they want me to give them a series of poems with drawings in color for them to produce at their own expense.

The terra-cotta bust of Pushkin at Orengo's, a *sublime object.* Wonderful little ram's head.* The bust comes from the wardrobe of Tsarskoye Selo. The master of the robes had slipped it out on the eve of the revolution. When he left the Riviera, he sold it to Orengo. I would give anything for it. I've asked Orengo to photograph it for me from different angles. When you see Pushkin's face, you understand how the love of his work transcends every crisis, every regime. No need to read him (besides, he's untranslatable), you only need to look at him.

For the printers and engravers of *Le Bal*, I'd like to illustrate (from a certain distance) the latest poems under the title *Clair-Obscur*.

Chamfort: From all evidence, long reigns are deplorable. God is eternal. Judge for yourself . . .

Picasso: People say I couldn't care less about the world. Absolutely. Like everyone else, like God himself.

Looking at Picasso's latest landscape, Braque said nothing. That evening, in the cafe, Picasso praised Juan Gris's austere attitude, with that genius for revenge of his. He supported it by a panegyric of Matisse.

Aragon asks me to sign a petition for the rehabilitation of the Rosenbergs. I tell him that no one except a Communist can sign his text. I correct it. He publishes it under this title: "An Initiative of Jean Cocteau."

---

*"Homage to Pushkin" in *Clair-Obscur* begins with this line: "Of this young ram, the untranslatable absence. . . ." Cocteau also published an article on Pushkin in *Ce Soir*, on March 30, 1937, and made a poster for the Paris exhibition for Pushkin's centenary that year.

At Versailles my voice has been replaced by actors, and my text has been cut and changed out of all recognition.

All of which encourages my misanthropy. I am sick of spicing up every sauce except the one I like.

. . . .

JUNE 25

Dr. R. from Beaulieu tells me that during the Occupation he and Professor P. hid a Jewish colleague in their cellar. They fed him through an air shaft. The day the Americans came, he was released. Now he has been given the Legion of Honor, the croix de guerre, the Cross of the Liberation. His clientele has tripled. He is high-handed with his saviors.

It has now been officially determined that Picasso is the devil, that he disintegrates the human countenance, destroys beauty, etc. As if every genius hadn't done as much—incarnated the devil from the point of view of Saint-Sulpice. From this perspective, God too is the devil. Isn't his reign destructive? According to the morning papers, God has never proceeded otherwise than by catastrophes.

I haven't much use for anecdotes, but last night, talking with friends, I recalled some entertaining ones.

Jacqueline de Pourtalès, who married Vladimir Rehbinder,* was looking at a photograph of Princess Lucien Murat, whom she loathed. "You can see," she told me, "how ugly she must have been!"

I remember the duke de Rohan, who prided himself on his wit, saying one evening in my presence, to his daughter the Princess Lucien Murat, who arrived for dinner very poorly dressed: "Marie, if you weren't what you are, you might be taken for what you're not." And then he would glance around with all the satisfaction

---

*Rehbinder photographed Cocteau in the 1920s.

of a successful playwright. The duke looked like a chamber pot with an eye painted on the bottom. His wife, née Verteilhac,* wrote incredible verses. We used to know lots of them by heart, Max Jacob and I. The poor woman had a kind of genius for absurdity, *an infelicity of expression*. Once Auguste Dorchain, the critic for *Les Annales*, told these noble poetesses that only the countess de Noailles was a true poet, and that the rest of them were amateurs. "An amateur!" exclaimed the baroness de Baye, "why, I no longer count my feet!"

"You are staring at my breasts, Monsieur l'Abbé" said the old and corpulent Mme de Talleyrand to the abbé Mugnier. "Would you like to touch them? I have the impression that is what you are eager to do."

"Madame," the abbé replied, "I should not dare. They are not yet relics."

One rainy evening, when the abbé had dined at the place des États-Unis and the conversation had been exclusively of Church matters, Francis de Croisset thought he would walk the abbé out to his car. "Aren't you afraid of getting wet, Monsieur l'Abbé?" "I fear God, cher Abner, and have no other fear." (*Athalie*.) It was Francis himself who told me this—he adored such absurdities.

At a dinner at the Wedel-Jarlsbergs—Wedel was then the Norwegian ambassador—he announced to me that he made nothing of Picasso's painting. I asked him what he made of his chef's dessert. He didn't take it well at all. Matters became so nasty that I forgot I was his guest and asked him (this was 1917), "Your lectures on patriotism are too much for me—have you done anything for France?" And he exclaimed, "I have sent three hundred young men to ski in the Vosges," and since he pronounced *skier*

---

*Herminie de la Brousse de Verteilhac (1853–1926), wife of the prince de Léon, who became, upon the death of his father in 1893, the eleventh duke de Rohan. A member of the Société des gens de lettres, a poet, and watercolorist, the duchess was a great friend of Robert de Montesquiou. Cocteau frequently made fun of her verses.

"chier" (shit), a burst of laughter around the table brought the disagreeable scene to an end.

Princess Murat had married Charles de Chambrun, and both of them were quite senile. At one dinner at their house, the princess farted. Chambrun, who was talking to the lady next to him, turned toward his wife: "Be still, Marie. You always talk when you have nothing to say."

At the Académie française, just before he died, Chambrun was so gaga that he introduced himself to one of his colleagues from the provinces by bowing and murmuring his telephone number.

Gaston Palewski is a great ladies' man. At the end of a party, he came up to a lady and murmured, "I understand you don't have your car—let me take you home in mine." To which she replied: "Very kind, but I'm rather tired this evening. I prefer to walk."

On the opening night of one of his plays, which was an evident flop, Mauriac was standing in the wings next to Henry Bernstein, who had come backstage to see him. "Are you pleased?" Bernstein asked Mauriac, who answered, "Not so much as you are."

. . . .

June 27

Reread Malraux's *La Condition humaine* (*Man's Fate*). At least tried to reread it: hateful as Claude Farrère. This is an example of what the "*école du soir*" has to offer!

Sent off the preface to the *Cent rimes* and the text for the homage to Marcel Herrand.

Lunch tomorrow at Vallauris.

Received the copy of the new edition of *Portraits-Souvenir* from Grasset. Cover very well printed. Printer's error on page 86, reversed lines making the text incomprehensible.

. . . .

JUNE 28

Lunch at Juan-les-Pins with the Picassos, Penrose, Lee Miller,* whom I almost failed to recognize. Picasso describes how at a Cannes dinner, van Dongen had made up a table of painters. He had included the bootmaker Greco.

Obscurity enjoys great privileges. (And the discretion which imposes it upon us bears its immediate reward.) Zorzi, sending me the proofs of *Le Sacre* from Venice, writes, "Your admirable poem." If the poem were not obscure, he would write, "Your charming, your delicious poem." The way people talk when they see Picasso's portraits of Paulo dressed as a harlequin or on his donkey. They would not dare speak so in the presence of his monsters.

Picasso the demiurge. The devil performs with fake gentleness— he deceives. Only God dares perform by crimes and catastrophes.

Sometimes I discern an almost divine stupidity in Picasso's cunning contraptions.

In Vence, at R.G.'s,† I lingered over the microscope, realizing once again that the dimensions do not exist and that if the idea of the "minuscule" were valid (it cannot be), these microbes more complex than a huge factory—the infusoria—could not satisfy the demands of their very complexity. Moreover, most of these beings are immortal (?). In other words, they live on another scale than ours. Consequently it is asserted that they are imported into us by error and that they endure this, but in reality belong to other systems where their existence is normal, healthy, and or-

---

*Lee Miller (1908–1977), American photographer, a student of Man Ray, wife of Sir Roland Penrose, art historian and British collector. She played the chief female part in Cocteau's film *Le Sang d'un poète*, 1930.

†Robert Gaillard, born 1909, a journalist, novelist, and biographer also interested in entomology and biology.

ganized. Hence the microbes are actually a sort of colony from an alien system, adapting themselves to ours where they live in order to fulfill their needs. It seems to me that this theory is absurd and that the famous "other worlds" are here, quite close, at incalculable distances. The giant factories invisible to the naked eye which I observe under the microscope relate to the problems I raise in my chapter "Of Distances" (in *Journal d'un inconnu*), which no one has yet understood.

Francine arrives at five-thirty this afternoon from Mortefontaine, where she was celebrating her daughter's birthday.

Did poems for *Clair-Obscur*. Homage to van Gogh—homage to Kafka—homage to Pushkin. Writing "clear" is dangerous now, when every sentence is misinterpreted. Secret weapon.

Overcast weather. These clouds must come from the polar ice melting. As you might expect, the Americans deny any connection to their atomic tests.

Who was the greatest star in the world? Stalin. He dies, and three months later nothing remains. No newspaper, even a Communist one, ever mentions his name.

Lucien Guitry would say to an author who had just read him a play, "Look here, my dear fellow, I know this will surprise you, but the role I'd really like to play is an ass, an ass-role." "Well . . . if you think about it," the author would always answer, "all in all, my character . . . *is* an ass, a real ass!"

What most people think the devil looks like is the Paganini statuette I've just bought in Nice. Down to the devil's violin in *Histoire du soldat*.* His detachment, his mandrake resonance.

---

*Ballet by Charles Ferdinand Ramuz and Igor Stravinsky (1918), for which Cocteau narrated in the Geneva performance of 1934 and the Vevey performance in 1962.

. . . .

JUNE 30

Worked all day yesterday on the colored drawings for *Clair-Obscur*.

x x x

Paragraph crossed out because I was writing about politics. No future interest—even for the people I'm speaking to.

Benda says that France seeks [an] equilibrium between her conformist mentality and her revolutionary spirit, and that our best periods are those when these two combine—when neither one massacres or imprisons the other. This is what I would call (in my jargon) the points of contradiction from which France draws her singular electricity.

Since I've been able to write some poems and illustrate them, my obsession with emptiness has passed. No doubt these poems wanted to come, had to come . . .

Nothing is deadlier than these arrests, these stops and starts. Picasso used to say, "You have to start all over, as if it were the first time." Which is why he never stops working and moves on from one thing to the next. As a result, a kind of inflation, an incredible avalanche of works making their way around the world.

Picasso is resented less for his genius than for the money he makes. He has toppled that old idol, the neglected artist starving to death. The gold of his genius remains invisible to French avarice, but the gold he exchanges it for is quite visible. This gold is more scandalous than the work. Even in Rome a lady came up to me at the exhibition and pointed to one of his canvases and asked me, "What's that one worth?"

. . . .

JULY 1 · 1953

An hour's flight to Barcelona. Journalists. Questions it is impossible
to answer. And the wall of languages. The *Orphée II* won't dock
until tomorrow. Lucien* is here with the car. We're staying at
the Ritz. A little stroll. Amazing 1900 architecture. One house near
the hotel looks as if it were built by Dali. Tomorrow, if the weather
is good, a bullfight. Reserved the seats. The journalist interviewing
me at the hotel remarks, "There are five or six people in the
stadium who know what's going on." Hellish racket of the trams.
Bought a red Burgos sausage, which we eat in the room.

The journalist asks, "Do you consider this period of atomic
disintegration to be a favorable one for poetry?" I answer: "That's
as if you asked me if some period of Spanish history is favorable
or unfavorable to bullfights. There will always be poets, painters,
and bullfights. Especially since you tell me that five or six people
out of four thousand are the only ones capable of understanding
them. This proves that the corrida is a kind of violent poetry. In
our poets' corrida, the public is the bull. Our profession conjugates
a spectacle with a science. But it's one in which the bull does the
killing. You have to work with the cape and not be afraid of death.
There is one death for each fight, which is ours. I no longer even
count my own deaths. Dying doesn't scare me. I've got into the
habit."

Notes written on the plane:

It's not our contemporaries who misunderstand us, it's humanity.

Valéry's weakness is the little margin he allows thoughts, the
unexpected contacts analogous to those of our dreams. He provokes
them, directs them more than he allows himself to be directed by
them.

---

*One of Francine Weisweiller's two chauffeurs.

148

It's by the exegeses it provokes that the poet's obscurity triumphs.

"When you write, are you thinking about yourself or other people?" "I am other people."

What people call thinking consists of discovering relations between objects close to one another, never discovering relations between objects remote from one another (alien to one another).

If they read aphorisms, people like what they could have said, what helps them to express it . . . Their laziness keeps them away from what they could never have said, from what they might risk *learning*.

A good aphorism is not reversible.

Thinking about something is a way of condemning yourself to solitude. "Do you think sometimes?" the curé of Milly asked his old housekeeper. "Oh yes, Monsieur le curé." "And when you think, what is it you think about?" "Oh, nothing."

Admirable old lady.

The reporter from the Barcelona paper (distributed throughout Spain): "They say you're a Communist. Is that so?" "No. I am not a Communist, but I have Communist friends. It's not the same thing."

In 1916 in Paris, politics had no role to play. There was only art politics. I didn't stop to think if Picasso was Spanish, Modigliani Italian, Stravinsky Russian. We were all from Montparnasse.

Now if I go to Paul Éluard's funeral, I become a Communist. The frenzy of labels. A free man is a circus freak, the creature of a vanished species.

The first question the Spanish journalists asked: "Would you like to be asked to form the government?"

The reporter who came to the hotel says, "The Spanish are even more individualistic than the French." I answer that from a distance this is difficult to discern, since the genius of their nation is declared, more than ours, by a general coloration, by a sort of flame that appears to be shared by all of them. One is wrongly led to suppose that there are several Frenchmen and only one Spaniard.

. . . .

JULY 2

Grand hotels. Funereal. The same in every city the world over. A
kind of no-man's-land with the same orchestra playing the same
pieces. The suite from *l'Arlésienne*, the waltz from *Faust*. The same
families around the tables. The same cuisine. The same waiters
with their long skirts made out of a napkin. The same lobby, the
same chandeliers. In a corner of this Ritz lobby, there's an old
gentleman under a shawl who looks like George V. He prides
himself on doing so, it would seem. After dinner the reporters
bring us the articles announcing my arrival. "The same articles."
The world seems to be increasingly impersonal. The reporters call
the night spots where you can see flamenco dances: Carco's Barcelona (*sic*). I woke up this morning after a nightmare in which
there had been an accident—a servant of my grandfather's had
had an ear cut off while he was dragging me behind him on a
motorcycle, an embassy where I had gone for help, ladies climbing
stairs in long gowns and not listening to me. I was shouting on
the sidewalk: "I wasn't made to live on this earth! I don't want
to live on this earth any longer!"

Puig arrives today from France. He will save us from this Ritz.
He has Gypsy friends. It was in his house that the Aurics saw such
fine dancing.

Dali is ridiculed—they deal with him as if he were a clown.
Picasso—they still hope he will come. He is respected, but his
recent canvases are decried. (I am talking about the reporters—
the same, I repeat, the world over.) Great freedom of speech with
regard to politics. I ask if taxes are high. I am told that every
lawyer in Spain is working to keep them down and to avoid the
laws. No one pays what he is asked.

The corrida is very useful for my answers. It is a spectacle and
a science. Very few people understand it, which doesn't keep the

crowds away. "But you're so famous"—"Famous and misunderstood, like your corridas."

COCTEAU: There have never been so many young poets in France.
REPORTER: Why just now?
COCTEAU: Youth must sing its despair.

After a paella we visited everything in Barcelona that shows the sources of Dali's inspiration and of Miró's. The extraordinary and inspired crag of the Sagrada Familia and the other buildings by Gaudi. The Parc Güell, its esplanade with the Egyptian temple and the slanting pillars, the rippled benches with their crockery mosaic so splendidly set in the cement. Gaudi suggests Gustave Doré and certain drawings by Victor Hugo. He's a sort of Facteur Cheval with all the skill and knowledge of an architect.

At six the corrida in the largest bullring. The bulls are too young, and weak. The spectacle of the corrida means something, for those who do not understand its true language, only if the bull is terrible and the matador superb. The corrida must be a drama. Here it was only a comedy (a slaughter). The boy who jumps down into the ring, the toreros who throw him out, the police who take him away. At the beginning of the fight, they draped one of the matador's blue capes in front of me. I didn't know that Puig had requested this homage—I only found out about it that evening.

Once Alberto Puig got to Barcelona, everything changed. The pomegranate opened and revealed its heart. Until three in the morning, we observed a sublime spectacle likely to reconcile anyone with the human race. Flamenco dancing and singing. This river of Gypsies comes from so far away. You wonder if its source isn't actually Egyptian, as they claim. They dance in a tiny whitewashed space with the violence and the nobility of certain nervous fits, a mysterious struggle against an angel of epilepsy. Moreover, they are great actors, and they know it. The star of the little troupe is a girl of fourteen. She has the profile of Seti I.

All these splendid people adore Alberto and compliment him between each number. Every one of them has his or her "genius," his or her own gestures, his or her rhythm, movements of the hands and feet, discoveries. And their fixed grimace when they're sitting in their chairs around the edges of the performing space seems to fling them into their number with a kind of sob. Each in turn stands up, enters the circle, stamps his feet, and such movements help me understand the source of the curves and broken rhythms, tragic or grotesque, the mechanism of Picasso's lines and forms—who paints the way they dance.

They sob and spit up fiery flowers [,which] they stamp out, as soon as they burst into flame. It's as if they were trying to stamp out themselves, stamping and clapping their hands, clapping their belly, their thighs, their feet, lifting their jacket as though to protect it against the flame of the flamenco. As soon as the fire is out, they sit down.

News of the *Orphée II*: The sailors have had to put in at Port-Vendres because of a storm. They won't be here till Sunday.

Serrano has sent me a tricolor bouquet. We went out with him last night. All our memories of the place de la Madeleine . . .

Los Caracoles, the restaurant run by Bofarull, whom I had known in Cannes. Food is served between the wine barrels, under strings of onions, peppers, dried herbs.

Lucien Defawes, director of Cinescola, has sent his apologies: he's at Pamplona and didn't even know I was in Barcelona. In fact, his apologies are sent by his secretaries. I had forgotten I was an honorary member of this academy.

At the corrida, a bullfighting reporter, sitting to my right and who didn't know me, decided that all the honors being shown me were for him. He tugged so hard at the blue cape that I never suspected it was meant for me. I kept out of the way as best I could, assuming he was the one being photographed. This business caused a lot of laughter among the other journalists and Puig's brother, who was sitting not far away from us.

. . . .

JULY 3

More photographers this morning, and those caricaturists who make me look like Sabartés.

Will visit Picasso's sister around seven this evening, with Alberto Puig.

Visit to the Ruiz family, but Mme Vilato is too ill to receive us. The whole family in an apartment very much like Picasso's. Sordid and royal. I'll visit her Sunday.

Dinner on the waterfront, in a dive like the one in Istanbul.

. . . .

JULY 4

Visit to the Museum of Modern Art. What I love is the bad painting. Visit to the exhibit of Romanesque art which is superb and which interests no one here. In the past, one did not go to museums to see these works, one went to churches. Now at the Matisse chapel, one does not go to church, one goes to see Matisse.

. . . .

JULY 5

My birthday. Sixty-four. At one in the morning at the Yacht Club, Puig and the flamenco troupe come into the little dining room carrying a cake with sixty-four candles, which I manage to blow out. Clapping, singing, dancing, stamping until five. At three, according to Yacht Club sources, the *Orphée II* sailed into harbor.

The Gypsies don't clap the rhythm, they applaud it.

Corrida. Today's is as various and splendid as the first one was dreary and ugly. The bulls may not have been first class, but the (new) matadors had a theatrical heroism. You felt they were ready to do anything to show their worth. One of them was tossed on the horns, another knocked down. In the last fight, the matador dedicated his bull to me.

· ·

JULY 6

Dinner last night with Serrano, at a friend's house. Another birthday cake, with the same sixty-four fatal candles. Which makes me 128. The pastry chef told them, "It must be for the same gentleman."

News at last of the *Orphée II*. Francine was able to telephone the sailors. Paul was sick at Port-de-Bouc, near Marseilles. He's better, and the boat could be in Barcelona the day after tomorrow.

Visit to the Naval Museum with Carlès and the director. Amazing architecture, of a simplicity which in most cases can be achieved only by ruins. Endless arcades and pillars. This was the shipyard. The sea came up to the ramp from which they launched the ships.

Did a lot of drawings of the flamenco for Puig. (Pronounced "Putch").

· ·

JULY 7

Visit to the Picasso family. His sister very plump and pink and young looking, with a little brioche-chignon. She is an invalid, sitting in the corner of a tiny room where the children and grand-children cluster around her, all talking at once. Paul plays the guitar. They sing, stamp, and clap. But I must leave early because the Puigs are waiting for me at the hotel. I promise to come back

Wednesday at eight and to stay until ten (when they take dinner).
We dine tonight in the markets. And I go to bed. (In Barcelona,
people are out walking and talking on the *ramblas* until six in the
morning.)

Must visit the consul at eleven. Afterward, out into the country
to visit the Puigs.

When the Spaniards shout *olé*, they draw out the *o*.

. . . .

JULY 8

Went to the Puigs' at Palamós. Long road. Good smell of the
countryside (the smell of a child's hair). Alberto's sister has bought
Sert's house, overlooking the gulf. Alberto had broken up the estate
into two parts. His is on the left and facing the sea, down to the
steep point, above which the Greek village had been built in a
semicircle. We visited the excavations. Back to Barcelona around
eleven. Telegram from Paul, still sick. We'll have to drive over to
Madrid and back to Málaga through Andalusia. We'll know today
whether the boat can join us there.

It's at Palamós (Castel) that Alberto gave those great Gypsy
festivals that Nora Auric kept urging us not to miss.

Visit to the consul, who complains, like all consuls. They've
been cut back, and the embassy in Madrid enlarged. And it costs
more to live in Barcelona than in Madrid, etc., etc.

The French Cinema Week collapsed at the Barcelona Trade Fair
because of sabotage of the machinery. You couldn't hear a thing,
and the audience hissed. The program had to be given up after
insoluble problems with machinery and customs. It seems to me
that the consul (M. Périer) went to none of the important people
in Barcelona (because he doesn't know any of them). He was
struggling with the gangsters of the trade. The films sent were:

Allégret's *La Jeune folle*, Tati's *Jour de fête*, Becker's *Casque d'or*, and Clouzot's *Salaire de la peur*.

Lingered a while longer in Barcelona because of this tiresome business with the yacht. But everything went off well because of the Puigs' kindness.

Puig shows me the copy of *Le Potomak* with my dedication to Misia. Sert had asked him to bring it to Castel.

The Gypsies drink a great deal during the dancing. (Several bottles of whiskey). They don't seem to get drunk. They work themselves up to the flamenco crisis. They wear fine shirts and suits of very good cut. Depending on the dance, they keep their shirt tucked in or else pull it out and knot it around their waist. They take off their street shoes and put on high-heeled dancing slippers. The women put on dresses with polka dots and pleated skirts. Their loose hair sometimes hides their faces altogether. Occasionally they pull off the scarf from around their neck and wave it around them while they stamp their feet in one place. The dancing takes place in tiny bars in the streets Genet describes in *The Thief's Journal* (Barrio Chino).

People here believe that Lorca was the victim of personal grudges. He was living with some Communist friends in Granada, and these friends, afraid he would be found with them, were foolish enough to take him to a village instead of a big city, where he could never be found. Nothing was done in Granada to rescue him. His enemies found him easily in that village, and the execution took place under an olive tree. Lorca asked for a priest—this was refused, and he was told he could not hope to save his soul.

I've just recorded some poems downstairs, on tape, for the university centers.

Saw Antonio de Cabo Tuero, director of the Teatro de Camara of Barcelona. Almost all foreign plays here are censored. The Chamber Theater does a single performance with the best Spanish actors. They have put on *La Voix humaine* and *Le Bel indifférent.* They are going to do *Les Parents terribles.*

On the radio, I said—among other things—*"To invent* is to bring together two objects so different and so remote from each other that no one would ever imagine their connection. *To under-stand* is to acknowledge this unexpected connection and immediately to see the meaning of the new object born of this marriage."

Impossible to create a thing without destroying another. This is why we are called destructive. Nature proceeds in the same way. In order to perpetuate herself, she devours herself.

Beauty continually displaces its lines. A beautiful object is a brief pause in a perpetual motion.

Example of a thing well said and misunderstood. I had written in *Cock and Harlequin* (1918), "There are no precursors, there are only latecomers," by which I meant that invention cannot be "ahead of its time" though it is supposed so because the public is "behind." Reverdy was wild with rage over this little sentence, which he took for a personal insult. *I was calling him a latecomer.* The sentence was too fast for his slow mind.

I've always been the victim of this kind of misunderstanding. I used to believe—I still do—that good manners consist in regarding those we speak to as capable of understanding the concision of our formulas. The French language permits these dangerous short-cuts. Only rarely can they be translated into another tongue.

Alberto brings me the issue of the *Revista* that comes out to-morrow. The whole first page is taken up by my photograph in front of Picasso's harlequin at the Museum of Modern Art, the whole last page by an article by Tharrats and by scenes from my films and from *Le Jeune Homme et la mort.**

---

*Cocteau's mimodrama to music by Bach, with choreography by Roland Petit, created in Paris by Jean Babilée and Nathalie Philippart in 1946.

It is likely that the poet's prestige derives from the waves he emits and which spread faster than his work.

Once I move away from the center, my wheel can be seen turning.

What the world calls dispersion is its misunderstanding of a man's work and the unity it forms. Knowing only certain points on the itinerary and not connecting them, people deduce that these points are made at random on our map.

Spanish censorship. It keeps minds from breathing and nips life in the bud. The censors do not realize that any cut in a work is like a torero's mistake and costs the life of a work.

The blood of our struggle is not seen. We are smeared with it. If it were visible, we would scare people, and we could be tracked.

When I was very young, I was close to the torero Bombita at Saint-Jean-de-Luz. He still wore the real coleta, a little braid at the back of his head that amazed me. It was a mistake to have substituted for this braid an artificial one. Every singularity suppressed is a mistake. The first hole in a fine fabric. The hole quickly grows bigger. So big that it takes up all the space, and the fabric vanishes. It is this feeling which last year in Spain provoked the scandal of the blunted horns. Public scandal managed to overcome this tendency to *blunt everything*. The horns are no longer blunted.

Sensitive souls who are upset by killing the bull forget to be upset by killing the chicken and the steer that they eat. Almost everyone can take the spectacle of the corrida; almost no one can take the spectacle of the slaughterhouses in Franju's film *Le Sang des bêtes*. Which does not keep these same souls from finding the slaughterhouses less inhuman than the bullring.

Picasso once said to me, "I've worked a miracle." "What?" "An old lady, an invalid in a wheelchair, came to see one of my shows. She ran away as fast as her legs could carry her."

I was very struck by seeing that the people at a corrida left the ring before the end, like the theater public. I had thought our modern rudeness was incompatible with this ceremony.

When *espontáneos* jump down into the ring, the public on the *sun* side of the ring laughs, and the public on the *shade* side is annoyed. People shout at them, the toreros throw them out, and the police take them away. They are released after twenty-four hours. Any number of famous matadors began by being espontáneos. They obstruct the drama. They risk their necks for no purpose, and if they succeed they discredit the *"sangre torera,"* which corresponds to the blue blood of nobility.

The picador is detested, hissed, whatever he does. He is the clown of the fight. If he falls off his horse, the bull is cheered. The picador is a wretched Saint George.

. . . .

JULY 9

Tonight *Paris-Presse* telephoned that Rosemonde Gérard has died.* I had feared this for Maurice. The end of that family, comparable in its style to the families of Gypsies. A big caravan, Cambo,† and the various Paris hotel rooms where the family camped out.

I never heard Rosemonde or Maurice speak ill of anyone. They were always to be found together, like two birds on the same perch. Maurice may die of this death. Lucien Daudet—Nel Boudot-Lamotte‡—Maurice. Theirs is a widower's mourning: the umbilical cord was never cut.

---

*The poet Rosemonde Gérard (1866–1953) in 1889 married Edmond Rostand (1868–1918); her children were Maurice Rostand (1891–1968), poet, novelist, and playwright, and Jean Rostand (1894–1977), biologist and writer.

†At Cambo, in the Basque country, Edmond Rostand had built the Villa Arnaga, where young Cocteau had stayed as a guest in October 1912.

‡Emmanuel Boudot-Lamotte (1908–1981), art critic, disciple of Henri Focillon,

Six-thirty. *Toros.* (Little ring.) In the big rings there is a sense of ice skating.

Splendid corrida. But the young matadors were foolhardy. It was a miracle no one was killed. The public is badly behaved, as everywhere. The least mistake, and all the prowess cheered is forgotten. The last fight—the ring emptying. Man and bull are left to fight it out alone.

If the fight before last was a drama, yesterday's was a magnificent tragedy. Toreros tossed, torn trousers mended with safety pins, huge bulls like war machines imagined by Leonardo, jackets blazing with silver and gold, matador borne in triumph by the young spectators. Even a picador was applauded, which I'd never seen.

The slow progress of the matador, dragging his feet, his body arched, watched by the motionless bull from a distance. Then, "Hey, hey, Toro!" And the matador provokes him, excites him, and the slow walk continues until the duel begins.

The bulls have been cared for, polished, fed in the best pastures. They will be eaten tomorrow all over Barcelona. In the past, sandwiches were served during the fights, made out of the meat from the first bull killed.

Night. We are walking through a charcuterie. A bric-a-brac like some of the old night spots of Montmartre, like the Hôtel Saint-Yves* distorted by a dream. On a tiny stage a pianist turns his back to us. He accompanies monsters who can neither dance nor sing, and who dance and sing. There was one quite toothless old gentleman who seemed to be suffering from an earache. He sang songs of Trenet and Ulmer, Strauss waltzes accompanied with castanets. A fat old crone utters a few squawks which appear to be *Madama Butterfly*. Then a very thin one with a long nose and a

---

photographer, translator of Stephen Hudson; Gaston Gallimard's private secretary from 1930 to 1944, then director of Éditions J. B. Janin.

    *A small Paris hotel at 4, rue de l'Université, now demolished. It was frequented between the wars by artists and writers (Maurice Sachs stayed there).

L. Picador est diablé, sifflé quand il passe
le gignol de la course. J'ai hurlé le cheval
acclame toréador le taureau. Le Picador et +
Sain g

twitching mouth performs an "oriental dance." They all know they're absurd but still feel they are "artists." The public extremely respectful of these grotesques. Serious young people, openmouthed.

Picasso's sister has given me a big box containing a whole corrida. The entire family has signed it all around the sides. We sang, danced, clapped, and stamped.

Tonight the *Orphée II* arrives (?).

. . . .

JULY 10

Manolete himself was occasionally hissed, yet he was a god of the bullring, just as Nijinsky was a god of the dance. He was borne in triumph all the way to his hotel. (The Hotel Oriente, on the Rambla). Manolete's death was an occasion for national mourning. He was killed in a tiny village ring. He might have been saved in a big city. But perhaps it was better this way. They would doubtless have had to amputate the leg. There are allegorical images of his death in the tiniest inns.

Tomorrow we'll be seeing a corrida fought on horseback.

If the corridas were forbidden, we would be thinking, "Imagine, such a thing once was, and is no longer; that we might have seen such a spectacle!"

In Portugal the spectacle is mimed—there is no killing. The horns are capped, and the toreros can only be knocked down. The deathblow is simulated with a stick.

In Spain Church censorship forbids *everything*. Plays can be put on for a single performance (by the Chamber Theater), and even then the Church must give permission. Great actors agree to perform for a single evening because they have no roles to work in, classical or modern.

The result of this Church censorship is precisely the opposite of what the Church calculates. This violent people, greedy for violent spectacles, not finding them in the theater, seek them out in life and in politics. The Church accepts the corridas because they keep the public from thinking. To prevent thinking, as the Cardinal in *Bacchus* says, is the Church's great affair.

Dali's corrida, where the dead bull was taken away by helicopter. Dominguin went along with it (he has no hatred of publicity). A great deal of talk about this—it never happened.

Thanks to the crew of the *Orphée II*, we have married Barcelona.

After the revolution, the Church sought to make itself feared. It managed only to make itself hated. The Spanish people are superstitious, but they hate the priests. This is why they get slaughtered in the first uprising.

Tennessee Williams arrived this morning. We saw the flamenco troupe this evening. Williams always a little grasping—a little remote from whatever isn't sexual.

Worked on the poem "Homage to Manolete." Last night the manager gave me the folk image of the dead Manolete which I had admired on the wall.

. . . .

JULY 13

We've got into their rhythm: Lunch at four in the afternoon, dinner at eleven. Tennessee was dead tired. He had got up at seven, gone to the beach.

The young intellectuals of Barcelona claim to despise the corrida. I have great difficulty explaining to them that I am not an intellectual.

Corrida. The first bullfight on horseback. If you haven't seen such a thing, you cannot imagine its elegance. The horse out of Velázquez, the rider who controls him with his knees, those turns and that sudden, arrowlike flight when the bull charges. A boy with a stick and a red rag jumped into the ring in the penultimate fight. He was tossed and trampled by the bull. Everyone thought he was dead. Except for one fight, when a picador's clumsiness forced the matador to work with an exhausted animal amid the boos of the crowd, the fights were splendid. All the matadors were awarded ears.

With Tennessee Williams last night while he was being interviewed for the national radio. The wall of languages produced extraordinary misunderstandings. No one understood anyone else, but we ended by understanding each other very well. I then tried to explain what he had said. But I didn't do any better. Besides, it didn't matter, since in this kind of interview nothing remains of what one meant to say. They asked him who he felt were the two greatest American actors. He answered, Marlon Brando and Greta Garbo. He added that Garbo had never acted on a stage, but that she would be the greatest stage actress if she wanted to be. Then I said that Garbo had passed through the wall of fame and that she was disintegrating. That she would never appear again, either in a film or on stage. It was my bad luck that she wanted to do *The Eagle Has Two Heads* when Tallulah turned it into a disaster in New York.

. . . .

JULY 14

Went to see the blacks play basketball. A big circus number which leaves you with nothing. During the half, an extraordinary Mexican juggler. The stadium so steep that you could make out, in the darkness, a dizzying espalier of faces. Worked all night on the poem to Manolete—added two stanzas. Had to stop at nine in the morning. Each time I change a word, the rest unravels, and I must begin the whole thing over. Mixture of halting verses and regular ones. I may be able to perfect the mechanism, but not too much or it will go dead.

Last night after the performance, Alberto showed me the proofs of the poem on Góngora, surrounded by my drawings of the corrida and the flamenco dancers. The untranslatable poem is translated underneath, word for word and with no attempt to follow the rhythm. Neville has sent from Madrid his translation of the poem to Lorca.

I'd like to add to my "Homages" one to Antonio Gaudi, the Barcelona architect.

Still no *Orphée II.* The joke is a little protracted. If it isn't here by tonight, we'll leave for Madrid.

Next to V. at the corrida, on Sunday, a Frenchwoman was scared to death when the crowd booed the picador. She thought the revolution was starting.

It is true that the anger of a Spanish crowd is a fearful thing. Even when they are excited in fun, the Spanish go to extremes. The other night the Gypsies set fire to the posters of the little wooden hall we were in, the way the mob set fire to the churches. I mean that an excited Spanish crowd might just as easily set fire to the churches as to the bullfight posters.

Beria arrested. The journalists speculate as to the reason: "If the Kremlin," they say, "hadn't executed Beria, Beria would have executed the Kremlin." (Robespierre.)

The real reason is that Beria was honored by Stalin. To accuse him of treason right now is the only way the regime has of denying Stalin (of condemning his policies). It would be logical to accuse Beria of having killed Stalin with the complicity of the doctors.

Margarita, Alberto's sister, has sent us a huge tricolor basket for July 14.

. . . .

JULY 15

We'll take the plane to Madrid tomorrow. The car will meet us there.

I realize more and more that the Mediterraneans form a race which has no relation to the others.

In a corrida, the wind is a terrible thing if it flaps the muleta. Matadors' skeleton: Belmonte had scoliosis, Manolete a slight deviation of the vertebral column. This helped form the curve through which the bull passed. Ultimately the bull is not trying to kill but to obey the man who speaks to him, who rules him. Dominguín had this power of speaking to animals and of charming them, compelling them to obey him.

The newspaper with my "Homage to Góngora," was brought to me just now, while I was having a glass with Tennessee Williams. He asks, "Who is Góngora?" Incredible. Another American, speaking of Sancho, says to Alberto, "Don Quixote's secretary."

. . . .

JULY 16

Lunch with Tennessee Williams and Cabo. This morning I was visited by a young author almost driven to suicide by Torquemadism. In Barcelona you're free to say whatever you like—you can't ever publish it. In Madrid, you must say nothing.

. . . .

JULY 19

Flew to Madrid. Rough flight. The descent to a pink, tawny, beige, pale green earth. Palace Hotel (the Ritz full). Wretched caravansary.

Lunch at Horcher's (calle de Alfonso XII, no. 6). Horcher himself cooks for us and invites us for lunch tomorrow.

That evening to Don Luis Escobar. Dominguín arrives with his dwarf, dressed as a little boy (short-sleeved open shirt, shorts). Dinner near the Plaza Mayor. In the center of this fine square, a statue now replaces the Inquisition's stakes. Down some steps under an archway and into a tiny inn (Las Cuevas de Luis Candelas). Dinner in the back room lined with bullfight engravings. Black bull's head. A glass case with a magnificent suit of some famous torero, covered with gold and coral beads.

It's likely that Luis Miguel Dominguín will stop fighting. The crowd resists him, for all his fame—which would lead him to all kinds of imprudent bravado. Don Luis advises him to be done with the ring. He has seen him sit on the barrier to place the banderillas and have the bull pin him between its horns. "Such spectacles," he says, "are not to be borne." I suppose that Manolete, who didn't have Dominguín's beauty, had what he lacks—the sangre torera. He gleamed, and possessed the adoration of the crowd. Dominguín possesses beauty, knowledge, grace. He doesn't gleam. His killing hand seems not to know his face, to live far from it, in another world. His face lives too much in "the world." Only his hand lives in the world of killers. I was hoping to see bullfights, but the Spaniards say that in summer the corrida turns to soccer.

We were supposed to go to Dominguín's, in the country, on Monday. The roads too crowded. Besides, Neville (who telephones from Galicia and returns tonight) advises against going to Toledo on a Sunday. No doubt we'll go there on Monday.

Two days a week with no electricity in Madrid. You shave in the dark.

Dominguín scarred and seamed from head to toe. After one fight, when he had his thigh ripped open, he was flung into a taxi which a lady gave up to him. He was wearing his bullfighter's suit covered with blood. The lady asked him, "Are you a torero?"

They know my new poems—my records that can no longer be found. Don Luis says, "I don't know yet in what form, but I think Spain is the country that will give you a lot." He's right. If one doesn't yield to the picturesque, which conceals what is important, Spain corresponds to the broken rhythm and inner fire of poets. In Madrid I find the same freedom of dialogue as in Barcelona. That same intensity of a banked fire struggling not to become a conflagration.

The duke of ————, jailed by the Reds. He tells me that the Reds said to him, "You sleep with your wife and with her maids." "Manners," he says, "made up for my courage. I only resent one thing. They asked twice as much to free my wife as they asked for me."

On the whole it's the terror of a conflagration (the real Red terror) which makes the regime accepted. In revolutionary crises, what's worst in the people rises against what's worst in the monarchy. Hence it is the best people who pay on both sides, when they are blamed for mistakes which are not committed by exceptional beings.

In bullfighting what is most feared is that a bull will leave the ring alive and give away the game. I'm told about a bull raised on the bottle, adored by all Spain—saved because all the women cried and begged for his release. A little girl came down into the ring and came to pet him; he licked her hand. Also feared are the boys who practice in secret with the bulls on farms, for they risk teaching the bulls the secret of the cape.

Yesterday Dominguín's dwarf was wearing his arm in a sling. Wounded by a bull.

Dominguín's secret: his power over all animals. He talks to them and they obey him. Strange that this power doesn't work on that animal the public. He charms the bull. It's a superiority which annoys this jealous Spain. Too much superiority in a matador corresponds to the physical advantages which rouse our public against certain actors. Some crowds say of Dominguín (in Seville, for instance), "He's a ballerina." His heroism has nothing to do with it. Tjhey say of Marais, "He's a pinup boy," which they will never say about Gérard Philipe. On the other hand, if Marais works against his physique and happens to play a father, he's blamed for that.

In short, a torero must never leave his milieu. If he does, he's lost for the crowd. He belongs to it. If he belongs to others, his popularity goes.

Prado. In front of certain canvases, Goya especially, which are like famous people you wanted to know and of whom you knew only photographs, or from whom you've had only letters, tears come to your eyes and blur your vision. There are canvases (for example, the rebels being shot) which are astounding for their size or their colors, which never show up properly in reproduction. The director of the museum despises El Greco. As a result his paintings are very poorly lit, in a small room. Moreover, all the lighting in the Prado is detestable.

Lunch with Mme Horcher. Abel Bonnard* lives in Madrid. She talks about him. It's always very embarrassing when anyone talks about those sentenced to death in absentia. After having sent back Laval, Franco dared not release anyone else.

Saw Sirerol at the hotel, for the film†—Llovet‡—Luis Escobar. Dinner at the Golf Club with Escobar and Llovet. Neville

---

*Abel Bonnard (born in Poitiers in 1883, died in Madrid in 1968), writer and journalist. Minister of national education in the Vichy government, he was initially condemned to death in absentia after the Liberation, then to ten years' banishment when he appeared before the High Court of Justice. In 1908–1909, when Cocteau was living in the Hôtel Biron (today the Rodin Museum), Bonnard was among the friends the young poet received there.

†Miguel Sirerol, cinema agent. The film was *Orphée*.

‡Enrique Llovet, a journalist.

was to join us, but he's driven from Galicia and must have fallen asleep. We're having lunch with him tomorrow.

Telegram from Port-de-Bouc. The boat can't come. Storms. We'll have to make the best of it—finish the trip half by plane, half by car.

Each friend or admirer of Lorca gives a different version of his death. Yesterday the reporter told me that he was taken to a labor camp and killed there by one man, not by a group.

The Spaniard lives within the moment. Sensation dominates him. He is always at some extremity—that is the source of his intensity.

Corridas. Last night Llovet explained that man and bull each live within a separate zone. The game consists in neither one's ever venturing into the other's zone.*

Sirerol offers to show me the Spanish-language version of *Orphée.* He claims the sound track is a wonder, that the work was entrusted to poets, etc. I have my doubts.

I know that there are several Spains and several dialects. But there is much more likely to be one Spain than one France. We have nothing national that corresponds to the corridas or to fla-menco. The internationalized Spaniard judges himself, even criti-cizes himself. I do not intend to follow him on this path.

. . . .

JULY 20

The flamenco dancer—the matador—one and the same person. My great discovery in Spain: Flamenco is not a rhythm, it is a syntax. The expression of suffering, a lover's complaint. The Arabs moan; the Spaniards articulate. The flamenco and the translation of certain Spanish poems have given me a syntax—that of my

---

*Theory of the *terrenos* ("terrains") of the bull and of the torero, essential to bullfighting.

latest poems. To the point where the Spanish cannot believe, for instance, that my farewell to Federico, translated by Neville, wasn't thought and written in Spanish.

Last night, at Neville's, I was listening to the pianist play flamenco music. One thing struck me. After the trip to Majorca, Chopin's style changed. He seems to have come under the influence of flamenco.

Prado. I believe that there exists no painting finer than in the rooms of Goya's tapestry cartoons. There are painter-painters, and painter-poets. Goya is a painter-painter *and* a great poet. He is also a chronicler. He says everything as if he were making light of it. As if he were visiting future centuries on the broomstick of his witches, enjoying himself there, *being influenced by those he will influence.* As if he were robbing his thieves, profiting from his profiteers, discovering himself in those who will imitate him in Manet's period, in Renoir's. His brush narrates, testifies. On the Castile roads we pass groups of these charming characters, but they no longer wear the showy costumes of Goya's young people. Something remains: the color of a skirt, a handkerchief around a head, the silver mist surrounding them. We went back upstairs to see the last canvas he painted, *The Milk Seller.* All of Renoir comes out of it. Astonishing that such boldness, such discoveries were accepted—that his commissions were approved. No doubt the court was yielding to a certain snobbery—like an elegant woman who commissions Picasso to do her portrait. In Goya's court portraits there is no insistence on caricature—rather, the caricature comes from the incredible exactitude of his eye. His malice is expressed without his knowing it.

Bosch. Here we are at the source of Dali and the surrealists. It is true that in Bosch's day, all this *told,* was read like a book. Now these symbols show only the imagination which has made them renowned. *The Garden of Earthly Delights* astounds us by the abundance of its erotic, playful, sadistic discoveries, by a madness of details whose lyricism and precision are incomparable. *Other* he is. *Other* like Goya, like Nijinsky, like Al Brown, like Manolete—like all the beings marked with a sign. Since every painter produces his own portrait, Bosch's multiple portrait brings us into contact with a man we would have liked to know. His behavior in life could only have been exceptional, extraordinary.

The treasures of the Prado are overwhelming. You have to walk through fast—not wear yourself out in front of the minor canvases. Run from one miracle to the next. From the *Maja* to *Las Meninas* and from the Velázquez *Infantes* to the little room where the Grecos are. And then keep coming back to bathe in the joyous pool of Goya's cartoons. Here you wash off the fatigue of the religious subjects.

Now and again a religious subject is transcended by the genius which handles it and loses the conventional style.

Escobar's alarming resemblance to the Spanish Bourbons. At the Escorial you have the impression that he is walking through his own house. You see his portraits everywhere.

The Escorial. After three-quarters of an hour's drive through a chaos of stones, of tawny plains, of blue mountains, you come face to face with virtue made stone. The Escorial is a city, a terrifying, magnificent prison. We were expected, and every door was opened. Many doors open with difficulty, reject all keys. We seemed to be burglars. Llovet says that having visited the Escorial at night, he was afraid that the electric lights would make it seem from outside that burglars were moving through the corridors. The priests who accompany us are, like everyone in Spain, very outspoken. They open the pantheon, the royal necropolis. A steep staircase leads down to this famous little cellar. Halfway down, the door of the decomposition room. In the round cellar, hivelike cells contain the gold-and-black marble sarcophagi. It is a funereal hive. Kings on the left; on the right, queens, mothers of kings. One empty sarcophagus awaits Alfonso XIII. He has signed his name on the plaque with the point of his sword. Above the door two other sarcophagi await future kings. All Spain rests on this underground pedestal. Those who lie embalmed and those of whom there remains only a handful of dust have believed in this poor earth and in the glory to be harvested from it. They have proudly thrust into it a talon like those supporting their sarcophagi. Of that world they ruled and organized to their will, nothing remains. Nothing but the terrible huge barracks where they lived and heard Mass from their bedrooms and from that tiny choir loft where Philip II slipped through a secret door in order not to disturb the ceremony.

In the church, facing the altar and by papal authorization, Jose Antonio is lying under a slab. Shot by the Reds in Alicante, he was brought on men's backs to the Escorial. Every ten kilometers the procession stopped and set up a marker.

The library (whose door refused to open) is a world. Thousands of volumes and in the center, in cases, the manuscripts of Saint Theresa, Bibles in Hebrew, Korans speckled with gold.

The whole Escorial smells of the boxwood of countless austere cloister-gardens and the pinewood of beams. Wood in which the resin has been left.

From whatever window you look out, a mountain looms up over the walls and the long sheds framing the entrance to the Escorial. To the right the palace surmounts a pool which irrigates the monks' vegetable gardens, above a Castile as harsh as the architecture it took twenty-one years to complete. But this palace doesn't show its age. It's a hard, unsmiling old man standing on a rock, encased in armor and his hands joined in prayer.

If you commit suicide in Spain, don't do it by halves. If you do, it's prison—you're guilty of having tried *to kill someone.*

Village corridas. A ring is made out of carts tipped over. A barrier of young men on their knees, armed with pikes, closes the ring. When the bull comes too close to the crowd, they hit him with clubs and also club the torero if he jumps out of the ring.

At the end the ring is left to the women. A very young bull with tiny horns is let in, but the women jostle one another and keep one another from working the bull. Finally they carry him out in triumph.

Here everyone is against something other than what he seems to be against.

Spain is not like anything that is said about it. Madrid is luxury within everyone's reach. The parks are splendid. The restaurants countless. Whereas in France the French can no longer afford to eat in restaurants, the Madrid restaurants are crowded with Spaniards of every class. Five hotels are being built. And without a penny of American money. At present the Spanish are all incendiaries on holiday.

It is Lorca's family that forbids his plays to be performed. Miguel Utrillo* says: "Now the family rules over his glory. When he was alive, they knew nothing of that glory and did nothing for it or him."

Saw Jose Luis Alonso. He's translating *Les Monstres sacrés*. The title sounds wrong in Spanish. I suggest *Le Théâtre chez soi*, and to end the play with "After we die, we'll ask Shakespeare to write us a play and we'll all act in it."

N.b. After all, Escobar thinks *Les Monstres sacrés* is better.

People question me about Picasso. Impossible to answer. I say, "Picasso is the first Communist king." And "In Nîmes he never misses a corrida."

Seven o'clock. Just saw *Orphée*, the Spanish-language version, first class. Respect for every word. Édouard heard himself speaking Spanish in a very young voice, very different from his own, as was his blond hair.

Belmonte's secret. He arrived at the ring weak, ill. People pitied

---

*Maurice Utrillo's half brother (his father had acknowledged the son of Suzanne Valadon).

him, cheered him to give him strength. He was inspired and scored a triumph.

The Spanish say about Luis Miguel, "He's perfect. There is no better matador on earth. He performs the most difficult passes, the most dangerous . . ." They cheer him. Then they try to recall this moment, and they fail. This is because he possesses considerable talent but lacks genius. When Manolete died he thought, "I have no rival now—it's my turn." But two young matadors were already taking the place Manolete had left. It is terrible to be a torero under the sway of a Manolete. Terrible to be a painter under the sway of a Goya, of a Picasso.

Everyone in Madrid makes fun of the American ambassadress to the Vatican. "Are you a Catholic?" she asks every Spaniard she meets. "Do you take communion?" She hasn't a clue that Spain is superstitious but loathes the Church. "Do you take communion?" she asked Edgar Neville. "No," he answered, "I'm overweight already."

. . . .

JULY 22

In the plane from Madrid to Málaga.

Toledo is an arrogant Arab and Jewish furnace bathed by the Tagus. Swords are plunged into it. No doubt it's the oldest Jewish city in Europe. But the yellow blood that feeds its tortuous entrails flows from a heart: the house of the strange foreigner with its sleeping garden in the curve of the road. Here is where he hung up his laundry, which the sun's rays froze into statues. They fill the city where ghost sheets and mandrake shirts are still drying.

We reached Toledo through torrid fields. Saw a boy fallen off his mule and left for dead on the side of the road amid a splash of red. We thought it was blood. He had broken his wine flask.

A French ambassador once wrote, "A squirrel could get from

Perpignan to Gibraltar without ever leaving the trees." Spain lacks coal. Every tree has been cut down and burned, the way Spain burns everything. The nakedness of the soil is that of a martyr, of a man flayed alive, of a Christ in the sepulcher.

The crag of Toledo is overshadowed by the ruins of the alcazar, where without food or water those men held out against the Reds, their leader (Moscardo) sacrificing his son rather than surrender. This ruin adds a new and Homeric pride to the old arrogance of Castile.

My first visit was to the palace of the duchess of Lerma and the hospice. The duchess is rarely there. The rooms are ready, alive and welcoming. The palace is of a great magnificence, but one magnificence devours all the rest: the last canvas Greco painted, *The Baptism of Christ*. Around the edges the painter wiped his brushes, which produces the only frame worthy of such a marvel. Greco is seventy. He no longer takes orders from anyone. Neither from the Church nor from the Orgaz family. He is free. He plunges deep into the submarine glory where his stormy waters distort limbs, where strange oyster shells reveal pearls which are angels with noses like trumpets of the Apocalypse, where Greek eroticism lovingly caresses the slender legs with huge thighs and calves, where the ecclesiastic tribunal no longer functions.

A door separates this dazzling work from the *Cardinal Tavera*, whose white horse I once told Picasso resembles the one in his *War and Peace*. Greco painted this portrait from a death mask. The Reds pillaged the place, cut the picture into ribbons. I've seen the photographs of this massacre. It has been restored. *The Burial of Count Orgaz* was leaving for Moscow. We found it in the station. In the Kremlin can be found the robe of the Black Virgin, decorated with eighty thousand pearls. (This mantle has been seen in the Kremlin by a French diplomat.) I have no love for the Church. Only, blind men for blind men, I prefer the blind men who amass to those who pillage. The visit to the cathedral will horrify me.

One used to go to churches to pray, not to see masterpieces. The tourists shock me, and the masterpieces that have nothing to do with worship exhaust me. Temples are not made for tourists. They are made for the faithful. So that instead of reading and discussing it, the faithful may kneel on the proud funeral slab where a cardinal had this inscription carved in Latin: *Here lies dust and ashes, nothing more.*

Greco's house is not tiring—it is restorative. Here he shut himself up, never opened the windows, organized livid scenes by candlelight. Friends came to see him, gossiped, posed (they all appear in *Count Orgaz*), drank chilled red wine with a peach in it.

In the alleys of Toledo, you meet his little pages. Around the Lerma Palace, the merest telegraph pole has the look of a Calvary. Toledo is scorching, livid, tortuous as the bodies tangled between heaven and earth which Greco superimposes, clutters with banners and a horrifying laundry. It is likely that the Toledans have no particular opinion of their treasures—that they make use of them the way the faithful worship. The women respect them without trying to understand, amazed that the tourists worship them instead of God.

After, the cathedral, its sacristy dishonored by a portrait of the last bishop which, amid Goyas and Grecos, betrays the level of the Church today. We couldn't take any more. Went to lie down on the hillside, at Dr. Marañon's.* With Unamuno and Ortega, Dr. Marañon is the most capacious and most venerated mind in Spain. I saw him in Barcelona the day he left for Brazil. He praised my translation of the Góngora sonnet. He's read everything, learned everything. Rich with what he's learned and read, he teaches. Neville opens his empty house for us. The housekeeper brings us

---

*Gregorio Marañon y Posadillo (1888–1960), writer and physician, one of the founders of endocrinology.

pitchers of red wine with peaches in it. We nap, and Neville sleeps so heavily that his chaise longue collapses.

We return to Madrid at about eight o'clock. The hotel bathrooms are lit by fluorescent light. The last Greco we see is nothing but our own face in the mirror.

One-forty. We fly over the sea, arriving in Málaga. And so to bed.

Torremolinos. On the beach—the inn run by Neville's sons. The grandmother owns the entire estate, which used to be worth very little and is still not worth much compared to the Riviera. To build is cheap enough. The inn is enchanting. We cross the road and take lunch, bathing at the club they have set up on the beach.

Édouard bathes, but not knowing that we are friends of the family, they make him get out of the water on the pretext that he is wearing a bikini and one must bathe in trunks. I see other bikinis. Only, either the bather is younger or the bikini is a few centimeters wider over the buttocks. The pools and clubs are afraid of being closed by the governor. That is the Church. That is the indecency of a clergy which harries life in all its forms and sees evil where there is no such thing. I could understand the clergy forbidding any bathing at all or insisting that people bathe in armor—but to count the centimeters of bathing suits remains a revolting enigma. It is true that this regime forbids bikinis and that the other would have closed the pools. Which is why the adversaries of the regime endure it. The Reds were defeated because instead of occupying the hotels they burned them down. They have burned themselves.

Greco's Evangelists. San Mateo and his unfinished left hand. The chapped sketch of that hand reminds me of something. And suddenly it shows me the origin of the huge shapeless hands by Picasso, which look like leaves. Picasso's eye swallows and digests everything.

Never would today's Church have commissioned Picasso or Dali to do the portrait of the last bishop. Which is what had to be done if the portrait were to deserve its place beside the earlier ones.

One wonders how the modern Spanish Church preserves the image of a naked god. How does it regard the Christ of El Greco, terrible in its Greek sensuality . . . I am told that the Church is reluctant to accept these nudes. On certain Romanesque frescoes it scratches out and adds loincloths. In Spain, as in Rome, it seems that Christ is not dead for humanity but for the artist. Nothing stranger than Hieronymus Bosch's Black Masses at the Escorial. If most of these works were not worth a fortune, they would be burned. And as I said, the opposing regime ultimately did destroy *Cardinal Tavera*. Between two evils, the Spaniard tolerates the lesser. This is the secret of Franco's success—Franco, whom everyone condemns for being at the orders of the Church, his enemy.

Terrible heat. Impossible to go out except at night. Around six we visit Málaga. We have extended the trip to include Gibraltar and Granada. If we go to Jerez, Alberto will join us. He has Gypsies on his estates there and hopes to organize a celebration for us.

During the war Neville had driven to the outskirts of Madrid to pick up a young man who was ill and bring him back to his family. He was returning with the sick boy and Conchita Manes when they were stopped, arrested, and sentenced to die. Neville protested and compelled the mayor to telephone the Ministry of War, which still had some prestige and where he knew some official or other. This was just to gain time, and, without much hope of success. At the Ministry of War, the telephone rang in an anteroom. A film designer, who was waiting for an audience there, picked up the phone. He was questioned. He said, "Release Neville." And Neville was released. Before going to the mayor's office, they had wanted to execute him on the spot and had blindfolded him. He said to the Reds: "First put your handkerchief in the mouth of the lady who is with me. She's going to scream, and that will be very unpleasant." He owed his first good luck to this piece of nerve. He was frightened to death. If he had shown it, he was a dead man.

Spain is one. One even when it is divided against itself, when it turns against itself. At night, in the trenches around Madrid, the propaganda loudspeakers played flamenco. Reds and Falangists shouted ¡olé! together.

Louis Aragon himself fired the cannon aimed at the alcazar of Toledo. Which no Spaniard has forgotten. Whereas everyone awaits Picasso's return.

You open a newspaper: "Protest of the Teachers' Conference of Alsace-Lorraine against the teaching of German in the schools." I wonder if France has not become the stupidest country of all.

Delicious coolness at nightfall. Air much lighter than on the Riviera.

Grace. Here grace animates everything, great or small. Houses, people, language have grace. The Sierra Nevada protects this gracious Africa where every season is clement, where the architecture, the trees, the workers' straw hats, the way the women walk delight a mind reluctant to respond to elegance and corrupted by the vileness of the time. The very inn kept by Neville's sons is full of grace. You feel neither in a hotel nor with strangers. You feel at home.

We return here with delight after a visit to the alcazar of Málaga: an Arab labyrinth rising among hanging gardens where peacocks perch on the trellises and eat the green grapes. It is eight o'clock. The clock of the Hotel des Postes shows 4:15. This simple detail sums up Andalusia's indifferences to the exactitudes and the constraints of time.

Neville is no longer with his wife. He remains her friend and takes us to dinner in a little bistro she has opened. Workers are as welcome here as the rich. No awkwardness in the mixture. Grace, grace everywhere. As aristocrats, father, mother, and son show no standoffishness whatever. Neville does not use his title, and his wife asks for nothing better than to be taken for a charming *patronne* of her bistro.

Is it not strange and incomprehensible that Manet-Renoir-Cézanne were regarded as scandalous, whereas Goya and Greco had already—long since—been successful with completely new and audacious ventures which generated those of the French? Our impressionist painters in a sense suffered and gained from a long period when Greco, for example, had lost all credence, even in Spain. They plundered artists in exile, expended a currency which was momentarily blocked. Baudelaire almost bought the *Maja* in Paris for a thousand francs, which was still dear, and Zuloaga,* when I was young, bought splendid Grecos for nothing. Which is astonishing, given that Goya was always valued in Spain, did not scandalize his times, and painted official portraits of incredible boldness (including the royal family), and that Greco received commissions from Philip II and from the Orgaz and Tavera families. No doubt we must attribute the ignorance of the sources of our painters and the blindness of our critics in the face of a false French Revolution (which was only a reprise of the Spanish one) to the frivolity of the eighteenth century and the mediocrity of the nineteenth. For all the genius of Manet, of Renoir, of Cézanne—Manet is *La Maja*, Cézanne the little scene embroidered on the left-hand chasuble in *The Burial of Count Orgaz*, Renoir is Goya's *Milk Seller*. Without what crowds the Prado, no impressionism in France (and by impressionism, I mean the figures who dominate this school). The honor of our painters is to have copied true masters during the period when false ones triumphed.

Admirable that Doménikos Theotokópouli should have lived on the site of a former school of magic, should have lived and painted

---

*The Spanish painter Ignacio Zuloaga y Zabaleta (1870–1945), a great admirer of El Greco.

above deep cellars where the millionaire Jew Samuel Ha-Levy hid his treasures, where the marqués de Villena used to say his Black Mass. Here is the true pedestal of his religious painting.

Make no mistake about it. According to the guidebooks, you can see clearly that Greco is forgiven his genius by *The Burial of Count Orgaz* in which he is executing an official commission, and even so only by the bottom of the picture, since the top part is described as "much questioned"—i.e., the strip of canvas where Greco, having agreed to reveal his genius even to ordinary eyes, signs his canvas—much more evidently than on the tip of the page's kerchief—by that zone of freedom crowning his masterpiece and legitimizing it in his own eyes. Greco is the perfect example of Delacroix's aphorism: *One is never understood. One is accepted.*

By means of commissions and of the *Evangelists* (through the clergy), Greco was able to escape the flames of stupidity and to compel that stupidity to tolerate works which would otherwise have harvested only outrage. He avoided the stake by siding with the iconoclasts, which is precisely the Spanish attitude in 1953. The destruction of the Tavera portrait by the Reds is the human proof of what I am saying. If this canvas had been a naked woman instead of the portrait of a cardinal, the Church would have made it suffer the same fate as the Reds did.

Spain detests the Church, detests Franco, detests the right and the left. Spain loves only Spain, which assures the continuity of its greatness. The Church and Franco detest one another. But Franco must obey the orders of his enemy, the clergy. He would be loved instead of accepted if he disobeyed the Church.

More than the salamander that lives in fire, Spain resembles the phoenix. It must continually burn itself up in order to be reborn.

In all of Spain the only thing you can hear (even on the barrel organs in the street) are French popular songs.

I've always compared Spain to China. Now I learn that Ortega said, "We are Chinese."

. . . .

JULY 25

Santiago. Return to Torremolinos.

The Málaga-Granada road: steep curves among a chaos of rocks, an old cataclysm—a submarine disorder of pale and tawny mountains. Sometimes on the empty road you pass a woman with a net of provisions. Where is she coming from? Where is she going? There's nothing for miles. Before the war the roads were good. Unamuno was in charge of them. Franco leaves them in poor condition.

Few cars except for French ones. Neville says, "There haven't been so many French in Spain since Napoleon." Someone asks him, "Are there still bandits?" He answers, "Now they run the hotels."

Amazing Spain—country of great poets without an audience. A handful of men publish admirable works. These men die unknown. The works must wait to be discovered and translated abroad.

All Spain endures the Church with difficulty but can paraphrase Henri IV's remark: "Spain is well worth a Mass."

Granada. We arrive after dark. The hotel in the Alhambra has not reserved our rooms. We find ourselves at the Alhambra Palace Hotel, a huge pale village with façades like sheets drying under earth-colored tiles.

And rising from the suburbs of the sky
Amazing sounds, cries of another Marseilles.

It is these old lines of mine I am reminded of at the window overlooking the Albaicín and the Sacro Monte where the Gypsies live. They live in caves hollowed out of the living rock. Cool in summer, warm in winter, some have bathrooms and telephones.

Neville takes us to the Alhambra, closed at night. He plans to bribe the guard or to telephone the prefecture. It is one in the morning. We are denied entrance, but Neville succeeds, after a phone call. The gates are opened for us. This nocturnal promenade gives the empty Alhambra a strangeness it no longer possesses by day. Earthquakes threaten its fragile architecture. The columns tilt. At night the decorative spells vanish, and the perfumes of flowers create others. Once the wonder of such refinement in the twelfth century is granted, you weary of a carcass of vanished luxuries. Before the state took it over, the Alhambra was populated by Gypsies. They camped out in it. Washington Irving rented a room from them. Today tourists invade the harem and behave as shockingly as they do in the churches.

The Generalife could be a rich villa on the Côte d'Azur if bad taste had not contaminated the modern world. There is only one instance of genius here: the watercourses. Water from the mountains flows through tiles on either side of the steps. You climb the steps between two icy little cascades which pour down and cool your hands.

What strikes me in Granada, more than its proud and gracious fortresses, is the city vaguely lit by lanterns, its murmur produced by a mysterious mixture of bells, hand clapping, barking dogs, braying donkeys. Granada is "flamenca." *To be flamenco, to be flamenca* does not necessarily mean that you dance. Flamenco is a certain way of behaving, a certain posture, a certain gait. The term comes from Flanders, from the Flemish country from which the soldiers of the War of Succession returned with a style of royal insolence. It was said of them, "He's a flamenco." Charles V preferred his Flemish subjects to the Spanish ones. For example, the Spanish censure Franco for not being flamenco. If he were, he would be loved. He is a Galician through and through. He is not flamenco.

A poet, a matador, a street boy, a whore, a duchess may or may not be flamenco. An indispensable nuance to grasp in order to understand the Spanish.

Visit to the cousins of Carmen Amaya.* The Amaya tribe lives in several caves dug into the mountainside. They dance in the first cave. Its door opens onto an alley where the children run around naked, where the men and women ask for alms habitually, professionally; they do not grumble if you refuse.

At the Amayas, the women (young and old) are seated around the little cave. Their hair dressed *à la chinoise*, a flower stuck at the top, they wait with their hands in their laps until the guitarists have tuned up. Once one begins and rattles his stormy guitar, they clap their hands so loud you hear the echo from the hill of the Generalife. A woman stands up, stamps, flings around her the flames of her polka-dot dress, loosens her wrists, kneels, tosses her hair in all directions. The flower stuck into it drops. Her friends pick it up and hand it back to her when she sits down again, giving way to a young cousin or to the mother, for it is the older women who dance best. They maintain a solemn, dry, fierce style which the tourists dislike, to the tribe's consternation, though they are gradually being influenced toward a less pure style. Pastora Imperio* was the first, forty years ago, to dance with her arms and hands high in the air. This produces a certain grace which is actually abused by today's Gypsies. But all of them preserve the irreproachable syntax of this language, which the slightest mistake in spelling would render unintelligible for the ear and for the eye.

Sometimes a young Gypsy fellow slips in from somewhere, perches behind the woman, and executes with her a series of mathematically

---

*Carmen Amaya (born in Barcelona in 1913, died in Cabo Bagur in 1963), a famous Gypsy dancer.

*Pastora Imperio (1890–1961), a famous Gypsy singer and dancer who in 1915 created Manuel de Falla's *El Amor brujo*.

precise turns. He wears a soft full shirt with the tails knotted over tight black pants that come up to his chest.

Along the alleys of the Sacro Monte, all the caves echo with a cannonade of castanets, clapping hands, stamping feet, and the eternal Olé that accompanies them. In front of the caves, the young people solicit trade—like one of the old streets in the oldest neighborhood of Marseilles. Only here they solicit for the dancing, and the Church cannot intervene in this prostitution-by-rhythm. (The archbishop of Seville condemns dancing. He cannot condemn flamenco.)

Visit to the Chapel Royal. Four lead coffins set down there like baggage in a waiting room. Two kings and two queens (Isabella and Joanna the Mad) occupy them. Above this hole (a supreme pride required this simplicity, as Hugo demanded a pauper's hearse) rise the four marble tombs. The effigies lie there, heads on a double cushion. Under the husbands' heads, the cushion remains stiff. Isabella's head sinks into hers. Joanna the Mad hollows hers only a little. The sculptor's intention is quite visible. These ladies had stronger heads than their husbands.

The cathedral wears me out, as usual. The gold organ looks like furniture bought by Sert. I need nothing but that view over the pale city and its lanterns. It's not the treasures of the past which move me in Granada—but that it is the city of Lorca, of Falla, of exquisite souls whom the perfumes of the Generalife shower with praise and whom a thousand Gypsy palms applaud night and day.

The insolent luxury of cathedrals. That insult to the doctrines of Christ. Who believes in God will not find him under these arrogant vaults. Hence the exhaustion that overcomes us, that sucks the marrow out of our bones.

When Diaghilev brought the *Cuadro flamenco** to Paris with the

---

*A series of Andalusian dances created at the Théâtre de la Gaîté-Lyrique in May 1921, with set and costumes by Picasso.

singer Maria Dalbaicin—we imagined it was a famous troupe and a singer renowned throughout Spain. And it was the ordinary family of a Granada cave—as if one said: Troupe X with Marie de Montmartre.

The Amaya family, speaking of the old mother, says: "The mistress—*the mistress of flamenco. The one who teaches us and dances better than we do.*"

A Gypsy woman never claps limply, is never distracted in her work, never shows disapproval or mockery toward another Gypsy or toward the strangers who are watching them. This is the whole difference from the bordellos, where insult prevails, where the oldest, fattest, ugliest women swathe themselves in "the eternal feminine" to insult the men who reject them. There is a relation between the Gypsy woman and the geisha. A nobility, a reserve, an incomparable bearing. The Gypsies are the converse of vulgarity. Greedy, thieving, liars,—but proud, but splendid. Among the Gypsies there is no such thing as a man who cheats on a woman. If the thing occurs, a tribunal is formed. A sentence is passed, as though for a crime.

"Spain scorns what she does not know," says one of her great poets.

Returning from Granada, after a dreadful road (at each jolt, we thought the car would break down), we lunched on the beach at Málaga. The gazpacho was made at the table because Francine wanted the recipe. With a blender, this exquisite cold soup is ready in five minutes. These women work with their hands all day long. *"You eat poorly in Spain. Watch out for the oil, etc."* Legends. You eat wonderfully. But you must not eat just anywhere. The Spaniard prefers cooking in oil. If you ask for butter, he'll cook in butter.

Spain's only fear in 1953: American dollars. Neville: "If we wanted to be rid of Franco, we would deal with that ourselves. We wouldn't let anyone else get involved."

The other night, in my hotel room in Granada, I heard, over the strange murmur of the city, the voice of Édith Piaf. How easily it became part of the city. Piaf should come to Spain. She would have a tremendous success here. She sings with her guts. Very flamenco.

To be or not to be flamenco. During the Occupation, Trenet told me, "Marshal Pétain isn't Zazou." This crack came to mind when Neville said, "Franco is not flamenco." Profound meaning of certain wisecracks, so much more important than the stupid gravity of our thinkers.

Francine buys old jewels in Granada. I buy mirrors for Milly.

During the civil war, in an Andalusian province, the bishop was pushed into the bullring stark naked. They stuck banderillas into him and charged him until he fell on all fours. The *espada* was stuck into him for the kill, and horses dragged his body, to a chorus of boos, around the ring.

The Lorca drama was the personal revenge of a political enemy of his brother-in-law. This man had arranged to arrest and execute Lorca before he was found out. When Lorca's whereabouts were discovered that evening, the governor was sound asleep, exhausted. They said, "He gets up at seven and will give orders for Federico to be released." At seven the crime had already taken place.

The English established themselves in Gibraltar to help the Spanish defend it. Then they never left. There is not the slightest treaty which legitimates their presence.

It is quite normal that the Spanish should love neither England nor France—the policies of both countries having always been to weaken and to dispossess Spain. The Spanish say to me: "It was easy for us to attack you from behind after '40. We were encouraged to do it. We don't do such things in Spain."

The Vatican took its revenge on Hitler, who hadn't kept his promises, by telling Franco to deny him free passage through Gibraltar. This denial determined his defeat.

The extreme kindness shown me by the Spaniards comes from the fact that they find me flamenco. This overcomes all the grievances that render the French suspect in Spain.

I was flamenco long before learning this term and what it represents. Perhaps Picasso has served as an example. It is what turns the monstrous French vulgarity against me. Alas, nothing is less flamenco than Paris.

France is a rich country that is poor. Spain is a poor country that is rich.

Now that I have some sense of the Spanish soul, I almost regret not having agreed to be ambassador when Spain had me offered the post through Sert. At the time, Franco struck me as a criminal. I probably wouldn't have served long in such a position. But I would have left a great memory.

The Communists have threatened Neville's wife, who on Corpus Christi always organizes a procession in honor of the Madonna. The day of Corpus Christi, all those who had threatened her fell to their knees.

This morning at Torremolinos an amazing scene with the young electrician who has made a halo for the Madonna. He argues with the curé, to whom he owes some money. He takes back his halo, shouting, *"She can light her own, if she's the Madonna!"* Rafael Neville shows me the halo which the electrician had thrown in front of his house.

Belmonte has changed the style of the corrida. He has made it into an exact science. Before him, one fought at a distance. He invented the idea of fighting without moving, as if enveloped by death. Then came Manolete. He would actually fight standing on his handkerchief.

Pleasant to write a posthumous diary—that way I can chatter in peace to the friends my work may make for me. Actually, I'd rather write this diary and poems than bother with the theater and films.

Amazing Spanish liberalism. People say to you quite openly: "How does Franco manage to write his name on the walls of villages lost in the mountains? No one would write it there if he didn't do it for himself." And a thousand other jokes which would send any Russian to the salt mines if he dared crack them in Russia. I repeat: The Spanish are against everything except Spain. Against the regime they defend—against the regime they accept, against the monarchy, against democracy, against the aristocrats they treat as imbeciles, and against the people they treat as cretins. Against the toreros they cheer. Against Pastora Imperio, a veritable queen of Spain, about whom they say, "She's always danced badly." They add: "Only she's sublime. All she has to do is move her hand." They are against the Madonna if she isn't the one from their parish. Even Manolete complained about the public. Since he was God, he was asked to work miracles. They no longer asked him to be better than the others—they asked him to be better than himself. And if he wasn't better than himself, they hissed him.

Modesty is as little approved in Spain as vanity in France. The journalists ask you, "Do you have genius?" You can answer, "A poet without genius is inconceivable—it's as if you asked a Gypsy if he can dance." Dali, in a lecture in Madrid, declares, "Picasso has genius and I have genius." No one dreams of taking this badly.

Genius is as natural to the Spaniard as heroism to the torero. Pastora Imperio's son-in-law is a matador, but he is afraid. Fear keeps him from fighting. No one dreams of blaming him for it. His genius consists in being afraid and in saying so.

Dali's exact words: "Picasso is a genius. So am I. Picasso is a Communist. Neither am I."

. . . .

JULY 26

A sudden fit, tonight, of the futility of everything—sudden collapse into that morass where I see only death as a way out. Everything in me withers. Nothing specific indicates when such fits are likely to occur.

We were to leave in a little while for a stopover before Gibraltar. We decide not to leave until tomorrow morning. Essential that we be in Gibraltar tomorrow. It's on Monday that the stores remain open—in every country in the world.

I wonder if this terrible fit of futility doesn't have a source out of all proportion to its strength. Rafael had taken us to have dinner with a lady of Torremolinos. This contact with people of no particular interest always encourages my tendency toward the void—pessimism—the feeling of being outside life. The mediocre minimize us. Idiots make us idiots.

Spaniards speak of Cardinal Segura* of Seville as of a madman. Incredible lack of psychology with which the clergy prepares the dramas of which it will always be the victim in Spain. In 1931 (May 12 and 13) forty-three churches and convents in Málaga were burned down, on the pretext that the old ideas were against the interests of the people. The truth is that the Church is smothering Spain until the country explodes. No lesson has been learned. Once again Franco's obligatory support makes the Church blind.

The Gypsy people is quite cerebral without the shadow of intellectualism. The intellectual Gypsy dances Rimsky-Korsakov, falls into the pantomime-artist genre and ceases speaking his own idiom, which is as pure, bitter, and dry as the yellow metal of Jerez. The flamenco idiom does not tolerate the slightest grammatical error.

---

*This prelate had just given evidence of a traditionalism astonishing even for the Spain of that period.

This is why a Gypsy man or woman can dance with more or less genius but cannot be mediocre.

Like childhood, Spain lives entirely within the moment, beautiful and cruel. "Draped in its rags—scorning what it knows not." Spain rejects offers from America but will not resist the temptation of superhighways. Hitherto protected by her bad roads, she will naively open herself to her ruin. Already Cardinal Segura is gradually despoiling Andalusia of its charm. America will do the rest. It is true that Spain, like France, devours those who invade her.

Franco, encouraged by the Vatican, must bow before the stupidities of the Church. But he does not measure the real danger because he is a Galician—a kind of Spanish Breton. "Ah! If he were flamenco!" That is the sigh of the Spanish people.

The Arabs have forgotten their elegance in Andalusia.

It is here, as in Venice, that one divines what they were and what they have ceased being.

Those jacket sleeves I turn up (so scandalously)—I find them all over Andalusia. To the point where I seem to be following an Andalusian fashion. People would ask me: "Why do you turn up your sleeves?" I never knew what to answer—usually it was something like "An old family habit," as the marquis of Aracena told me yesterday: "My grandfather turned up his sleeves, and I turn up mine." Flamenco instinct for style. A certain negligence, the correct corrected by an incorrect, unexpected detail.

Flamenco style is always uneven. The triumph of 1-3-7. To the point where the Gypsies wear only one sleeve and roll up one trouser leg to the knee. What I call *poetic lameness* is flamenco.

What I've learned in Spain is not to describe it but to borrow its syntax, which remains a dead letter to tourists in love with the picturesque.

Peking—Venice—Seville—Jerez are the last bastions of profound elegance. The age's vulgarity removes its shoes on the threshold.

. . . .

July 30

Gibraltar is an old dead tooth of a vanished Atlantis. The British have drilled and filled this tooth with gold. They have stuffed this terrible plum pudding with cannons and machine guns. Their incapacity to adapt has made this peninsula an English city where British soldiers speak Spanish with a pure Andalusian accent. They claim you can find in Gibraltar merchandise available nowhere else. This is not true. You find the same merchandise in Algeciras and in Seville. What I am smuggling back is a bronchitis caught in the British draft and added to the Spanish variety, a wind from the open sea which freezes the sweat in your shirt.

We buy Indian materials, and Neville buys a radio which the customs officer discovers under the bench. This might have gone badly (Neville being a diplomat) if miraculously enough the Spanish consul hadn't passed by, recognized Neville, and arranged matters.

We sleep at the hotel in Algeciras and leave for Jerez.

Jerez, which used to be written Xérès, and which the Spanish pronounce "Hérès" and the French "Kérès," is a town of a luxury and grace scarcely imaginable in a period when depersonalization makes all cities resemble one another. Not one house like another. Not one window indifferent. Not one balcony, not one patio without flowers, plants. The wretched neon has not yet transformed Andalusia into a danse macabre. As in Granada and as we shall see in Seville, the old lanterns gently illuminate the mysterious doors surmounted by their coats of arms. We take a horse-drawn carriage. These fiacres which resemble musical instruments are just the width of the streets. Seville will delight us in the same way with its look of a royal village and a splendid market town, with its little squares roofed by a ceiling of vines and jasmine, with its labyrinth of alleyways which by civil ordinance must be whitewashed over and over, producing that astonishing pallor of Granada

as of the tiniest Andalusian farm. In the evening we took a glass
with one of those flamenco wine merchants whose house is stuffed
with relics of Manolete, portraits, posters, and the last pink program
of Linares. Workmen and truck drivers drink standing at the
counter. Suddenly on this counter a hand claps out the inimitable
uneven rhythm of the flamenco. Every hand joins in, clapping the
counterrhythm. Neither guitar nor castanets. The hands go on
clapping until one of the workers clutches a shoulder as if he felt
an epileptic attack coming on, as if he were suffering from ap-
pendicitis, and sings his pain. It emerges from him in jerks, this
long, complicated complaint which his comrades encourage like
that of a woman in labor. They help him get it out by the olés
which escape from their mouths with the indolence of cigar smoke.
(While I am writing these lines in the plane, we pass over Toledo.
The Tagus sparkles like the steel of its sword blades.)

One of the workmen recognized me. They all offered us a drink
and refused to let us treat them. In turn, they transmit that grimace
of apostles leaning over the dead Christ, and [they] sob. They sob,
they tell *themselves*, they seem to call us to witness a wound of love
which is killing them. Once the complaint is spoken, their demon
releases them and they again become good fellows who put on no
airs. They amuse themselves by getting into this state, bewitching
themselves, beguiling the others by the embellishments of their
despair.

Visit the next day to one of the vast wine cellars of Jerez. (It
belongs to Don Fernando Gonzalez Gordon.) The black casks are
piled up to form avenues around us. A royal cellar. The casks with
kings' arms and those of infantas. I sign one cask, between the
matadors and poets of Spain. You sign with chalk. The signature
will be in this cellar as long as the scrolls of the sarcophagi in the
Escorial. Of some vintages, there is only one cask left. An old
specialist draws out some wine with what looks like a candlesnuffer
and fills the glasses. The Jerez, or Xeres, that travels changes taste.

At its source, it is a ferruginous blood that goes right to your head. The treasure of these treasures is a tiny cask of sherry—the one that Falstaff drank. Blood again, almost black. This is why I wrote above my signature, "Here I drank the blood of kings." It is as if these grand seigneurs of wine religiously preserve the blue blood, the "sangre torera," and all the dramatic blood of Castille.

Seville. We wander through the city by night with the marquis of Aracena, who came two hundred kilometers from his country place in answer to a phone call from Neville telling him we were here. It is quite normal for any Andalusian to be proud to present this accumulation of magnificences, so human and intimate that the streets, as narrow as those of Venice, do not let us step back and admire the composition of the facades. We end the night in a stable in the new section, where Gypsies dance and sing. They wear high, close-fitting black trousers, short jackets, and white ruffled shirts. Some of them look about fourteen and say they are eighteen because the cardinal and the prefect have forbidden dancers under eighteen to exhibit themselves. One young Gypsy girl in a white dress with a train: she looks like a furious madonna, an angry queen, an Arab Thoroughbred in the corrida braving the bull. She astonishes Aracena and Neville. They say: "You always think it's over, that there will be no more great dancers. And you're always wrong. New ones appear." The word *sublime* is the only appropriate one to describe this girl's dancing. She triumphs over the men who usually win out because her skirts conceal a woman's legwork, whereas in the men's dancing all the detail of the inventive mechanism can be seen. There is never anything murky about flamenco. The real flamenco dancing is as chaste, as precise, as grave, and as solitary as the passes of a matador. Cerebral without intellectuality. The Gypsy, with his whole body, *speaks a language.* If he tries for a new style, tries to embellish this language, he is lost. Such things are good for New York. Moreover, they are very rare. When an old man from the audience gets up onto the dancing floor, the whole troupe steps back, claps, and accompanies him with cries of ¡olé! and the greatest respect.

This morning Joaquin Romero Murube shows us the alcazar. The city has appointed a poet to the position of curator. We pass through the (intact) Arab rooms too fast, and the garden where, through invisible holes, water jets up between the tiles. Another exquisite invention, analogous to the watercourses of the Alhambra. Everything is perfumed. As soon as you brush against a leaf, the scent is overpowering.

Romero accompanies us to the cathedral, but it is closed. We're going to miss the plane. Neville can't be found. He was at Iberia, changing our tickets for seats on the four o'clock plane. The bags are taken off, and we lunch at the sumptuous Alfonso XIII (which reminds me of a huge Mena House).* I took these notes between Seville and Madrid.

Madrid. In the chaos of memories, I had forgotten a visit with Don Alvaro Domecq (mayor of Jerez) and the first mounted torero in Spain. He gave up the ring after the drama of Linares: Manolete was his best friend. He takes us into the stables and tells us the special features of each horse. It takes two years to train the horses, and all the work is useless if the horse turns out to be afraid in the ring.

In his house a tall case set into the wall contains the white cape embroidered with red roses which Manolete wore the day of his death. Under the cape, a banderilla and his sunglasses.

It was after this visit, where we drank the gazpacho, that we took the Jerez-Seville road that crosses Belmonte's huge estate.

Very difficult for me to describe this trip because we kept doubling back from one place to another, when I would take no

---

*An Egyptian hotel near the Pyramids, where Cocteau stayed in 1936, in the course of his trip round the world in eighty days.

notes, and then I would have to use nothing but superlatives, the words *admirable—marvelous—magnificent—splendid*—the only ones that come to mind as soon as I recall the slightest details of Andalusia, where nothing jars, everything delights. I had been told, "You will die of the heat." Now we were almost cold in the evenings, and the heat was never painful. It was the ventilators and the drafts that disturbed me. I had been told, "Watch out for rancid oil." I never smelled or tasted rancid oil. I had been told, "You will eat poorly." The cooking was excellent. I had been told, "The hotels are filthy." The hotels were impeccable. Everything I had been told about Spain was nonsense. To be fair, it seems that the temperature this summer of 1953 was exceptional.

Alberto meets us in Madrid. Dinner at Edgar's, where I meet Belmonte.* After dinner Alberto alerts the Gypsies. Some dozen appear (including Pastora Imperio's son-in-law). Until four in the morning, they sing and dance. This time, it is a lively, even gay flamenco. They have a good time. Their faces, often quite grim, brighten as soon as they stand up and improvise, each in turn.

Countess de Yebes points out one Gypsy wearing a brown shirt with a yellow braid for a necktie. This shirt, she tells me, is the result of a vow. You have to live a long time in the Gypsy world to understand it, for it is a world that does not understand itself.

I think of Genet, who once lived in Barcelona and who thinks for those who do not think—who attributes to the human animal a fabulist's language. Impossible that men who externalize themselves by gestures and rhythms of such grace and intelligence should not possess a psychology quite unrelated to that of a class equivalent to theirs. Everyone seems heavy, clumsy, vulgar beside them, whatever they do.

My cold must have got worse in the plane; Francine says it was

---

*In Edgar Neville's film *Flamenco*, Juan Belmonte gives a demonstration of his *toreo*.

freezing. I was writing and didn't realize it. We'll leave tomorrow morning for Nice. I have had nothing forwarded, and I am terrified in advance by what I will find at the villa.

The biggest-selling newspaper in Spain is the *ABC*. Another article by Llovet about me. He offers a rather confused reflection of the very specific things I said about the Prado, about bullfighting and flamenco dancing. After an article in the *ABC*, everyone here bows very low indeed.

This week a funicular taking pilgrims on a pilgrimage of the Virgin broke its cable. Everyone was killed or hurt. A priest publishes a dreadful article, "A Miracle of the Virgin." All the victims, by this method, are entitled to heaven. The families of the wounded must be deeply satisfied by this article.

Summary of this trip. Did not see all the artists I wanted to see. Many are out of town, at the beaches. Saw the places I wanted to see (except for Cádiz and Córdoba). And saw quickly, which, contrary to what people think, is the right way to see. Spain does not love Franco, it accepts him. He is the schoolmaster who controls a dangerous uproar. The Spaniard fears himself and the violence by which he contrives to ruin others and himself as well. The Spaniard is superstitious. The Church takes advantage of this. It rules. Freedom of speech stops at the written word. Spanish pride is a patriotism which permits opposing everything which is Spanish. Difficult to understand what a Spaniard is against. He is against everything, except the nucleus which constitutes the whole. The public is terrible, "despising what it does not know," believing the torero is paid for the bull to kill him. In the ring the public is the fiercest element of the three. The animal and the man defend themselves. The public pays dear to watch their death. Manolete's glory, beyond his genius, comes from the fact that the animal and the man died together.

At Linares a famous matador killed the bull. A famous bull killed the matador. That is what gives free rein to the mourners, to the flamenco elegies, to that vast sob which shakes all Spain between two conflagrations. The Spanish dream of massacring the priests, but they know that if they do, the second round will be won by the Church, powerful in its martyrs. All of which momentarily calms these incendiaries. Their only fear is American aid, which they reject. But they will not resist the offer of new roads. They do not realize that they are threatened by *Flamencocacola*.

. . . .

AUGUST 1

Plane between Madrid and Nice. Last night Edgar came up to my room to take notes. He is preparing two articles on our trip, and since misunderstood and mistranslated words risk causing all sorts of problems, I dictate very specific sentences to him and have him translate them in my presence.

Yesterday at the hotel I had a visit from young K., who is shooting a film in Estremadura. Of all those who want to do a film about me, he is the only one to whom I do not present a categorical no. His ideas please me. He can recognize my own work in films where I have worked with other directors. I tell him I may not have anything more to do with cinema; he objects that if I surrender certain projects, others will exploit and ruin them, which would be too bad. But if I were to make a film, I would make sure that it would be unexploitable, would have only the resource of the film clubs, and would not even pay back the advances. *The Blood of a Poet* and *The Age of Gold* were possible only because Charles de Noailles expected no profit or return. Who nowadays would risk considerable sums for the expression of an invisible poetry which would become visible only much later? Film is dying because of the immediate success demanded by the money it costs. I had decided on the preparations for *Sleeping Beauty* for

Korda; I am withdrawing. Technicolor would offer too many obstacles, and besides, the result would be merely a lovely film, a
balance between individualism and the industry's demands. This
balance no longer corresponds to my syntax.

We've passed Barcelona. We'll be in Nice in half an hour. Lucien,
after having driven us to the airport, will return to Madrid for a
letter from the Foreign Affairs Ministry so that he won't have
difficulties at the border with customs. (He's bringing back my
mirrors from Granada and the fabrics from Gibraltar.)

Rapidity of the journey. I was thinking of Chopin and that grim
trip to Majorca with the Sand woman. It would be interesting to
publish a true study of that journey and the one to Venice. The
Musset-Sand arrival. The strange couple: a bearded lady and a man
in skirts, and the consequences of this misunderstanding, such
consequences having nothing to do with the erotic romanticism
with which the ignorance of sexual problems tricks it out. Pagello
falling among these tourist ladies. The lady pederastically smitten
with this Pagello after her lesbian disappointments with a pseudo-
woman wearing a blond beard. And this trio understanding nothing
about what is happening to them.

The same business with Chopin. It often happens that these
dark women who imagine themselves normal because they seek
out men, but seek them out only the way men seek out one
another, choose, being so masculine, feminine men who correspond
to their male instincts and make them believe they are real women
loving real men—Whereas they are attracted by a man-woman
who, being homosexual, finds no satisfaction with them. Even Freud
has never ventured into this quagmire.*

---

*Cocteau develops here one of his assertions from *Le Livre blanc*, 1928: "There
exist pederastic women, women who look like lesbians but seek out men in the particular
way in which men seek each other."

· ·

AUGUST 3 · 1953

My return. It exceeds in horror all I imagined. Such a disgust for everything that I would do away with myself were it not for Francine and Édouard. Most likely I'll put my affairs in order with Orengo and then renounce any contact with my contemporaries. I don't speak their language. They don't understand mine. Silence is better. I wanted no such thing as fame, neither palpable nor posthumous. I wanted a little respect for my work. Not having gained this, I withdrew.

Forty years now that I have gone to bed to forget this world and force myself, getting up, to perform the farce of good humor. I no longer have the strength for it. I have never insulted anyone. I find most works that are praised mediocre and absurd. I have made the mistake of supposing that a sort of justice would be created, unknown to the justice of men. I was wrong. If I still write, it will be a matter of personal hygiene and without expecting any response to what I have to say.

In 1953 there is not a single periodical which, either by silences or by mockery, by insult, does not eliminate me from the scale of values constructed by its group. My solitude is all the more terrifying in that these various groups proclaim, if I happen to encounter them somewhere, the greatest affection in my regard.

My suffering would indeed like to die, but to die, it must kill me first.

· ·

AUGUST 5

On the roads of Spain, everyone is completely dressed. On ours, everyone walks naked. Nothing is stranger than this difference when you move quickly, by plane, from one country to the next.

Saw James Lord. Visit from Genet last evening.

It is most likely that what fame I have comes from my mistakes, and that what should be my authentic fame—my glory—remains invisible. So if I persist in writing, I must make fewer and fewer mistakes, and become more and more invisible.

Truth about the *Orphée II*: a grim business. The sailors lied and elaborated their lie. They stole the boat to go on a spree from port to port. Moreover, they stole motors and sails. The boat is in wretched condition. Francine is receiving bills from all over the coast. Paul, one of the sailors, concocted receipts and did not pay. And appearances were in his favor. Smuggling cigarettes adds to this scandal. Lucky that customs hasn't confiscated the boat and held Francine responsible as captain.

. . . .

AUGUST 6

Visit from Julian Green and Robert de Saint-Jean, staying in Saint-Tropez. Green is writing a new play* which takes place in France at the end of the eighteenth century. He asks my advice about set and costumes. How to answer? With Bérard, we have lost everything for the time being. Escoffier† remains (costumes), but he's the only one, and uneven.

Pasquini this evening brings me the poster of the Cézanne exhibition. James Lord shames France with our sordid bargainings after he obtained 5,000,000 francs from America to buy Cézanne's studio.

Pasquini tells me he was among the seven young men chosen by lot to execute Darlan.‡ (Algiers.) Death was also the fate of

---

*L'Ennemi.

†Marcel Escoffier, born 1910, originally Christian Bérard's assistant, then a costume designer.

‡Cocteau was related to Admiral François Darlan (1881–1942).

La Chapelle, to whom safety was promised. Until he was put up against the wall, he believed it.

The serious thing is that we end up believing those who minimize us. Beethoven wrote nothing more for the theater after *Fidelio*, because of the critics.

If you don't work for Lord knows what—you must resign yourself to work for Lord knows whom.

Bronchitis no better. Ears improved. But the least draft drenches me with sweat. Yesterday I had 6,000 units of bipenicillin. They begin again this morning. I don't think I can go to the Cézanne exhibition. I explained to the mayor of Menton, who had invited me to the festival.

This morning Édouard is at Monte Carlo for the formalities of his Monacan registration.

Wrote the poem "Fleuve du Tage," in which I combine the duchess of Langeais with Toledo. This secret writing must be a consequence of my extreme disgust for contacts these days. I work without any desire to be read.

Spain has lost her pelt of trees, her pilose system. She has been depilated. Nothing conceals her skinny body, all bones and muscles. France, all belly and nerves—incapable of reacting. Electricity, gas, postal service, trains are paralyzed. Last night travelers were immobilized in the middle of the countryside. Letters neither leave nor arrive. The British spending their vacations in Paris cannot get back to England and remain, penniless.

Young R. comes to see me with his wife and says: "This is what I propose. When you die they will murder your corpse. Name me your defender, and in exchange help me launch my books." (Youth of 1953.) The young woman seems to find all this quite natural.

It is this boy who has "sold" a hundred thousand copies of his first book by a system of peddling by hand. He is an example of those anarchists-in-words whom their actions contradict. I tell him, "Your comrades will soon add to the peddling of the books

you write and publish, the peddling of toothbrushes and brassieres."
"They already have," he answers. "We all camp near Juan-les-
Pins, and I've given up trying to prevent their schemes." This boy
is not without talent. He is astonished by what he calls my "in-
feriority complex," by which he means my doubts about my work
and my resistance to my noisy legend. "If I were you . . . ," he
tells me, not realizing that I would not have become what I am
by his methods.

. . . .

AUGUST 9

Postal service and telegraph still out. Still sick. Countless dreams
caricaturing my anxieties, my discomforts.

During this drama of France, all the magazines show Christian
Dior measuring a woman's skirt with a ruler. They all speak of
the "war of the skirts" with the greatest seriousness.

Perhaps one should have adopted Picasso's attitude, saying to
James Lord yesterday: "Ah! You're buying Cézanne's studio. I knew
it. Who cares about Cézanne's studio?" knowing very well ahead
of time that his own studios will be bought, cataloged, visited, and
littered with plaques. He never shifts the light he has trained on
his person. No doubt I have loved others, helped others too much.
I have wasted the strength I should have kept for myself.

The Art of Poetry. Poetry is a language apart, which poets can
speak without fear, since the crowd is in the habit of mistaking
for this language a certain way of using their own. Poetry compels
knotting the thread of speech in such a way that the spool never
unwinds until it gets out into the street.

Genet's strength is not to be the victim of his legend. He came
here in a splendid car and said to me quite proudly, "In Barcelona
now I'm living at the Ritz."

Cézanne finds in us every path except the road to our heart.

But he finds no path in those who visited his exhibition in Nice yesterday. These are the same persons who considered him ridiculous. Time has humbled them without making any other progress. They no longer dare say what they think, that's all. Picasso takes advantage of this fear which paralyzes them.

Very likely I am a good Frenchman all the same—for I am as sick as France.

A magazine article says that Sacha has invented everything, even *The Human Voice*. The full-color spread shows him as Louis XIV*— a Louis XIV *who thinks*. For Chamfort describes a game at Versailles which consisted in betting whether or not Louis was the stupidest man in the kingdom. In the royal council, when Louis had just uttered some enormous stupidity, the duke de B. forgot himself and exclaimed, "You see!," for he had bet on Louis XIV.

There are seven walls. I have passed through six. The seventh I have not managed to pass through.

All these young people who print poetic things and call themselves poets. In Seville, after the Gypsies perform, couples come out on the floor and dance together. *They think they are dancing.* They are stammering a language the Gypsies speak. What struck me about Spain is that the country isn't poetic. It is a poet.

. . . .

AUGUST 10

Improvement. It seems that penicillin has played the role of some atom bomb or some plague. Now my microbes have had their ages of civilization and their wars, which must correspond, within a couple of months, to our period.

The doctor asks me how I am. "Doctor, the mail isn't being delivered yet, but a few trains are in service."

------

*In *Si Versailles m'était conté*, a film Sacha Guitry (1885–1957) was then making.

Warning strike. One imagines what threatens the government, all for lack of the right man. All France can be paralyzed in a single day (and in winter).* I once asked Eisenstein, "When did you feel that the revolution had begun?" "The day when the faucets and toilets no longer worked."

Guitry as Louis XIV. His nylon wig. The beadwork embroidery on his costume. It is possible (I didn't know *Faisons un rêve*) that he used the telephone before I did throughout a whole act.† But in art "invention" counts only to the degree you can sculpt it. Racine, Molière copied the Greeks, the Italians, and the Spanish. It is where the copy diverges from the original that genius is proved. Even if I had known *Faisons un rêve*, I would have written my play. I would never have said to myself, "It's already been done." Everything has already been done. And the Chinese are wise men who have only three or four fixed themes around which they create their entire theater.

. . . .

AUGUST 11

Penicillin makes me feel as if I were fainting. This morning Dr. Ricoux gave me a third shot.

At Saint-Jean the drama of ————. The duchess tried to kill the sleeping duke with a silver candlestick. The duke suddenly awakened, flung himself to the foot of the bed, and his pillow received the blow. The duchess fainted. These families still use the vocabulary of 1900. The duchess reproaches the duke for having a "cocotte." This is the third time she has tried to kill herself with

---

*In August 1953 occurred one of the major strikes of the postwar period. All France was without transportation, mail, interurban telephone service, and other services.

†A comedy by Sacha Guitry written in September 1914, created by Raimu and the author in 1916. During the second act, a man uses the telephone to seduce a woman he desires.

Veronal. The young prince de B. sleeps in front of her door on a doormat. The duke says: "He's a servant. I pay him." He pays him, I imagine, not to watch over the duchess and keep her from killing herself, but so that she can get hold of enough Veronal to be rid of her.

The duchess goes to confession at Agay and leaves letters specifying that if she is discovered dead, it is not suicide but the consequences of the Veronal she must take in order to be able to sleep. She is cheating God. (I was reminded of Max Jacob saying, "I have got quite good at cheating God.") In reality it is only her fear of not being buried properly.

Yesterday the dose of Veronal was too strong. She was found at eleven, black in the face. They took her to the British hospital, where Ricoux is taking care of her. He doesn't think she can be saved. The duke, with tears in his eyes, hopes not.

. . . .

AUGUST 13

The duchess still in a coma. Four doctors, on the pretext of "tests," are struggling to revive a wretched woman who wants to die and who is lying in death's waiting room. None of these doctors would take it upon himself not to do exactly what should be done, while saying he has tried to do the impossible.

Still not well. Incredibly weak. I virtually can't get out of the bedroom. Francine wants to call in Durupt. Despite the strikes there is telephone service to Paris from Ricoux's office, when the call is from doctor to doctor and of a medical nature. If it is not of a strictly medical nature, the call is cut off. (Air France on strike).

I learn, when I wake up from the doctor who comes to take my blood, that the strike is a general one throughout France (all the department stores).

Strange that I picked up by chance and read Gobineau's tales about the Greek islands and the earthquake of Santorin* just when the horrible catastrophe of Cephalonia and Zante occurred. We might have decided to make our trip this year instead of the one before. To go to Spain last year, and this year to the Greek islands. Everything is going wrong, and I am going with it.

During these strikes and catastrophes, that duchess of ———, covered with tubes and needles, the spasms of her sleep breaking her teeth on the metal tube which keeps her from swallowing her tongue, neither alive nor dead. Her glassy eyes wide open, and the yacht and the steamer trunks and the gowns arriving. The villa filled with princes and queens in exile fearing, like the duke, that she might recover.

. . . .

AUGUST 14

I am writing lying on my back, immobilized by an intense pain near the left hip. Last night I tried to stand up, and it was impossible to get back into bed by myself. I called. Édouard heard me from his room. He came and carried me. This morning the slightest movement, the slightest cough wrenches this hideous pain from me.

No one ever believes I am sick. Yesterday Sadoul† and a crew insisted on seeing me. Though they were told I was ill, they replied to Thérèse, "Let him know that we'll be there all the same." One lady saying, "It must be a little cold."

Since the doctor had told me about purchasing a new machine which stops nervous pains ultrasonically, I have a call put in telling

---

*Akrivie Phrangopoulo (Naxos), 1867, and Le Mouchoir rouge (Cephalonia), 1868.

†Robert Sadoul, of the Radiodiffusion française, secretary of the association Les Amis de Vence.

him to bring it, but the poor man never sleeps at home because of the duchess, and I wonder when he'll be able to come. The blood analysis is, on the whole, negative. No doubt I'm suffering from a fit of sciatica. It sometimes happens that strong doses of penicillin cause this.

This year is a year of poems. They organize themselves in my mind without my having any say in the matter. Despite this crisis, I've almost finished the series for the "Homage to Manolete."

Montaigne says that we suffer more from the representation of pain than from pain itself and that we must learn to master this pain.

The duchess is dead. They brought her back up to the surface so that she could feel herself sink to the bottom. The duke, who had brought clothes to bury her on the eve of her death, thinks of only one thing: "If this is talked about in Saint-Jean, our family will be dishonored."

Another duchess in the doctor's care deplores the "fact" that her young chambermaid has been discovered sleeping with the gardener's son. "Such things happen," the doctor says, "and she's not your daughter." "I don't understand it," says the duchess. "A chambermaid! What kind of feelings can she have?"

Chamfort: "The dauphin of France said to his governess, 'Look, you have five fingers, just like me!' "

Francine brings the paper. The catastrophe of the Greek islands exceeds anything imaginable. They are falling to pieces into the sea. Agostolion, Lixoúrion, Zante are destroyed. The mountains collapse, the earth explodes.

The strikes are spreading, and France affords the world the pathetic spectacle of an island creating its own catastrophe.

This morning Dr. Ricoux came to give me the ultrasonic treatment. Treatment by means of a cry the human ear cannot hear. This silent scream manages to suppress a shoulder sciatica in one session. For lumbago it would take three five-minute sessions. I can already make several movements I couldn't achieve this morning. I have managed to get up, and I can sit up in bed.

Human Realm. Sartre quotes my saying that as a child I didn't think foreigners actually spoke a language. I believed they were pretending. With regard to poetry, this is the common opinion.

I've always inverted my expressions. Perhaps even more in *Clair-Obscur.* Though *L'Ange Heurtebise** remains the typical example of this defense against a certain vulgarity which so readily threatens the French language today.

It seems that poetry flourishes best in secret, protected by those who despise it, since the complicated poet demands exegeses. Góngora, an inverted, complex poet if ever there was one, remains one of the greatest in Spain. Pushkin is untranslatable, which does not hamper his prestige. (Copy this out as a note for *Clair-Obscur.*)

Today is when Luis Miguel Domingúin and his friends were to arrive at the Cap Estel, the hotel where I reserved rooms for them. But most likely the strikes will prevent them from coming.

Italy is profiting from our crisis. Full of tourists. France is emptying, except for the tourists who can't get out and haven't a penny. In Spain the foreigners who are stuck there are sleeping in the parks.

After this nice work our ruin will be complete, and we shall be bled by new taxes which will vanish down a hole. I was right to note, while I was in Spain, that France had become the stupidest country in the world.

Working people are splendid-looking here in the Alpes-Maritimes. Magnificent youngsters moving from place to place or working on the roads. The inferior race is the one which clutters up the place in August—petits bourgeois of a repellent vulgarity.

Despite this horror in the Greek islands, my hideous coreligionists find a way to say that a miracle has spared the church of

---

*Poem by Cocteau published in 1925.

Saint Denis. In the circumstances, Saint Denis hasn't lost his head—he's made sure to protect himself.

Moreover, the scandal of the miracles continues: pilgrimage trains derailed, pilgrimage funiculars crashing . . . All so many cheap miracles.

I can see it now, some naive reader thinking, if these notes ever appear, "He keeps talking about the vanity of human affairs, and yet he's oddly interested in them." Of course I live in a tiny zone of this chaotic age. Of course I am interested in that tiny zone, the way a villager is interested in his village. But without forgetting that this tiny zone is an illusion.

In the course of this dark business of writing, to enliven a chapter by some luminous sentence from a book seems delicious to me. It would always be nice to illuminate one's texts with the lanterns of Montaigne, each of whose sentences is a companion in one's solitude.

Blood analysis this morning. Doctor surprised. All the results are positive and as normal as Miss Europe. No doubt it's this equilibrium of my blood that accounts for my astonishing strength.

The Ionian islands continue collapsing into the sea, and the British ships cannot approach because of the tidal waves. Those who escape are dying of hunger and thirst. Supplies are being parachuted in. But the poor devils expect new quakes.

And while these islands are dying, and the tourists are besieging any vehicle that can carry them, and France is being ruined, the Venetian Nights, the White Fairylands, the galas of the Riviera continue.

People are always so surprised that I am hesitant about answering letters that ask for advice. I notice in the papers that a young woman has committed suicide because an orchestra conductor advised her not to pursue her studies as a singer.

This morning the inaudible cry that seems to have frightened off my pains was the kind Gide once mentioned to me, the kind fish utter from the depths of the sea, the kind they utter when they're caught and it suits us not to hear them. Christ believed that God created fish to be eaten by men, and the Romans believed that Jupiter created Christians to be eaten by lions.

Civilization consists in this: Morally, men are cannibals.

Tomorrow, August 15, is the worst day on the Riviera. An invasion of grubs, the lees of humanity.

Malraux, Montherlant, Sartre, Camus, Anouilh, etc.—they are figured in . . . I am disfigured.

. . . .

AUGUST 15

It rained this morning. It rains quite often for the holidays. I am suffering less than at first, but I cough, and each fit of coughing is a dagger. I'm waiting for the doctor with the ultrasonic machine—it helped yesterday.

The drama of the Ionian islands continues. Ours too. How do they dare ruin France, for the retirement benefits of white-collar workers . . . It all has a meaning only if the problem of irresponsibility is faced: perhaps these disorders obey deeper reasons than those which seem to motivate them.

One even wonders if France hasn't a secret advantage in remaining on the margin of the abyss and of international conflicts.

Spanish friends, expected between the fifteenth and the eighteenth. But since foreign journalists doubtless exaggerate the critical nature of events, it's possible that the Spaniards will postpone their trip. Moreover, I would be dreadfully sorry if they arrived while I'm sick.

Second ultrasonic session. The machine is made in Vence. No doubt this is the first time a German discovery has been perfected in this country. The cure (Austria—Germany) first took place in great secrecy. The patients were treated in a dark room. The machines were enormous. The French development is chiefly in what is called the probe (which is what costs the most), the sealed capsule which plays the role of a loudspeaker and focuses the sound. With this machine Ricoux can treat a sprained ankle in five minutes. Which doesn't keep other machines from being invented or Ricoux from buying them, or ever managing to amortize the sums invested (on credit) in the machines made obsolete by progress.

Guy Boncourt's discovery (thanks to Swiss funding) outstrips all present television equipment. It gets rid of the relays, the way the automobile has got rid of the stagecoach relays. It combines images and radio waves, which the specialists said was impossible. It clarifies and stabilizes the image.

Soon this discovery will pass for an American or a Russian one, France having the privilege of being inventive without deriving any advantage from it. The world accuses us of being in confusion—helter-skelter. It forgets our individualism and that a modest engineer of thirty-nine comes along in the middle of a general strike and a governmental crisis and puts to shame the vast enterprises of which the world is so proud. For France to prevail and prove herself, it is sufficient that there be one man who makes all the knowledge of the great industrial nations child's play. Who will say so in France? No one. Who will profit by it in France? No one. France had a magnificent chance of growing rich and recouping her losses. But she would rather founder in family quarrels while her possessions are taken from her.

One imagines what the Russians would have done with so considerable a discovery. Malenkov would have announced it along with the H-bomb. Actually, it's a bomb more powerful than the H-bomb, since it has just destroyed in a minute all the television sets the world over. A French bomb which is worth more than the atom bomb.

I'd like to begin the book *Clair-Obscur* and end it *en clair*, to show that my syntax grows complex and inverted according to the necessity I encounter. And so that people can say, the way they do for Picasso, "You see, he's perfectly clear when he wants to be!" Then they would have to say, "You see, he's not clear when he wants to be!" *Clair-Obscur* should be, in my oeuvre, an anarchic and aristocratic insult to a period which supposes itself capable of understanding everything and treats as ridiculous whatever it fails to understand. Montaigne is difficult to read at close range. But what delight one takes, what savor one relishes after having reached the fresh and tortuous kernel of his writing.

If in the poems of *Clair-Obscur* I change the natural order of words, it's so that the mind won't slide over them, but stop, reflect, and put them where they belong. During this effort, the mind becomes familiar with the meaning and, proud of having collaborated in the work, is more interested and becomes more sensitive to why these differences occur. I am speaking, of course, of the rare minds that know how to read.

The syntax of the poems of *Clair-Obscur*, like that of *L'Ange Heurtebise*, is the contrary of Mallarmé's syntax. It is solely intended to harden and corrugate a language likely to flow too readily and to spoil the charm by grandiloquence. Valéry realized the danger of a language which flows and of grandiloquence, but, not being a poet, he indulged in a sort of alchemy, deceived everyone and made gold out of gold. Besides, he very shrewdly realized that a thinker—if I dare use this word—finds great power in the use of verse and rhymes . . . Valéry uses nothing but ideas and images, nothing précieux in his stanza, which has the exact meaning of numbers. Nothing is missing, except that "everything" Apollinaire had. In Apollinaire the lines are not only a faultless object—they are something which cannot be explained: a poem, with space around it. As Alfred, the Potomak's guard, would say, "They elude analysis."

James Lord says, "At Vallauris, Picasso is under house arrest."

. . . .

AUGUST 16

Louis Mountbatten declares that the whole world must collaborate in the effort to relieve the Ionian islands. Three tiny islands on the map. The whole world takes less trouble about destroying vast territories and then offering them relief.

Despite this Greek disaster, despite the drama of Morocco changing its religious leaders, despite the continuing strikes, Nice last night held its "Earthly Paradise" carnival. The absurdity of this festival was aggravated by a visible proof of the lack of imagination, of taste, of the least glimmer of intelligence. I am judging from the photographs of this monstrous imbecility.

I remember the old festivals of flowers—already so comical. You could read in the papers: "Widely noticed, in his float, Count Gautier-Vignal, president of the Fencing Club and the Skeet-Shooting Circle. The wheels iris, the whip a sunflower." I was living in Villefranche. Paul Morand had cut out the piece and sent it to me.

Francine reports that at the Cézanne exhibition, Chagall told Pasquini that these Nice carnivals were humiliating, that such ruinous and embarrassing nonsense should be stopped.

When you think that all sense of proportion is lost in the realm of art and architecture, and that a few inches less in women's skirts are revolutionizing the world in 1953 . . . No one even thinks of smiling. People talk about the Dior bomb quite as seriously as about the atom bomb.

The "Earthly Paradise" festival (costumes of the period) has apparently earned the city of Nice some 7,000,000 francs, which seems scarcely credible, since the hotels are empty and soup kitchens are being opened to feed the tourists stuck in Nice without a penny. Now it's possible that any number of idiots have come from Cannes and Antibes to see "naked women," forgetting that they see them every day. It's likely that the phrase "in costumes of the period" was a real find.

After the third ultrasonic session, intense pain has given way to a sort of very tolerable ache. I can get up and climb stairs, which was impossible for me the day before yesterday.

Genet is coming to dinner. Fernand went to Cannes to pick him up.

Strikes. The advantage of being cut off from everything Paris supposes to be of extreme importance, which I can do without quite nicely. Almost finished the poem "Suis-je Clair?," which should end the book *Clair-Obscur*, which will be mostly the Spanish poems.*

James Lord brings me from Mme Guynet the box of drawings she was keeping at the Musée Masséna. I plan to use the drawings made of blots and to add colors for the limited edition which will precede the commercial one. (Poems from *Clair-Obscur*.) Orengo comes tomorrow to decide on the order of the "Oeuvres complètes" which I don't want to call that, but maybe "Oeuvres de J. C. (from this date to that)." Orengo thinks it will take four volumes on Bible paper and plans to begin with the novels and plays. Grasset has signed up young Dubourg (his book on my plays and films).

Leonardo da Vinci's obsessive researches led to failures in the fabrication of his colors. In his lifetime he saw his works crack, become covered with patches, fall into dust. None of his machines was executed. While he was painting his very tiresome *Last Supper*, the duchess† kept interrupting him, sending for him to repair her plumbing, regarding him much more as a sort of handyman than as a painter. He must have lived better at the court of François I.

---

*This poem was not included in *Clair-Obscur*, which ends with "Hommages et poèmes espagnols."

†Beatrice d'Este, wife of Ludovico Sforza, duke of Milan.

Yet he was asked to do quite a lot of plumbing there too. Too bad. Nothing is left of the automatons and moving jewels he created for festivities, which must have been wonders. I would have preferred them to that Gioconda whose glory remains inexplicable to me. It's true that this picture is so filthy, so black (perhaps due to the defective colors) that it's difficult to realize its charms. The picture interests me as a taboo, as a mysterious fortune of an object which engenders legends and becomes a cult object. It is the type of work that passes through the wall which confronts all works. There can no longer be any question of judging the Gioconda. It is there. The Louvre, if it happened to destroy it in restoration, could exhibit a good copy without anyone's knowing. It is no longer the picture, it is the idea one forms of the picture which counts. Very likely this Mona Lisa draws its strength from the countless works Leonardo destroyed. If he were alive today, no doubt he would be quite astonished at what had happened to him. He might say: "Who is that Mona Lisa? That Gioconda? I never painted any such thing." With his own eyes Leonardo saw his *Leda* flung into the *purifying flames* by Savonarola's boy scouts. It showed Castor and Pollux hatching from an egg.

I imagine that the majority of singular works from all periods have vanished, either on account of the monks or because of the difficulty young artists have in obtaining durable materials. Of Greece there must survive only fragments of official art. Very rare are the works that attest to a disobedience of the rules. And it is likely that the mutilations and lacerations of certain statues add to that look of audacity which struck me in Munich when I saw the Rodin bronzes which had been lacerated by bombs. The same bronzes intact seemed almost insipid when I saw them again in Paris. It's true that the wreck of a work makes it singular only if that work is beautiful to begin with. If it lacks strangeness, its ruin may bestow that quality on it, as happened to a bronze in the Louvre (the youth) which one might call a capricious work of lightning (in the rotunda, over or under the one where the Venus de Milo is).

If you are reading this diary after my death, you are probably wondering why the paragraphs inexplicably jump from one subject to the next. It is because I am gossiping to myself here; between any two paragraphs I may receive a visit which changes my ideas and orients them in an unexpected direction. Moreover, I advise those who edit these diaries to cut what I jot down for reference and the repetitions which occur, because I don't remember if I've already described the things I've described.

. . . .

AUGUST 18

Jean Genet came for lunch. He looks fine, and resembles Lucien* more and more. He's working now and gives himself orders, strict rules for the composition of his book. Each chapter or stanza, he says, must be complete at that moment, and must fit onto what precedes it. The book must create its own form as it goes along. It will be called *La Mort*. He says, "We write to unite ourselves— otherwise we would be scattered." He talks about Picasso: "I admire him, but I don't love him. He's even trickier than I am. In front of the Rembrandt in London, it's easy to see he must have known he could never be a god of painting. And because he knew, he decided to be the devil. He's putting all his effort into destroying the scale of values, so that no one will realize he's incapable of rising to such heights."

He talks about Sartre. When I say: "Sartre will be pleased with your new method of working. He'll think you've listened to him. He'll speak of the Mallarméan suicide . . . " Genet answers: "I'm

---

*Lucien Sénémaud. See Genet's *Thief's Journal* and his poem "Le Pêcheur de Suquet."

the one who explained all that to him. His book about me is very intelligent, but he's merely repeated what I said. He's given me nothing new."

He describes Lourdes to me, where he's spent a few days. The tradespeople despise you because you look as if you've come asking alms from the Virgin. They treat you like beggars. He wanted to buy some jars with the Virgin painted on them, to send them to Lucien. "With or without halo?" the saleswoman asked him. "It's thirty francs more with." One evening he was out walking and happened to be whistling. He passed an old lady who said to him, "You're mighty cheerful!"

He says: "The pederast is without continuity. He gathers himself up, he collects himself in the moment. You could put each one of my footsteps under glass." Everything Genet says would be admirable if you didn't feel it was dictated by insane pride. This egocentricity impels him to express the same things as a soul newly arrived at sanctity: Everything is vain in this world (*except him*). Everything is merely vanity (*except his*).

Yesterday I received three telegrams dated two weeks ago.

A slow mind puts a great deal of trust in "speed." On the highway it is the fools who must pass the others. In our age, people say of a writer that he has been "passed by."

Last night Jean Marais was able to telephone me from Paris, by special authorization, in order to receive information about a sick man.

Dr. Ricoux has just given me a fourth ultrasonic session.

Here is how he summarizes the ———— case: The duchess (unable to find anything of interest except herself) had decided that the duke would have to die first and then she would follow him. But the duke was unwilling and refused to take the Veronal. That was why the duchess tried to kill him with the candlestick. Failing, she determined to take revenge by killing herself and causing a scandal which would disgrace the duke. She took poison.

The duke gave her a very simple and noble funeral. Low Mass in the Beaulieu chapel with the queens in exile (all except the queen of Spain, who had wired that she couldn't come because of the strikes). The duke obtained from the physicians a rather vague death certificate and from the pope the right to bury his wife in religion. So in the long run, the duchess rests in the shroud of her stupidity and her egotism. There remains the new yacht, on board which the duke will breathe his "whew!" on the high seas, accompanied by his "cocotte."

The sultan of Morocco refuses to give up his spiritual powers. He regards the Glaoui's action as a schism. France remains, according to her custom, between two stools, i.e., between two thrones ready to turn on each other and massacre the French.

Another miracle: As a consequence of the strikes, the great pilgrimage of Lourdes will not take place this year.

Treasure is the name of the lost dog Monsieur and Madame picked up in Montrouge. Treasure never barked. He was a real thoroughbred. One day when Monsieur was walking Treasure, he met the veterinarian, who said, "You'd better keep your jackal on a leash." Monsieur turned pale and called the police. Treasure had escaped from a circus. He was returned to his cage. (This morning's paper.)

. . . .

AUGUST 20

The date the Great Pyramid gives for "great changes in world affairs." What is happening everywhere certainly doesn't contradict the prediction. Still, we'd have to know how the dates of the pyramid correspond to our calendar. And there are the Egyptologists living at the Great Pyramid today, waiting . . .

A sick man is bored and reads the newspaper. Nothing is more deadly than this kind of reading, which deceives you as to the truth and paralyzes your intellectual forces by the illusion that you're excluded from an active world.

Blacks from Harlem attack the White House. President Eisenhower assassinated. The Red Army sets fire to the Kremlin. Sixty thousand flying saucers over Paris, sending down a rain of gold. Berber troops give General Guillaume a victory parade. Nice announces the Carnival of Naked Postmen. In Cannes, election of Miss End of the World, Miss Catastrophe, and Miss Earth.

Incredible thrones to which fate raises Picasso. Someone sends me the catalog of the Lyons exhibition, under the presidency of *all the ministers and all the ambassadors (including the American ambassador).*

Riviera taboos. Matisse chapel. Such absence of genius demanded talent. Matisse counted only on genius.

Write nothing henceforth except what is of interest to my own universe. The only one ever likely to interest anyone someday.

I've just realized that I must paint the inner courtyard of the villa. (Begin by the wall with the mosaic niche. I've made the sketch of a centaur, but to do the thing itself, I must regain my strength.)

Have colored in gouache the drawings that were at the Musée Masséna. (For the limited edition.)

Yesterday I met with Orengo here and told him that a writer's work has to be regarded as posthumous, that it should be edited and arranged without his intervention.

Once I know that things are in order, my mind will be free to start new work—if there is going to be new work. Orengo immediately found the person capable of arranging the material for the four volumes.

In my oeuvre, the poem *L'Ange Heurtebise* has the importance of *Les Demoiselles d'Avignon* in Picasso's. Unfortunately, no eye has managed to see, no ear to hear—but that is the fact. Éluard is an impressionist poet. He made you squint your ears the way the impressionists made you squint your eyes. Nothing is stranger and less comprehensible than his collaboration with Picasso. It is true that works succeed to the degree that they are considered imitable. Now Éluard opened a door to anything and everything, which he managed with incredible charm. *L'Ange Heurtebise* is so inimitable that I myself couldn't imitate it. I am often tempted to try, and I always abandon the effort. It is an object of solitude, separated by a pane of glass from poetry as it is "practiced."

Poetry is not a way of using the written language. It is a language, an idiom apart. It has no purpose except to create a void around itself. Since I've been ill, I've rediscovered, without at all expecting it, the vein of *Plain-Chant** with the theme of death substituted for the theme of sleep. This vein had never returned. The strange thing is that it returns now after the Gongoristic style of the Spanish poems. As if my fatigue from being ill had loosened the links, kept me from knotting up the threads.

You must be suspicious of a "vein." Very little separates it from a tendency to imitate that vein. Once you imitate yourself it is crucial to stop, no longer write, try other methods. You slip quickly from the vein to automatism.

Nothing sadder than that discovery which deprives us of a work and thrusts us back into the void.

A great lesson from Kafka's diary. He wrote it during the First World War, which he never mentions. Not a single line refers to it.

. . . .

AUGUST 21

The Pyramid was right. Yesterday produced some tremendous spectacles.

---

*Cocteau's poems in a classical manner, composed at Pramousquier (Var), where Cocteau was staying with Radiguet, in October 1922.

Finished the poem "L'Autre Paul," in which I describe Éluard on his deathbed.

Poems on death. In this sense my lack of connection with events manages to touch events after all. Nothing but death in the press.

Peace has become synonymous with war: that is the paradox of 1953.

. . . .

AUGUST 22

Turn myself down to the least possible glow. Dim that ignoble need to "communicate." Health better since yesterday.

The postman came for letters this morning (letters written fifteen days ago).

Do not allow yourself to stop on any excuse. Continue under your own steam. Let yourself be splashed and spattered without discouragement, without being deceived by the lies of progress and speed.

Genet says that Sartre, meeting D. in Rome for the first time, took his pipe out of his mouth and stuck it in his pocket out of a purely automatic reaction of respect in the presence of beauty. (Which does not prevent Sartre from judging D. severely—he has done so in my presence.)—(Compare with this the story of Stravinsky saying to his son Theodore on the Nice road, "How dare you insult someone so handsome?") The notion of beauty higher than the notion of sex.

Gaxotte* very amusing about the despair of Saint-Germain-des-Prés. Despairing aperitifs. Despairing sweaters. Despairing beards. Despairing cars.

No doubt Genet is right to call Picasso a great despairing poet (a real one, the kind who doesn't show it) and [to say] that this

---

*Pierre Gaxotte (1895–1982), historian and journalist.

is the source of the huge favor he enjoys from a world overrun by a wave of despair. Only a despairing man struggles that much against despair. Only a despairing man takes active nihilism so far. Only a despairing man attaches—as Éluard's death has proved with regard to Picasso—no importance to life and to death. Only a despairing man turns against the human countenance to this degree. It is true that Picasso is borne on by a crushing success, which renders his despair both celebrated and comfortable.

. . . .

AUGUST 23

The duchess had told the doctor, who has managed to put aside 25,000 francs: "I've rented my yacht for 40,000,000. I didn't charge too much, do you think, doctor?"

Since the duchess's death, the duke has prowled around the hospital. He comes into the courtyard, doesn't park his car, but drives slowly round and round. Yesterday he parked. He asked to see the room where his wife died. He was told this was impossible, that another patient was now in that room. He begged to be permitted just to look in through the open door. Then, on the excuse that a wreath had been forgotten, he asked to have the chapel opened for him. It was explained that no wreath had been left there and that other bodies had passed through the chapel subsequently. Upon his insistence the chapel was opened, and the duke fell to his knees. He hated his wife, who hated him. No doubt he so longed for her death that he feared her vengeance. The doctor says, "He's returning to the scene of the crime."

Unable to sleep, and probably because I couldn't find a way to work out the penultimate stanza of the poem about Éluard. I finally dozed off toward morning. Waking, I found what was paralyzing the stanza.

Evening: Ink and mind spattered. If I were to write, I would merely imitate myself. Call a halt.

. . . .

AUGUST 24

There are men whom official honors compromise and men who compromise official honors. This is Picasso's case, and it would be mine if I became a member of the Académie française.

Excursion on the *Orphée II*. Lunch on board in the Gulf of La Garoupe.*

. . . .

AUGUST 25

Picasso—something of Voltaire and even more of the Barber of Seville. Picasso here, Picasso there . . . The abnormal and unique knot formed by Picasso between the here and now and something else. Impossible to open a newspaper without finding his name or his portrait. I haven't been able to bring him the news from Barcelona yet. James Lord will telephone to Vallauris so that I can go up there next week.

Chaplin and Oona have just had a son, in Lausanne. Telegraphed.

The strikes continue, especially in Paris.

The *Plain-Chant* vein seems exhausted. Since exploiting it, I haven't collected most of the almost illegible poems I wrote then. If the improvement in my health continues, I'll begin working on them.

Very few letters get through. Very little telephone communication possible. It is easier to get England than France and to receive mail from across the Channel.

———

*Bay on the east coast of the Cap d'Antibes.

All the discoveries of science and all the techniques of progress are useless if they are not put in the service of an ideology. If their ideology is limited to themselves, they can only use themselves up on the spot. (Which is happening.)

Reread *Monsieur Teste*. It seems to me that Valéry is speaking here of an indispensable ethic equivalent to technological progress.

I was right about the considerable discovery of Guy Boncourt, in Switzerland. No newspaper has mentioned it, and many people seem not even to have heard of it.

A visit from Mme Guynet and Georges Salles. Salles had dined with Claudel, Mauriac, and Pons.* Mauriac did his dance of the seven veils for young Pons. He asked him, "After Saint-Germain-des-Prés, where will it happen?" And Pons answered, "Where I am."

In Paris a shortage of bread. (Trains derailed. Acts of violence against those who work despite the strike.)

All these idiots who can see nothing on the earth and want to get to the moon. Luckily, if they do so—which I doubt—they will never return.

Sent the article for the theater issue of *Plaisir de France*.

People forget that France has always been in a bad way, stagnating except during the first euphoric years of the reign of Louis XIV. Famines, counterfeit coinage, etc. Nothing new about it. The horoscope on the radio declares that Sacha Guitry is Louis XIV. Paris, short of bread yesterday (no doubt because of blocked trains and the failure of flour shipments), should have gone to Versailles and asked Sacha Guitry for bread. (He's shooting his film in the château.)

James Lord asks me, "Does Picasso have a heart?" I answer, "Picasso has a heart—*in his hand*."

A journalist comes to the Louvre to watch Braque painting his

---

*The writer Maurice Pons (*Rosa*) was born in Strasbourg in 1927.

ceiling—a sky with two huge black birds. "Ah," he says, "you too—you're painting doves too!" Braque showed him the door.

A young photographer, assigned to photograph this ceiling, looks at it (it is an intense blue) a long while and says: "What a pity! I thought it was in color."

Prévert: they also thought that Béranger was a poet.

. . . .

AUGUST 28 · 1953 · ANNUS TERRIBILIS

Henceforth I must regard myself, and increasingly, as a simple private person, having never participated in the mechanisms of letters and not participating in the gains and losses of a marketplace. I must consider both the silence and the legends which envelop me as a protection of my work, withdrawn from the exchange and placed in a vault. Never let in, through any fissure whatever, a regret for being apart from a certain here and now of the mind. Anyone who comes to see me must have enough perspicacity to understand what a void separates the person I am from the person I have been made into. Never sleep or wake without realizing this and without drawing strength from it, instead of taking it for a sign of weakness.

If I were capable of pride, I would only be entitled to the pride of being an unexampled literary experiment. The typical victim of the conspiracy of noise, equivalent to the old conspiracy of silence.

. . . .

AUGUST 29

Picasso has the Ramié boy telephone to say he is going to Vichy and then on to Perpignan. From corrida to corrida. Picasso the Spaniard.

Swam yesterday and this morning. The weather we should have had in April.

Frank writes that the remake of *Les Parents terribles, Intimate Relations*, is a huge success in London. It's on for the eighth week, whereas Frank usually shows his films for only three. The house full all the time. I was convinced the film wouldn't work. Everything is slack in it—too open. No doubt that's what makes it more legible than mine to the London public.

The director of the Grenoble museum tells me he woke Picasso at La Galloise yesterday exactly one minute before the toreros arrived. They were to leave together for the Vichy bullfights. Picasso had them driven in his car by his son. According to the Ramié boy's telephone call, he's accompanying them to Vichy and on to Perpignan. Picasso's always gone to see all the corridas in France, but he's never seemed to me a victim of this tornado which is keeping him from painting. According to one newspaper, he wants to buy the Vallauris soccer field and build a bullring for Dominguín.

Before I left for Spain, he was quite calm. When he stopped painting, he gave life to his doves by wringing their necks and cooking them.

I've promised a canvas to the director of the Grenoble museum. He has turned up the cartoon I had once given the museum, on the request of the former director. This was in the Opera days (Villefranche). *Riders Attacked by Plaster Hands*—that was the title of the cartoon. I'd like to have it back in exchange for the canvas.* It miraculously escaped Maurice Sachs's thievery.†

Lorenzi has made the frame that will mount my tapestry *The Birth of Pegasus*. I'm not yet strong enough to paint it.

Francine has hired a new crew for the *Orphée II*.

---

*This pastel, one of Cocteau's most curious works, was exhibited in Paris in 1926. In 1929 Cocteau gave the work to the Grenoble museum.

†"One year when I was staying in Villefranche, Maurice Sachs stole everything he could find in my room in Paris" (*Journal d'un inconnu*).

. . . .

SEPTEMBER 1

Vallauris, or the waltz of the toreadors. Françoise telephones—
she's alone there. I'll go and have lunch with her tomorrow.

The poems. They must be cut like a diamond *so that they don't
sparkle.*

No sleep last night. I was trying to fit in three words. No question
of putting them where I wanted them to go, but where they
wanted to go. Yesterday rewrote the "Homage to Kafka."

. . . .

SEPTEMBER 2

Lunch at La Galloise. I was to lunch with Françoise, but Picasso
came back from Vichy at three in the morning. Françoise doesn't
seem to enjoy this waltz of the toreadors. (She doesn't like bullfights.) There was a shadow over her face, and when she was
alone with me she said: "Picasso is more Spanish than the Spanish
because he doesn't live in Spain. To love Spain, he has to leave
it forever." At table I don't talk too much about the trip (except about Barcelona and Picasso's family—who had written
to Vallauris: "Cocteau is a true Gypsy"). I even notice that Picasso is a little jealous, as if I were talking about a woman he no
longer sees.

This whole waltz of the toreadors is organized by Alberto. It's
a maneuver to get Picasso back to Spain. A maneuver Picasso
doesn't suspect, while telling me that his toreros speak only of
Puig.

Françoise tells me that she has known people who rented out
a little house on their property to some unfortunates subject to
all kinds of disasters—as a kind of lightning rod. She also says
that Picasso had made her get off before their station on the metro

because there was a young couple and a child all so lovely that Picasso said: "Those people are too happy. An accident is bound to happen." (Typical Spanish story.)

Picasso, speaking of Dominguín: "His real plaza is the Place Vendôme." And he adds, "You don't believe he's like the others, but he's exactly the same."

Last night Picasso stopped at a gas station. The attendant, assisted by a huge young fellow, said, "You look like Picasso." "I am." "Then you knew Misia." "Yes, of course." "Well, I'm the one who killed Mimi."* He was the fellow with whom Mimi had her fatal accident. "I spent the rest of the trip," Picasso said, "in complete unreality. I kept thinking that that gas station was a contact with reality itself. And there you are: you never get away from it."

He describes a family and a magnificent estate where he was received with his toreros. There were a lot of young people there. "They will talk about us," he says, "the way you talked about Catulle Mendès.† We won't be us any more, but what they decide we should be."

Françoise: "You must avoid having friends like yourself. They become accomplices."

. . . .

SEPTEMBER 5

The Paris-Nice (Nice-Saigon) plane crashes in the Alps. Fifty dead. Jacques Thibaud‡ on the list.

---

*Marie (Mimi) Godebska, ex-wife of Aimery Blacque-Belair, killed in an automobile accident in 1949, was the niece of Misia Sert.

†Before paying him homage in *Portraits-Souvenir*, Cocteau had written a caricatural portrait of Catulle Mendès (1841–1909) under the name Pygamon the Parnassian, in the "Letter to Persicaire" in *Le Potomak*.

‡The violinist Jacques Thibaud, born 1880.

The Cuevas ball. Cuevas accomplished in Biarritz what Beistegui botched in Venice. Mortal labor of the idle.

Another burglary at Warner's, in Antibes: 25,000,000 francs.

Alec is here with Carole.

"Poetry Congress." You wonder what it could mean. Rochefort announces the topics: "Must we kill the old poets?" "Poetry and the accordion . . ." Disgusting mixture of a poetic atmosphere à la Prévert and real poetry, a language apart. Living and dead, having no relation to what people take it for.

. . . .

SEPTEMBER 6

Alberto telephones from Spain. I am to ask Picasso if he would like Alberto to bring along his Gypsies next week—would it amuse Picasso's friends?

Edgar Neville telegraphs, asking us to send the car to Ventimiglia at one-thirty. Returning from Venice.

Thefts continue. This time it is two princesses (one née Guinness). Admirable, if the socialites imitate their burglars.

Édouard's misanthropy: "I'm always afraid of having to blush for being human."

In France since Encyclopedism, everyone meddles with everything, imagining he can outdo anything he hears, reads, sees. There is no longer a public—only colleagues. The great countries (China, Spain) have remained like our seventeenth century. A handful of men think for the rest. In Germany the ignorant public respects the primacy of an elite.

The thieving princesses: "We're as good as our burglars."

Worked a good deal on the poems. Mathematics of the word. A simplicity anything but simple. Invisibility of research. To say (apparently) simply and clearly the most difficult things, which require a whole chapter in a book. To say them in four lines. Use of greeting-card rhymes which wrest treasures out of the dark.

In *L'Espoir*, Mario Brun says I have been to see Michèle Morgan and Henri Vidal. Now, I had said to him, "Picasso is not working for the moment; he's traveling from corrida to corrida." This has become: "Picasso is engaged in a titanic work on bullfighting." The best journalists neither listen nor retain. Instinctive hatred of exactitude.

Yesterday a visit from Carleton Smith, director of the National Arts Foundation of New York(?). He's prospecting for a likely recipient of a kind of Nobel Prize which America is proposing to institute. I suggest: "A man who can really read and write." He doesn't speak a word of French and I speak his language very poorly. He makes this observation: "You must be untranslatable— for in English you have such a sense of exact formulation that it can only be a result of your style. Even your English sentences would be difficult to transfer to another language."

He never goes to the movies, nor to the theater. He's seen Garbo only once, long ago, in some film neither of us remembers.

I tell him: "America knows nothing about secrecy. Such a prize will only be given, like your Oscars, to a person to whom it will mean nothing. And moreover, if the prize were given to a van Gogh in his lifetime, it would be given to everything that America despises, to poverty and disorder. Your problem is not to find millions, but a reasonable sum. That would not inspire confidence. And of course millions are never given to an unknown or a young person."

Yesterday my "Notes on a First Trip to Spain" appeared in *Paris-Presse-L'Intransigeant*.

Regrettable psychosis. Neorealism—considered from a Communist perspective. In reality these films are those of Arab storytellers. In the *Arabian Nights*, the caliph disguises himself to prowl through his city. A Vittorio De Sica disguises himself as a camera to prowl through his, to creep into the houses and discover stories.

233

This is also (actors who are not actors) the tradition of street theater, of Goldoni. In short, the Italians loathe these films which they regard as presenting a poor propaganda.

At the last Cannes festival, I went to the films of two friends, Buñuel and De Sica. I was interviewed on the radio: "You've come to Cannes only twice?"

"That's correct."

"For Buñuel's film, and for De Sica's?"

"Correct."

"Those are Communist films."

"A question of phraseology. We used to say *humanitarian* films. And, I might add, Christian films: Love one another . . . Come unto me . . . The last shall be first . . . "

"M. Cocteau, you know the Milan cathedral."

"I do."

"Have you noticed which way it faces?"

"No, I never have—I have no sense of direction."

"At the end of the film—*Miracle in Milan*—all the poor fly off on broomsticks to a better world. Didn't you notice which way they flew?"

"_____"

"They flew east."

Destestable psychosis which is at its peak in America (as Smith confirmed yesterday).

Besides, it is not one ideology in opposition to another. It is, "My pocket is being threatened."

Edgar Neville our guest for two days. Tomorrow he returns to Madrid by way of Barcelona.

The Italians came yesterday to show me Sicilian periodicals and a book on Italy whose color reproductions equal the Swiss methods.

The sound barrier. There can be no sound barrier. The racket of the meeting the day before yesterday made the villa tremble.

To say, we are "separated from the invisible by a wall" would be absurd, since that wall is ourselves.

. . . .

SEPTEMBER 9

In California a hydroplane went wild, without its pilot being able to do anything about the "eccentricities" which were terrifying the crew. The crew parachuted out.

André Dubois* for lunch. He tells me about having been visited in Metz by the son of Mimi Blacque-Belair—Patrice. Patrice has taken orders. He doesn't wear the soutane but the insignia, a cross inside a heart. In Paris, not knowing where to go, he called on Pierre Brisson, who was living with his mother. Brisson sent him to Mauriac. And it was Patrice, an anticolonialist, who brought Mauriac to the defense of the Istiqlal.

Édouard brings back from Nice the books I had mentioned to him which had delighted my childhood. But what has he found? Tiny volumes familiar only because of their titles. Better that they vanish altogether. Cruel to find them cut, mutilated, weakened, without enough substance to live, being only the ghosts of what we had read. Those interminable books, companions of our sickness, I find reduced to a few pages and illustrated by absurd images. Including *The Mysteries of Paris* as little more than a pamphlet. A book to read standing up, as they say.

Lunch at Marie Cuttoli's. The curator of the Antibes museum (a Communist) says: After a thousand battles, I'm the one who is responsible for the Picasso Museum. The mayor loathes it and loathes me. I advised Picasso to give the city nothing. If there were

---

*Prefect of the Moselle and, in 1954, prefect of the Seine. André Dubois, born 1903, had married the journalist Carmen Tessier.

a stronger mayor and I should die, everything would be taken down."

I'm going to exhibit the *Judith* tapestry at this museum for a month or two.

The Communists say to the curator, "What social message do you find in such painting?"

My yellow frame is dry. Tomorrow I'll paint the black commas. Then I'll send the picture and the frame to Aubusson, so that Bouret can execute it. The sleazier the times, the more important to contradict them with luxury work.

The engineers of Los Alamos, after hideous experiments which the human carcass does not withstand: "Will man always be in the way of progress?" and "Considered from the perspective of future aeronautical technique, man at present is a flop." They might well add, "It is only from the perspective of art that man is not a flop." In mechanics, man can only be *replaced*. And what happened yesterday to that "wild" hydroplane will happen again. The machine will no longer accept human control.

At Marie Cuttoli's yesterday, there was a lady with gray hair at the table. This lady, née Polak, was none other than the little girl I had kissed on the mouth in Switzerland; I was eleven and she was twelve. There is a photograph of us on a seesaw. This memory was so intense for each of us that she dared not see me again. I remember having come back into the hotel dining room so red that my mother asked, "What's come over you?"

Last night I remembered the words of the charming old curé de Grenelle. We had dined together with the Maritains. He said: "I've seen the Holy Virgin three times. The first was in my little garden, where I was hoeing, and I was quite exhausted. I was just thinking that, and all of a sudden the Virgin was in front of me, between the beds. Before vanishing, she made a kind of playful curtsy and she said, 'I'm still hard at it.' The second time was in my sacristy. She seemed to come out of the wall, with an escort, and she was laughing. She said to someone in her escort, 'He doesn't look very comfortable.' Which was the truth. I must have been absurd. I had dropped my breviary. The third time I was saying Mass. The choirboy saw her, but the idiot was frightened. He ran away as fast as he could. At first there was a kind of flickering over our heads. Then that calmed down like dust settling, and I saw the Virgin's feet very clearly on the altar cloth. I noticed something like chalk in her toenails. She was standing between the devil's legs—thick black legs. She tapped one of his knees and said, 'He's not as bad as he looks.' "

The narrative of his visions was so simple and so lovable. There were no grottoes, none of those speeches and ridiculous gestures that children always attribute to the Virgin. "She was as tall as a bottle." "She clasped her hands." "She said, 'You don't pray enough' "—and other nonsense typical of our visionaries.

I can't understand how the Church, which is so discreet, accredits the scandal of Lourdes and its wretched commercial arrangements. The doctor told me that for each miracle, medicine records any number of dreadful diseases which the pilgrims bring back from that cold water, that microbe soup. It must be too late to intervene. It would be a serious matter to learn that Bernadette had surprised the pharmacist's wife sowing her wild oats in the grotto. She had played the role of the Virgin under a gauze scarf and repeated her performance without her partner (a captain in the reserves) to give credit to the legend and avoid suspicion. The truth was told later by the captain. The pharmacist had died, and the lovers moved away.

As I see it, there would be no scandal in telling the truth. The Church would lose some revenue, but would gain dignity. Moreover, it is finer that this impulse of faith should begin out of a joke and that heaven should gain by it. Such apparitions reduce divine omnipotence to little enough. It is not for children to spread the Virgin's *grievances* through the village. She is great enough to work her miracles directly and cannot complain without compromising her prestige and her invisibility. The children who indulge in *playing a part* that is more serious than the one they play in haunted houses should be punished. Hysteria has excuses. These wretched brats do not. In the case of Bernadette, it's something else. She was the victim of a vulgar and sacrilegious couple and could not anticipate the consequences of her action.

Moreover, no one would believe the retired captain, any more than they believed Esterhazy confessing to anyone who would listen (he even confessed to Oscar Wilde) that he was guilty. Dreyfus *had* to be guilty. The general staff knew what to do and must have told Esterhazy—like Dr. Verne to Thomas's aunt: "You are innocent. I order you to be."* Even after Dreyfus's (rather dim) rehabilitation, Esterhazy, despite the proofs Germany provided, never received the slightest reproach. His servant was taken away. This imbecile didn't confess out of remorse, but boastfully. He declared to Wilde: "Dreyfus was a weakling. If I had confessed, he would have said I was lying out of respect for his superiors."

Dreyfus once said to Morand, who was visiting him when he was back in the service: "You know, it wasn't me. It was that poor Esterhazy." And Paul Iribe, who had dined with Dreyfus at the time, used to say: "He would have confessed during dessert to make himself interesting. *But no one would have believed him.*"

Never has there been a victim less worthy of his drama. In the

---

*In *Thomas l'imposteur*, young Guillaume Thomas, born at Fontenoy, claims to be the nephew of Genral de Fontenoy. Dr. Verne persuades Guillaume's aunt to keep this imposture a secret: "He exclaimed, in the fashion of the mesmerizers, 'You are a Fontenoy, I command it.' " This injunction reappears in the last line of Radiguet's *Bal du comte d'Orgel*, a novel contemporary with Cocteau's *Thomas l'imposteur*, in which Cocteau (as we know from a letter to his mother of October 20, 1922) "supplied the last word": "He used, without realizing it, the hypnotists' order: 'And now, Mahaut, sleep! I command it.' "

midst of the affair, Mme Straus* used to say, according to Proust, "We ought to change innocents."

For a young man's culture, it's simple: he merely needs to read *The Princess of Cleves, The Red and the Black, Splendors and Miseries, The Idiot.* I cannot forget Marcel Khill,† a young creature quite without culture but a noble soul, reading *Splendors and Miseries* at Fourques and not being able to go on because he couldn't bear the scene where Rubempré denounces Collin. That gives the measure of a man.

Stranger still is Charles de Noailles, incapable of reading a book that ends badly and inquiring to find out first. For him the worst of the books that end badly was Irène Nemirovsky's *Bal* (1930)— which I didn't understand before learning that a botched ball is terrible for a socialite, even if he has Charles's spiritual elegance.

. . . .

SEPTEMBER 14

A lot of people come to Santo Sospir, but not for long—as if they realized the atmosphere of calm and of work which their visits disturb.

The jewel thefts are now occurring in Paris. The thieves are back from their vacation.

On the beach at Beaulieu, the doctor sees a woman bather with a pointed straw hat. "Doesn't that remind you of something?" he

---

*Geneviève Halévy (1849–1926), daughter of the composer Fromental Halévy, wife of the composer Georges Bizet (1869), then of the lawyer Émile Straus (1886).

†Mustapha Marcel Khelilou Belkacem ben Abdelkader, known as Marcel Khill, was born in 1912 of a Norman mother and a Kabyle father. Cocteau met him in 1932, and in 1934 Khill created the role of the Messenger from Corinth in *La Machine infernale*. In 1936 he was Cocteau's Passepartout in his *Tour du monde en 80 jours* and was the dedicatee of *Portraits-Souvenir*. He was killed in Alsace on June 18, 1940.

asks his wife. "Yes, *Beauty and the Beast*." The bather turns around. It was Mila Parély.* I'm having lunch with her today.

Today I was lucky enough to write. This does not always happen, and I force myself. The result is that I do not communicate life, but a silhouette of life. Even to my eyes, it is difficult to see the difference. It can be seen with much greater perspective.

Yesterday I finished the frame for the tapestry *Birth of Pegasus*. Gaxotte says very accurately, over his signature Pangloss, that young people are amazed by paintings and statues of mythological and even biblical inspiration, because they are unaware of the sources and no longer know about such things. How fortunate I am to be of an age when people read, when people learned. Otherwise I would be like those people who live in a street and haven't a clue about what constitutes the glory of the name it bears. I strongly doubt that the electronic brain can inform young people about a world which their ignorance depopulates of all signification.

. . . .

SEPTEMBER *17*

Telegram from the Puigs. Alberto suggests coming the twenty-fourth with Pastora Imperio and her little troupe.

Yesterday appeared two huge Swiss fellows with an enormous amount of recording equipment in their car (sound hunters). After everything was set up in the studio, they discover we are on a frequency of twenty-five. They pack up and we drive to Beaulieu. Twenty-five. I take them to Nice—to the Musée Masséna. Mme Guynet says the museum is still waiting for its frequency of fifty, but that certain districts of the city have this frequency already.

---

*In *Beauty and the Beast*, Mila Parély, wearing a conical hat, plays the role of Félicie, one of Beauty's two sisters.

She telephones to the Musée Chéret. They have fifty. We drive to the Musée Chéret, which looks like some sort of mad dream. Enormous, and marble throughout. Chéret's canvases and posters* are everywhere. We are given a room where the Nice carnival exhibits its plans and models. I record. And my Swiss return to Geneva, astounded by this hunt for electricity.

Parinaud telephones that Le Figaro is printing a poisonous account of my pieces on Spain and on certain things I said about Mauriac and the Spanish journalists. He asks if I want to answer. I tell him that where I am, Le Figaro seems a figment of the imagination. A diseased imagination.

I'll go to Nice this afternoon and choose the drawings for Bruckmann and have them photographed. Marie Cuttoli telephones that she herself will come for the Judith tapestry to install it in the Antibes museum.

Mary Hoeck writes that one of the Oxford ladies had mentioned their "adventure" to her parents forty years ago, but in those days, such an adventure did not seem "suitable" in England.

. . . .

SEPTEMBER 18

Visit from Hervé and Gérard Mille. Hervé says that there exist poems written by the electronic brain of which certain lines, produced entirely by chance, are quite remarkable. (Style 1924.) Hervé wanted to put on thirty performances of La Machine infernale at the Athénée before Jeannot leaves, but the dates don't work out. He talks of taking off whatever play is being done there when he returns and doing the thirty performances before Jeannot goes on at the Bouffes.

---

*Jules Chéret, born in Paris in 1836, a famous and productive poster artist of the turn of the century, died in Nice in 1932.

Always too fast. I should have kept *Bacchus* in a drawer till now and done it at the Bouffes.

Picasso has Marie Cuttoli call to say that the Spaniards should be put off because of Emmer's film. Since I have postponed the Puigs so many times, I suggest that they come without Pastora and her little troupe. The Rosens arrived at the hotel on the Cape yesterday; they'll come here for lunch today.

Took the Masséna drawings to the photographer. Monday I'll go to Antibes for lunch at Marie Cuttoli's and see how the tapestry is hung.

Picasso. I know no man more alien to the solution of the problems attributed to him. It's the story of the golden section, which supposedly determines certain artists' work, whereas it can only verify their instinctive equilibrium.

Heinz Rosen reports this bit of dialogue between an American sports fan and a German one:

AMERICAN: You won only the bronze medal at the Olympics. Too bad.

GERMAN: Yes, but in 1960 we'll win the gold medal, because *our* blacks will have grown up.

Dinner at Villefranche.* You can't live on your memories. I dined as if I were coming there for the third or fourth time. The young fishermen have grown old. The grandsons stroll along the quai as if they were grandfathers.

The better I know the language and the more I work with it, the more my vocabulary becomes limited to a few words which

---

*It was Marcelle Garros, widow of the aviator, who in 1924 introduced Cocteau to the tiny port of Villefranche-sur-Mer. Until 1929 the poet made numerous extended stays here, producing between 1925 and 1927 *Le Mystère de Jean l'oiseleur, Lettre à Jacques Maritain, Orphée, Oedipus Rex*, and others.

I shift about like letters of the alphabet, like bits of glass in a kaleidoscope.

. . . .

SEPTEMBER 20

When Raimu* asked Marcel Pagnol how many stars there were, Pagnol cited a number at random. "It's good to have been a schoolteacher," Raimu said, "something always sticks."

Other worlds must have developed civilizations in a direction very different from ours. I believe absolutely in what have been called "flying saucers," but it is likely we won't see them again, our form of civilization offering no interest for theirs.

This morning I went over to the hotel pool to see the Rosens, who want me to make a film with the materials from *La Dame à la licorne*—a film that could be better than *La Belle et la Bête* and would correspond to the ballet requirements of the London producers. Then and there came a phone call that the young Englishman putting on *Bacchus* in Cambridge is at the villa. I have him come to the pool and took him back to the villa where he left his bags. I sent him off to Nice after drawing for him the replicas of certain costumes for *Bacchus*. Nothing harder than to keep a Sunday free.

This young man tells me that Auden's translation, *The Knights of the Round Table*, is as far from my play as Ronald Duncan's of *L'Aigle à Deux Tetes*.

A poet is posthumous—dead—stone dead. He can do absolutely nothing about the way in which his works circulate in the world. Better to be unknown than betrayed. Unknown *and* betrayed, that is the poet's fate.

---

*Jules Muraire, known as Raimu (1883–1946), celebrated French stage and film actor.

These poems I've been working on have restored my equilibrium and a certain happiness. No doubt I was in that state I never manage to recognize, suffering those birth pangs I always mistake for an incapacity to write. What I dread is feeling this work become detached from me (no longer requiring my help). And I also fear extending the birth artificially, imitating myself to fool myself.

Two weeks ago I was already suspecting that the work was leaving me and that I was cheating. But it was only a pause. The vein was not exhausted.

. . . .

SEPTEMBER 23

Launay, at Marie Cuttoli's, gave me a book containing *All the Poems of Victor Hugo*. He had printed it for Canada. A fiasco. Terrible to reread. Hugo flows, torrential, ingenious, with no sense of the rare. Even "Olympio" no longer stands up. There are lines which stick in your mind and overwhelm the rest. But the accumulation is dreadful.

Jeannot is in Nice, where he is shooting *Monte-Cristo*. He called this morning.

Total lack of judgment with regard to my recent poems. I sometimes reread myself with the eyes of those who denigrate everything I do. I lose the sight of my own eyes.

. . . .

SEPTEMBER 25

Rain. I had to send away the color-film people from the Tourist Office. Visit from Charles MacArthur Hardy for the Australian press. He confirms the huge success of the remake of *Les Parents terribles*.

244

Did the drawing and sentence to be inscribed on the door of the television exhibit.

Did the salute to the magicians for Jean Weber.

Answered letters. Recopied poems. Phone call from Orengo, who says that the *Réalités* people plan to take over the journal *Arts* and will do my text "What Are You Working On?" only if this takeover is definitive.

Dinner with Jeannot last night in Villefranche, Chez Germain. He's shot the first takes of *Monte-Cristo* in the cloister of Cimiez and in the old part of Nice.

. . . .

SEPTEMBER 27

Telegram from the Puigs, who offer to come and visit either alone or with Pastora Imperio and the Gypsies.

(Letter from Marie-Laure.*) At the moment when, because of Marie-Laure's indiscretion (she was in Grasse at the time), the rumor got started about our marriage, and since Mme de Chevigné† seemed to be holding me responsible for it (taking me for a fortune hunter from one day to the next—I hadn't a clue what Marie-Laure was telling her girlfriends), my mother made this admirable remark, "I've told you over and over that you shouldn't see people who don't pay their debts." The triumphant bourgeoisie of those days held the fallen nobility in terrible scorn. When Chanel invited duchesses to a ball (and they came), my brother Paul prevented his wife from going on the excuse that one must not "frequent these tradespeople."

Radio. Beethoven had a lofty soul and a great vulgarity of means.

---

*Viscountess Marie-Laure de Noailles.

†Countess Adhéaume de Chevigné, née Laure de Sade (1859–1936), model for the duchess de Guermantes in Proust's novel. She was Marie-Laure's maternal grandmother and lived in the same Paris apartment house as Jean Cocteau and his mother.

Nietzsche contrasts him with Goethe: peasant and aristocrat. The means of Bach and Mozart are of an elegance comparable to their inventive genius. In Beethoven there is a sort of musical militarism I detest.

Misia Sert used to say about Ravel, "He puts in the punctuation, but he forgets to write in the words."

Satie's perfect elegance makes him invisible. As Brummel says, "If you have found me elegant, it is because I was no such thing: it is because you have *seen* me."

Greco sustained himself against Toledo's incomprehension only by his powerful personality. Immediately after his death, decadence relegated him to the bric-a-brac where our age discovered him and from which it rescued him.

To write "in verse," "with rhymes," to give a certain platitude a certain relief, to restore its nobility to the language (but without Valéry's preciosity). To unite Malherbe and Charles d'Orléans. The Malherbe of "In whose number I am placed / Is the source of such repute / As will stand eternally." True, Malherbe rarely sustains such perfection.

. . . .

SEPTEMBER 28

James Lord writes he has had lunch with Dora Maar.* She said about Picasso, "He would have liked to be Jean Marais, and he has succeeded in a way."

Received the copy of *Les Enfants terribles* in German (Desch)—*Kinder der Nacht*. Why this incredible delay with *Bacchus*? Church censorship? I shall ask Desch.

---

*A photographer of Yugoslav origin, born 1909, Picasso's companion from 1936 to 1946.

Pierre P. arrives tonight. I've telephoned Orengo to meet him here.

Rather stupid article about me in *L'Espoir*. Trying to be kind. Makes me say that I'm "entranced" with the title *Clair-Obscur*. How like me.

. . . .

SEPTEMBER 29

Two little boys, five and seven, have drowned a girl of three, after carefully planning their crime, of which they boast. They even said they undressed her first, though when the child's body was recovered, it was dressed.

Changeable weather, deplorable for shooting *Monte-Cristo* in color. According to what Jeannot tells me, and despite all my admiration for Georges Neveux,* it seems to me he has tried to make plausible a story whose whole charm is that it isn't any such thing.

Very interesting book by Philippe Erlanger on *Monsieur, frère de Louis XIV*. You realize, from the texts he quotes, that history skips everything that would bring it to life.

To Picasso might be applied what was said of Henrietta Maria of England: "She considered that duty was an absurd inconvenience."

First arrangement of poems for *Clair-Obscur*.

(The young today.) J.-P. Rosnay† asked me yesterday, "How did you go about becoming famous?" I answered, "By working every minute without ever thinking it would make me famous."

---

*Cocteau's admiration for the playwright Georges Neveux (1900–1982) dates to Neveux's 1930 play *Juliette, ou la Clé des songes*, for a film version of which Cocteau had written dialogue and Christian Bérard created sets and costumes (the film was never made).

†Jean-Pierre Rosnay, born 1926, poet and founder of the "Club des poètes"; producer of the radio program of the same name.

I don't know if I've already noted the delivery of Jacques-Emile Blanche's portrait of me. It is a sketch dated 1913 (Offranville), with a dedication to Marcelle Meyer.* The portrait itself is in the Cluny museum. At this remove, the sketch seems as good as a Vuillard. Leymarie, director of the Grenoble museum, had told me something of the kind in speaking of Blanche.

I told Rosnay yesterday, apropos of his manuscript, that by determining to be an anarchist and a revolutionary, he was sacrificing to fashion and that he would become invisible because of his craze for visibility. Very difficult to get this across to the young, hungry for the immediate.

Impossibility of judging what one writes for lack of comparison. Once you start approving what you do, there's the danger that it will be like other things you approve. Once there is something new, you're in the void.

People always take an exact definition for a piece of wit.

A certain formal perfection flattens out the relief. Malherbe amazes us by one or two perfect jewels in a grisaille of language. My difficulty now consists in achieving a certain lame perfection. (*Clair-Obscur.*)

Cover of *Les Enfants terribles* in German. Black canvas with my signature stamped in gold. This would be the best thing for the *Oeuvres complètes*. Great elegance. Title on the spine.

Nothing for nothing. Mlle Caussignac telephones yesterday that the prefect has ordered the villa next door to be put under surveillance while explosives are being used. But she adds that the prefect would be delighted to have one of my drawings.

Medieval times. Too many apparitions of the Virgin. The Church seems to be afraid of them and afraid that the scandal of exploitation will no longer be limited to Lourdes. The children who experience

---

*Marcelle Meyer (1897–1958), a pianist who was the favorite interpreter of the Groupe des Six and who appears in the center of the group portrait by Blanche.

these apparitions are tortured, and their answers to interrogation are almost always admirable. "Why did the Virgin show herself to you in particular?" The little girl answers, "Because she couldn't find anything lower than us."

Carole has been shown the film of *La Villa Santo Sospir*. I remembered what the projectionist of the Cinéma des Champs-Élysées said: "They should keep this film in a pyramid." This flawed film (an amateur's film) has already gained strength in the darkness. Keep it there as long as possible. One day it will be an extremely curious object. Today it can be only an indiscretion.

Orengo telephones; he'll come Friday morning.

.   .   .   .

SEPTEMBER 30

Sunshine. The Tourism film people came this morning. I shot scenes with the cartoon of *Birth of Pegasus* tapestry.

First arrangement of the poems in *Clair-Obscur* in groups.

.   .   .   .

OCTOBER 4

Mme Cuttoli stops in to see me. Françoise Gilot has just left Vallauris because of the hubbub that surrounds Picasso. She is reluctant, she says, for Claude to be brought up the way Paulo was.

Telegram from the Puigs. They are coming Sunday night, *with* Pastora and the Gypsies.

Saw Orengo with Pierre Peyraud. Planned the Monacan company . . .

Carole left last night, on the Blue Train, for her school. She was crying—she had a fine vacation.

Splendid weather yesterday. Overcast today. No *sequences*.

This morning Claude Roy telephoned. He wanted to come and

see me. Picasso had suddenly left Vallauris and gone to Paris. Claude Roy was leaving tomorrow, and since I was expecting my Spaniards, I couldn't meet him on the Cape. No doubt he wanted to talk to me about the drama at Vallauris, about which I had some suspicions from Françoise's face and from Mme Cuttoli's words the day before yesterday. Now it is Alberto who tells me what's happening. The whole troupe arrived at nine because Pastora Imperio began vomiting on the road. Alberto had dined with Picasso at the frontier a week ago. Picasso told him he was leaving Françoise and that she had arranged to keep Claude and Paloma.

I love Françoise and Picasso's friends don't. They find her "distant" and bourgeoise. This dread of a "bourgeois" calm always impels Picasso to destroy his households. After eight years he drops a young, lovely, charming woman because she rejects the tornado of freeloaders and parasites and because she doesn't want Claude to be brought up like Paulo. Picasso, besides the fact that he loves and respects no one, believes he remains loyal to a style of destruction by ruining the happiness of his successive families . . . Paloma seems to me to be his first love. (Note after the fact: All this is incorrect. I leave it as it stands.)

Alberto and Margarita Puig have come with Pastora Imperio, Luis Escobar, Pastora's son-in-law and two young Gypsies, little Dolores and a new fellow, who is apparently a remarkable dancer.

Pierre-Aimé Touchard publishes his memoirs as the administrator of the Comédie-Française in *Réalités*. He doesn't pull his punches. I am astonished that those ladies and gentlemen do not file suit, as the Foreign Affairs office did against Peyrefitte. Peyrefitte victorious. Mme Bidault's foolishness has managed to sell forty thousand copies of the book* in a week and has cost her husband the presidency of the Republic.

La Fin des ambassades. In this roman à clef, Mlle Crapote is Suzanne Borel, future wife of Georges Bidault.

Cuevas is suing Monseigneur Gerlier, primate of Gaul, for provocation to murder, Monseigneur Gerlier having declared he would consider it [to be] just that Cuevas be stoned by the people of Biarritz. Strange words from a priest. Never has the Roman Catholic Church opposed masquerades—quite the contrary. As the Cardinal in *Bacchus* says, "Carnivals keep the people from thinking." What is Cuevas's crime? He amuses himself and a host of others. He spends money and supports business. His frivolity is not that of an idler, since he sends huge spectacles around the world. France lives on foreigners and insults them as soon as they spend their money on her.

François de Vallombreuse, Jean-Pierre Lacloche's brother, was in charge of the material organization of the ball. He put everything in his own pocket, Jean-Pierre tells me, so that the buffet of this sumptuous affair offered nothing but beer and sausages.

.   .   .   .

OCTOBER 5

Lunch with our Spanish friends.

Picasso disdains intelligence because he has only genius, and he uses that (outside his art) without rhyme or reason.

Besides, since the goal of art has nothing to do with morality, he can pride himself on being a contagious disease.

Francine sets up the flamenco floor on the terrace. Pastora and the girl have sent their Gypsy dresses to be ironed. Jean Marais is coming, and the doctor with his camera and lights for color films. An exceptional celebration at Santo Sospir.

On Saturday Pierre, Orengo, Édouard, and I went to see lawyer Oreglia to get the company started. It's likely the company will share the apartment with Orengo, to extend the premises of Les Éditions du Rocher...

What would Picasso's power be if he suddenly calmed down and began to invoke a kind of realism capable of destroying him?

. . . .

OCTOBER 6

Last night the Spanish party—a success. Except that the number of Gypsies did not permit things to reach the point which transfigures them. But Pastora Imperio wielded her tragedienne's charm, stamped her inimitable feet in the crocodile tail of her red gown, seduced with her arms like an old snake charmer.

At two in the morning the little troupe, unaccustomed to real alcohol, was dead drunk. Only Pastora sat enthroned, dignified as a queen.

Alberto tells me today at lunch that the party went on last night at Nice, after the discovery of a little whores' bar. The whole troupe, except for the women, didn't get to bed until seven in the morning.

Sent off the China preface to Claude Roy (for the Guilde du livre suisse) and the Letter to the Center for Psycho-Pedagogic Studies (Belgium-Holland).

We're going in a few minutes to the Antibes museum with the Spaniards.

Back from Antibes and Vallauris. Fine weather. Showed the *Judith* tapestry at Antibes. At Vallauris visited Mme Ramié, who gave Picasso plates to Puig and Francine. I give Puig mine. I had been completely mistaken about the drama of Vallauris. It is not Picasso who is leaving Françoise, it is Françoise who is leaving. She can no longer put up with the endless storm of visitors and that mad dash from one bullring to the next. Perhaps there are even deeper and more specific reasons. (A young man?) Picasso is very unhappy. Françoise is not taking the children with her. She is keeping them to bring them up and will remain, if Picasso likes, his best friend. Sad. Françoise exerted the best influence. For the first time Picasso had a perfect wife. He has always left his wives. That Françoise should leave him wounds his heart and his pride. No doubt this is why he speaks of this break to Alberto as of a piece of monstrous behavior on the part of Françoise, who is "taking his children away from him." Tomorrow he comes back to Vallauris (at least so Mme Ramié supposes), where he has an appointment with Emmer and the Italian film people.

. . . .

OCTOBER 7

An evening with the Spaniards. I showed them the film of *Santo Sospir* and *Les Enfants terribles*. This morning we went, with Françoise, to say good-bye to them. Tonight Haddad and Colinet came to show me their work. At first glance it seemed good. Rereading, it is mediocre. I told Haddad that even if the film were to be done, he would not do the part. The film exists only if Thomas is a very pure enchanter . . .

. . . .

OCTOBER 8

The demon of understanding. No doubt the original sin of the paradise of árt. Especially since art has become its own end, which it didn't use to be.

Sun. No news from Madrid. We don't know yet when we will be going there.

Last night I had dreams of "translation" without any relation to my texts. D'Annunzio was mixed up in this series of nasty and confused episodes.

Outrageous publicity around the Virgin of Syracuse, reducing a supernatural power to nothing. Science will discover, soon perhaps, that the obsession with tears can be communicated to matter (which is alive). Why would the Virgin weep, since she can stop the tears of those who do? And why should her tears be human tears, as the laboratories prove? There is a sacrilege here from the purely Catholic point of view.

. . . .

OCTOBER 11

Claudel's *Christopher Columbus*. Enormous silliness. Triumph. The gala of *Irène*.*

Giraudoux. Claudel. The two disastrous victors of our age.

According to the phone call from Jean-Pierre Lacloche, Picasso is in Fontainebleau. If this is true, he's standing up Emmer and his whole team of filmmakers in Vallauris.

Since this diary will not be published till after my death, I can indulge in the luxury of speaking the truth. My tapestry at the Antibes museum overwhelms all the Picassos in the place. It explodes like a bomb on the second floor.

Redid five drawings for Orengo. Will send them tomorrow.

Anything and everything to keep from being turned into a statue. It is likely that my defensive instinct has led me to commit what I took for mistakes.

. . . .

OCTOBER 14

Rain and wind. Only Sunday was fine, when they were not shooting *Monte-Cristo*. Francine had gone to preside over the inauguration of the soccer field.

---

*On March 30, 1778, at the Comédie-Française, Voltaire—eighty-four years old and only two months from his death—attended the sixth performance of *Irène*, his last tragedy, and the triumphal crowning of his bust.

I saw the reproduction of the poem-object *Dentelle d'éternité* in *Les Lettres françaises*. The photograph of my decoupage was very well done.

Visit yesterday from one of those young poets who haven't a penny to their name and don't know where to go, where to stay. It was raining. He was coming from Cannes on a rented motorbike he had to return that night. We dried him out, gave him shoes and socks. I was ashamed to send him on his way. But what can you do? The Riviera will soon have swallowed up what little money I slipped into his pocket. I notice that most of these young fellows have a father or a mother who has remarried, a family eager to be rid of them without trying to find out much about what becomes of them.

Stopped the poems. *I was imitating myself.* Burned everything that didn't seem to me authentic. I still have to punctuate and arrange in the right order.

Birth of Pegasus. Panel and frames sent to Aubusson. Received the new proof for *Judith.* Seems to me as good as the other one.

I will have to make up my mind to dictate the whole passage of last year's journal concerning the trip to Greece and rereading Proust. The tedium of dictating makes me very reluctant to begin the work.

I gave Jeannot the cuts for *La Machine infernale.*

Letter from England. Another blow for Miss Hoeck. Her translation of *Les Enfants terribles* was judged poor, and the task has been given to Rosamond Lehmann. It is likely that Miss Hoeck, without even realizing it, introduces into her translations of my work a kind of softness which is her own affair and a lack of style which robs them of their acuity. This is what I gather from what I am told. Too bad she has taken all this trouble for nothing. Cambridge has had to retype her translation of *Bacchus.*

Jeannot came here last night for dinner. No shooting. The rain continues this morning.

A lacuna in work, in thought, in everything. Upset which corresponds, no doubt, to the peculiar weather. Spent the day yesterday answering letters. Telephone call from Lourau, who approves my project for a film on *La Dame à la licorne*.

I actually envy those who can control their work and don't have to wait until the work compels them to confront it. Apropos of Claudel's *Christopher Columbus*, I ponder the tremendous success of that clever adventurer who was wrong about everything, the glory of a man who knew nothing about navigation, thought the earth was pear-shaped, and believed he had discovered the islands of the Indies. It is likely that his splendid name has been more powerful than he and has gathered up the glory of others, the way a magnet gathers iron filings. He is the typical example of an impostor seated on the throne. We know that the letters he says he received are fakes; we know that he was not the one who managed the voyage; we know that he didn't pay the sums promised and that he obtained others on false pretenses; we know all that, but we accept the lie as a historical truth. The Church has set everything going for the solid installation of this impostor, and Claudel adds the flourish of the senile gamin.

Match speaks of "the triumph of Paul Claudel." Now you can like Claudel or not like Claudel, but you can't talk about "the triumph of Claudel" when an inspired staging saves an opera libretto scribbled down and recited without a single revision.

France should buttress herself with Germany, rearm her, make her into her own true line of defense. Instead of which France remains the prisoner of a Barrésian nationalism—Alsace-Lorraine and pointed helmets. Our true grievance is not Hitler but Bismarck.

Jeannot reports that he's seen Ophüls's film *Madame de** and was delighted by its grace. I imagine that its lack of success with

---

*A film by Max Ophüls from the novel by Louise de Vilmorin.

the critics is the consequence of a moral elegance which is detested and which is attributed to sentimentality. At the present time, it is almost impossible to succeed in nuance and without crudity. It is in this regard that my new poems are in conflict with the times and risk remaining invisible.

Jeannot also finds the film admirably made—which the critics cannot see, mistaking clumsiness for strength.

The morning paper. If its columns were real ones, you would see that the building cannot stand.

. . . .

OCTOBER 15

Dinner last night with Jeannot and Lulu Watier. Her plane had circled the field at Nice and gone back to Rome. Not understanding English or the stewardess's explanations, she thought she was getting off in Nice. In Rome she ran into Gérard Philipe, who was still waiting for his wife. (They are going to Tokyo.)

Lulu shows me a printed slip on the dressing table of her hotel room in Rome: *"For audiences with the pope, make an appointment with the concierge of the hotel."*

Jeannot glum, withdrawn, tense, inexplicable. I always wonder what he's thinking, what he *registers,* like his mother in her unfortunate memoir.

The film of the Gypsies came this morning. We'll see it tonight. Pastora Imperio, a phenomenon of collective hypnosis. She scarcely moves. Yet she rouses the soul of Spain. In the Seville procession, women kiss the hem of her dress, and she is escorted by people in convulsions.

New poem. I'll try to find a line, an order. Work for this day. Lorenzi has brought me the rag on which I wiped my brushes, stretched as a canvas. I would like to inscribe it with an homage to the impressionists. Women in a garden.*

First approximate arrangement of the poems in *Clair-Obscur*.

Saw the sixteen-millimeter film—Pastora—great nobility of her gestures in silence.

. . . .

OCTOBER 17

Dinner with Jeannot, Corbeau†—disconcerted by the film they are shooting. The more incompetent the director turns out to be, the more jealous of his prerogatives he becomes. All the images taken at sea could be done in Paris, and one wonders by what lack of imagination a crew has to go to an island to shoot the coast of an island. A fortune is spent renting an old ship you never see except from a distance and in silhouette. The actors are made up for shots where no one can see them. The whole troupe is brought to Antibes to shoot a scene in front of a wall. All this costs millions. And the producers go along with it, without a murmur . . . And you wonder why the cinema, as these people understand it, disgusts me.

Wrote the text for the *Gala des Six*.

Yesterday Francine found a young electrician, here to repair the wires, looking at the frescoes. She asked him some questions, and it turns out he knew all my books, all my plays, all my films. This morning he stood a long time in front of my latest canvas, *Mother and Daughter in a Garden*, and spoke about it as no one would speak . . .

---

*Mother and Daughter in a Garden, tapestry woven by the atelier of Marie Cuttoli. Collection Francine Weisweiller.

†The cameraman Roger Corbeau, born 1908, who had worked on Cocteau's films *Les Parents terribles* (1948) and *Orphée* (1949).

Sun this morning. I think I recognized the *Pharaoh* offshore. A boat on the left must contain the cameras and equipment. Jeannot had to be costumed and made up for these long-distance shots.

Ivernel, one of the actors in the film, says to Corbeau: "Jean Marais is so simple! It's embarrassing—he's the star. It makes it impossible for me to be difficult."

Philippe Hériat's play *Noces de deuil*. Postponed and postponed again because of house disputes at the Comédie-Française. Apparently the preview was stormy. The next night was the opening. There was a stagehands' strike which necessitated postponement. This morning the newspaper says that the minister is closing the national theaters. I shall not let anything more of mine be given in that house. And I shall withdraw *Renaud et Armide*.* Probably, later on, I'll also withdraw *La Voix humaine*.

Provisionally, *Clair-Obscur* is arranged as follows: Preface—stanzas (121 variations on familiar themes)—Miscellany—Homages and Spanish poems.

I am so fond of my picture *Mother and Daughter in a Garden* that I'd like to forget I painted it and be rich enough to buy it.

Francine says, "I won't prosecute Paul (the sailor) because I refuse to be responsible for putting a man in prison."

Lorenzi reports that all Beaulieu says the most incredible things about us: "What can they be doing since they don't play cards?" Impossible for the idle and the ignorant to understand that I work, and that Francine works to make that work pleasant. It is beyond their imagination. Besides, people envy Lorenzi and Dr. Ricoux because they come to see us frequently.

People stop Lorenzi when they see him coming here. "Since you see Cocteau, could you ask him to sign a book for me" (or

---

*Cocteau's tragedy in verse which he directed in 1943 at the Comédie-Française, with sets and costumes by Christian Bérard.

some other favor). Lorenzi answers, "I'm a tradesman, and since the people at the villa treat me as a friend, I'd be ashamed to ask them to do me a favor."

I answer about twenty letters a day (just to read them!—they're long and always want something). Work on my poems, correct proofs, take these notes, paint, prepare a tapestry, read the countless books and manuscripts that get sent me, and the day passes without my realizing it.

Francine spends her morning paying bills and signing checks for people she helps in secret. She goes to the beach if there's sun. She eats very little. She rests. Then she reads or paints flowers. But her crime is not to know how to play bridge. Alec actually thinks she's a little mad.

Édouard reads all the time—books on science—instructs himself, paints canvases which require incredible patience. In eight days I've seen the portrait of Carole become a wonder. His recreation is to play *boules* with Fernand the chauffeur.

It's likely that the things they say about life at the villa are pretty bad, since I've heard that the doctor wanted to complain about them to the mayor.

One lady, speaking of Francine. "Apparently she feeds and houses her servants on the same footing as herself. It must be to keep their mouths shut."

Francine's exquisite manners. She laughs at such gossip.

Example of a morning's work: this morning. Besides answering a dozen letters, I've had to write an article on Barrès, an article in support of a book by Maurice Raphael, an article on the Ballets Russes, additional notes for Bruckmann's biography, etc., etc. When would I have time to play cards?

· ·

OCTOBER 18

Nobel Prize to Churchill. Mauriac makes me laugh when he speaks of "posterity." Who reads Mistral and Sully Prudhomme?

The Old Man and the Sea. Called a masterpiece. A charming little tale.

On a desert island, there are reptiles and insects. Around our happy island, there are people who speculate about us in the shadows—and we speculate about no one except our friends. At five we were playing boules with François the electrician and Fernand the chauffeur when a woman, dead drunk, and her husband, a baker from Saint-Jean, burst into the garden brandishing Paul's countless debts. When Francine asked for information about the details of this very vague and very old bill, they began— especially the drunk woman—insulting her and shrieking and making a scene. Fernand and François throw them out, and we could hear them still screaming insults out on the road.

So it's not just the cardplayers who are creating legends about us but even the tradespeople of a town where Francine spends a fortune and keeps the *Cercle Sportif* alive.

I advised Francine to see the mayor. He has his secretary call and say he will stop by the villa tomorrow morning. And all this because Francine refuses to prosecute Paul. His forgeries could land him in jail. "I know about you!" the shrew was shrieking, "I saw how you behaved at the Fiorentina when I was a chambermaid there! I know all about you!" Francine was pale and stupefied. She had never set foot in the Fiorentina, typical of the pretentious places we avoid like the plague. One imagines what such a house can be like if this drunken shrew was a chambermaid there!

I can only speculate about the enterprises of the terrible English lady who is building down below the studio and whom the mayor and the prefect have forbidden to use dynamite. She must be wild with rage. Such ladies are not content to rage—they act.

It is the first time in three years that this secret nastiness has shown itself. We had naively suspected nothing of the kind.

Have had to write the burgomaster of Oldenburg that I won't be able to attend the opening of *Chevaliers de le table ronde** because of the conflict with dates for the concert of Les Six and of *Orphée* in Madrid.

The more I think about it, the more my eyes are opened. Marie-Blanche de Polignac and Antoinette d'Harcourt had telephoned they wanted to come and see me. Not being free that same day (I was going to Biot), I asked them to call back and come for lunch or dinner any day of the week. They did not get in touch again, being convinced by gossip—or at least so I imagine—that Francine would find some excuse not to receive them. I remember Marie-Laure's phrase when she came to the Cape later on: "So you're sequestering Jean." It was this phrase which gave me the notion for a play in which a young couple decide to live in the country, far away from everyone. People manage to convince the young woman that her husband whom she adores *is sequestering her.*

I had written in *Journal d'un inconnu* that the world wants a corrida with a death at the end and takes a happy household for a barnyard spectacle. I was rather counting on the world's disappointment when it is given no drama, no dispute to feed on. But I was wrong. If there's no corrida, the world invents one.

Luckily our discovery did not occur while I was working on the poems. It would have robbed me of all my enthusiasm, all my impulsive strength. On November 1, I'll go to Milly, where other gossip is doubtless waiting for me. Only good old Madeleine in

---

*A play by Cocteau, created in 1937 with costumes by Chanel and sets by the author, who directed it.

the rue de Montpensier has a heart solid as a rock; no one would dare touch a hair of my head, or of Francine's, in her presence.

. . . .

OCTOBER 20

I didn't hear *La Machine infernale* on the radio, but I have heard it praised a good deal. Better not to hear it; other people don't suffer from a thousand details that would distress me. Last night Jeannot asked me to add a few lines in the last act—he never has time enough to "become" a blind man and finish his makeup in the wings before the end of the Creon-Tiresias dialogue. I added the lines this morning.

Four new poems for *Clair-Obscur*.

Jeannot is leaving Nice tonight. I'll drive him to the airport and bring him the text for *La Machine*.

Our childhood dreams. "How did Haydée look," I asked Jean Marais, "when she boarded the yacht with you?" "Like a barrel." "Did she have golden necklaces?" "No." I wonder if filmmakers read the books they turn into films. They must leaf through them.

Lunched with our neighbor at the Villa Boutac, between us and Villefranche. The garden is very beautiful. The English and Americans around the table didn't seem much more pleased with their governments than we are with ours. They asked me the secret of the charm which makes them want to live in France. I answered that French decadence was the extreme tip of a great civilization. Lord ——— might have found asylum in France. He could have slept with a thousand Boy Scouts without being condemned to hard labor.

It has taken several centuries for the behavior of the court of Louis XIV to reach the public. What went on at Versailles was no prettier than what is to be found each morning in the newspapers.

. . . .

OCTOBER 21

Langlois* telephones for the poster for the Rome festival.

Emmer telephones that he's through shooting Picasso and will stop by here between five and six.

Went this morning to have a drink on the Villefranche waterfront with the troupe of *Quai des blondes*.† Michel Auclair comes in one of Alec's planes between performances of *Rope*.‡

Finished the "Homage to Rilke."

Did the frame for *Mother and Daughter in a Garden*. Lorenzi had stretched the paint-spattered old rags on wood for me. Fascinating struggle with chance.

Luciano Emmer came with his collaborators on the way to Milan. He did what had to be done at Antibes and Vallauris. "Picasso," he says, "is a great actor. No need to rehearse with him. He always takes the right camera angle."

. . . .

OCTOBER 22

I haven't been able to sleep, thinking about the lies being spread about us and our lives here. I am convinced it is better to let people believe we are like all the others. For if, by some misfortune, the world discovered our innocence, it would be all up with us. Stendhal used to say: "I am no lamb, therefore I'm nothing." Now we could say, "I am no crook, therefore I am nothing."

---

*Henri Langlois (1914–1977), founder of the French Cinémathèque and of the International Federation of Film Archives.

†A film by Paul Cadéac, with Michel Auclair.

‡Michel Auclair, born 1922, who played the role of Ludovic in *La Balle et la bête*, was performing Patrick Hamilton's *Rope* at the Théâtre de la Renaissance in Paris while shooting the film *Quai des blondes*.

Alexandre Dumas, as drawn on October 22, 1953.

Received Ferruccio Leiss's *Venise* with my preface.* On the cover, in color, a splendid shot of the horses of Saint Mark's. I discover that upside down, this image becomes a kind of young demon saluting Venice. I cut it out and sent it to Daria Guarnati, the publisher.

Churches *out of style*. The first mannequin at Lanvin tells us that when she was visiting the Matisse chapel at Venice the other day, she saw a woman come up to an elderly nun and ask her why there were no flowers on the altar. The nun shrugged and scornfully remarked that "flowers were no longer used." The good woman trotted behind her: "But sister, we use them at home, in our church." And the nun: "Possibly. But flowers are no longer used."

Dictated this morning my "Homage to the Mediterranean" for Radio Monte-Carlo, and the "Présentation du Groupe des Six."

That tremendous fatigue which doesn't come from within but from outside.

Peyrefitte's book, which I have just read. It adds to my discomfort. But it is not a book of gossip. It is history. It represents a great courage. Since Mme Bidault was foolish enough to recognize herself in it, sales have continued to increase.

Finished and sent off the drawing of Alexandre Dumas for Calmann-Lévy, with this phrase: "Le maître du plus vrai que le vrai."

. . . .

OCTOBER 25

Rain. I'll take advantage of it to do the poster for "Fifty Years of French Film," in Rome.

---

*Ferruccio Leiss, *Immagini di Venezia*, Jean Cocteau, "L'autre face de Venise ou Venise la gaie."

Telephone call from Mme Maeterlinck. Her style: "Good morning, dear magician." Will lunch Tuesday at Orlamonde.

Last night happened to hear by accident the Mogador Gala, where Isa Miranda recited *Anna la Bonne* with great success—but either because of where the microphone was or because of her accent, I had difficulty understanding. Except for the end, where she cut off the last line (I wonder why) and burst into hysterical laughter after "She must have taken her yacht to Java." Marianne Oswald has more style.* It's style that's missing in all the actresses who try *Anna* or *La Voix humaine*—without, moreover, ever informing me or asking my advice.

Worked a lot more on *Mother and Daughter in a Garden*. The vision or the impression of any poem or picture I've created depends entirely on the person I'm showing it to. It changes, fades, or grows illustrious depending on what that person feels.

Gave Meunier the drawing of my hand to accompany his article.

Reading the terrible paragraphs on Montherlant in Peyrefitte's book, I think of the many visits they paid me together in the rue de Montpensier, at the time of the Liberation. Montherlant was sick with anxiety about his fame. They were intimate friends at the time. Whenever a group of lycée boys passed under the arcades, they rushed to the window, where I saw nothing more than their two behinds.

Peyrefitte's book is based on the international role of diplomacy. What he calls *the end of embassies* results from the fact that patriotism and nationalism are perverting a métier whose cynical aspect Talleyrand never concealed. "I put myself," he once said, "at the service of events." And he added his famous sentence: "Treason is a matter of dates." Mlle Crapote is amusing, and Mme Bidault

---

*Marianne Oswald, 1903–1985, created in 1934 two monologues written for her by Cocteau, *Anna la bonne* and *La Dame de Monte-Carlo*.

even more so, but that is not the whole book, which seems to me to be the only true document on the German occupation.

Rhymes. A word rhyming with *geste* was what I was looking for. It had to express the fact that everything is scratched out on the parchment, so that it can be written on all over again. No other word but the one I could not find would do. Opening the dictionary, I fell upon *palimpseste.* I had forgotten the meaning.

Received more documents on Alexandre Dumas's face. Nadar's caricature is so curious, so powerful, so revealing, that it would be impossible to use it. Besides, the drawing I sent to Sigaux must have crossed in the mail with this new piece from Nadar's collection.

The young woman who was going to inherit 200,000,000 francs will no longer inherit. The papers were full of her. Now they are quite unconcerned. The mother, arriving in Nice, announces that she is not the daughter of the heir but of a musician.

Pasquini dinner. He is astounded because Francine tells the story of our dinner at the C.'s the day when, after Pétain's death, *Match* had published the marshal's kepi on its cover. I had just said, "I wonder why *Match* publishes a color photograph of the old fool's kepi?" This cast a pall (and Suzanne Blum, my lawyer, was there, and several pillars of the Resistance). I realized I had just made a horrible blunder. In a general's house, *I was offending the kepi.* Respect for the kepi prevails over all political opinions.

Pasquini, whom I try to persuade that all the deals he offers me on the Riviera are of no interest to me, is baffled when I tell him that I refused 7,000,000 francs from Brazil for three lectures because I preferred to take a few cruises on the *Orphée II.* That Édouard was shamed by Simone B.'s offering him, in secret, 500,000 francs if he could persuade me to write a play for her theater. Etc., etc. Like all others, Pasquini, a man of great rectitude, fails to understand what a private morality is (what it compels). He regards me as a fool and a dupe, exhausting myself doing favors for others and working for nothing.

Recorded the text for the Gala de la Méditerranée in Monte Carlo. (Another favor.) I was amazed that I was handed 20,000 francs "for travel expenses."

If I accepted all the deals I am offered, I would have to have the three legs of the Sicilian escutcheon, and I would be running to my moral ruin for amounts the fisc would take anyway. I prefer to do favors.

At the moment Pasquini was getting into his car, and I realized how dumbfounded he was. I said these words to him, more or less: "My dear friend, there is one thing you don't know and that I must teach you. Our profession has its heroes too, and I hope to be one, until my death. Our heroism consists in permitting ourselves to be taken for dupes, to serve our country without expecting the slightest comprehension or the slightest reward, refusing advantageous offers but proceeding in such a way that, as Genet says, we could put each of our footsteps under glass. You find me an intelligent man capable of a great number of enterprises, and you fear my pessimism. Now, I am no pessimist, but having realized what a farce the world is, I refuse to be its victim. Don't believe I'm burying my head in the sand. I have worked in an invisible zone, and I am making progress there as well as I can. I cannot be touched by insults because I believe that no one in the world is in a position to reward me according to my merits."

Pasquini got into his car, looking bemused. Through the window he said, "I think I'm beginning to understand you." Once the car was on the road, I thought of the thousands of Pasquinis who can make nothing out of my attitude and who are far from possessing his spiritual distinction.

. . . .

OCTOBER 26

Received my paper construction, *Dentelle d'éternité*. The paper behind the decoupage looks too light; it should have been darker.
But the thing as a whole is splendid.

I've redone the villa's large living room. A certain sloth was
keeping me from finishing it, from painting the blues which should
enhance the pale drawings. I spent the day on ladders, covered
with paint. Still missing the red of the three Phrygian caps. Lorenzi
hadn't prepared the colors for me.

Lunch yesterday with Mme Maeterlinck and Dr. Debat and his
wife. I hadn't seen Debat since his visit to the rue Vignon, about
fifteen years ago. He remembers it down to the smallest detail.
His wife has brick-red hair; his is sky blue. He speaks a good deal
about his flowers and about penicillin, thanks to which he saved
his son's life. "My work," he says, "consists in saving others in
memory of that misery." Mme Maeterlinck describes the lunch
Einstein and Maeterlinck had together in America. Saying good-
bye to Maeterlinck, Einstein remarked: "You didn't mention the
atom to me, and I didn't talk to you about bees. We're even."

At the F.'s, Nina de Polignac says to me: "I own *all your books*,
every one. But what a pity you haven't written any since *Thomas
l'imposteur*.*

A British publisher has commissioned a biography of me from
the lady who has published one of Colette. Marie Hoeck knows
the lady and says she's quite ignorant. She is on vacation, as it
happens, at Antibes, and wants to come and see me at five this
afternoon.

---

*I.e., since 1922.

. . . .

OCTOBER 27

Grotesque "poetic" voices on the radio. Descriptions of the Poitou region—like high school themes. Nightmare of our childhood.

Took Langlois the poster (for Rome). Splendid weather after diluvial rains last night.

Strange situation: Paris resents me, and loads me up with its tasks. Not a preface, not a poster, not a lecture which I am spared.

By and large Matisse is a mediocre draftsman. Picasso a great one, and avoids his talent with genius. How weak the abstract artists are. The writers no longer know the language. Anouilh passes for a genius. Prévert for a poet . . .

Most of the works that I see, and that are admired, would shame me to death if I had done them. And I shut up about it. I would seem worse than pretentious.

. . . .

OCTOBER 29

Deluge of letters and telegrams. I would have to give up earning my living and doing my work in order to devote myself to those of others.

Elio Zorzi writes me from the Biennale: "Your admirable poem on Picasso has been published in no. 15 of the *Biennale de Venise*." But his letter was sent by mistake to Milly instead of to the Cape.

This morning I finished the frescoes. The three Phrygian caps in sanguine. The painting was poor. Once dry, I sanded it off— which gives exactly the effect I want.

Hindemith and I have an old game we play together: an exchange

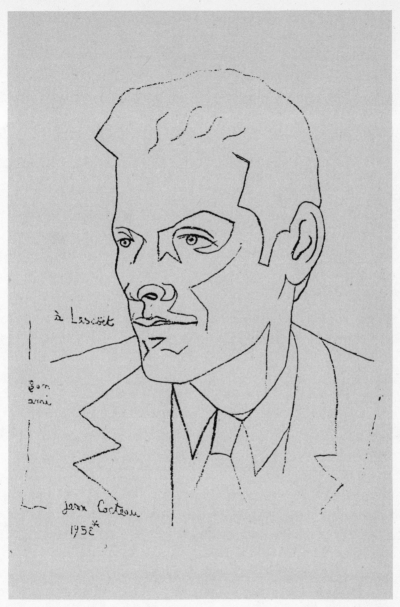

Henri de Lescoët, whose *Poésie ma solitude* was published in 1955, as drawn on
October 26, 1953.

of our great military careers. (Hindemith signs his letters "General Paul.") I wrote him this morning that I had managed to isolate the salt in seawater and make it explosive at the slightest contact. Thus all ships could be blown up without exception, and quite economically.

Ignoble vulgarity of the radio. When it's left on, I escape. It is possible that such constant vulgarity attacks the soul without our suspecting it and demoralizes us. Certain (admirable) atmospheres—Triebschen, for example—would not have been possible with a radio in the house.

Criticism. There are nothing but flops and masterpieces. Disasters or triumphs. Triumph of Claudel. Masterpiece by Anouilh. I haven't seen *The Lark*, but I'm positive it is not a masterpiece. No doubt a work of intelligence and charm. Just as Philippe Hériat does not deserve the scornful mud that is flung at him. *"Woe unto me, I am nuance,"* said Nietzsche.

. . . .

OCTOBER 30

I take out of the rooms upstairs a mountain of letters, prospectuses, pamphlets, manuscripts. After this massive housecleaning, the disorder does not seem appeased—it remains, one would say, the same.

The Glaoui has summoned our antique dealer from Beaulieu to furnish the lovenest of one of his mistresses. (Mahogany throughout.) The poor dealer arrived in Paris the day before yesterday with his truck and the furniture. The Glaoui's secretary was there: "We're leaving tomorrow," he said, "but unfortunately I forgot to tell you that the lady in question has dyed her hair a mahogany color. Mahogany, therefore, is impossible." The antique dealer has had to sell his truck in order to take the train.

. . . .
October 31

Thesis of Miss Elga Lippmann: "*Jean Cocteau: Graphic Poet,* for the degree of master of arts at Columbia University, New York." Like all the theses on me I have read, this one is insufficiently informed about my work and my life.

Four days ago I was visited by the lady who is to write the same sort of book about me as the one she published in England on Colette. Her husband is French. I warned her about the hopeless task on which she has embarked. She seems quite courageous about it all, but what use is courage? It is likely that even if she were to live with me for a year and questioned me every day, she would not bring off such a book.

Telegram from Madrid. The premiere of *Orphée* is scheduled for the ninth. We'll arrive the night before, a Sunday.

Monaco. Apartment next to the Orengo building free. Deal concluded.

I spoke again to Mme Maeterlinck about my rather vague project for a film of *Pelléas.* She asks me if Marais would be willing to play Golaud. Of course. But on the screen the play would regain all its subversive power, and the public would laugh at certain naive phrases that Mélisande speaks—as it laughed during the first performances. The Maeterlinck-Debussy marriage is like the marriage of praying mantises. A terribly feminine genius (Debussy) devours a terribly masculine one (Maeterlinck). Besides, Arkel's castle is not built in the clouds, and the music helps us to believe it is. What is sad is that the music begins to make quite long and boring a play which is neither one nor the other. (Problem of film music— and of music for this film.)

The caretaker who shows people around the absurd "Englishman's Castle" at Mont-Boron says, "This is where Cocteau made his film of *Beauty and the Beast*." I wonder who could have started such a piece of nonsense.

. . . .

NOVEMBER 3

Returned Sunday by car. Stopped at Feurs. (Very good stop at the Chapeau Rouge.) Milly. Sleep. Sun. Paris this morning. Véfour. Went to embrace Colette.

. . . .

NOVEMBER 5

The Concert des Six* a great success last night, as was the supper at Maxim's. Honegger too ill in Switzerland to come. There was a family spirit in the orchestra and a curious similitude in the use of the woodwinds and brass.

Deluge of telephone calls, visits, letters.

Germaine Tailleferre astonished me. Her orchestra is rich, full, lively. Her syntax clear and without the shadow of silliness. Odd how Durey "opposes" impressionism by the quintessence of impressionist orchestration. For the first time I *heard* Auric's *Phèdre*. At the Opera my set and costumes devoured the orchestra, for the eye overwhelms the ear in the theater. Moreover, the orchestra sound from the pit of the Opera was heavy and confused. Last night the work emerged with a true and grave brio. Arthur and

---

*On the program of this concert, given at the Théâtre des Champs-Élysées under the direction of Georges Tzipine: *Overture* by Germaine Tailleferre (1932); "Le Printemps au fond de la mer," poem by Cocteau, set by Louis Durey (1920); orchestral suite from *Phèdre* by Georges Auric (1950); *Secheresses* by Francis Poulenc (1937); *Prelude, Fugue, and Postlude* by Arthur Honegger (1948); and *Second Symphony* by Darius Milhaud (1944); address by Cocteau following the intermission.

Darius (especially Darius) orchestrate splendidly, but their syntax escapes me. The tender Darius seems to compose through some electronic brain. Poulenc triumphs with his orchestra and chorus. The soul of a musician. I realized last night to what degree orchestral music is in the hands of the conductor. The triumph of our *Oedipus Rex* in Vienna was because of the conductor. Last night nothing was heavy, nothing blurred. At Maxim's I asked our friends to give a concert with their first works: *Les Facheux,** *Les Biches,*† *Le Boeuf sur le toit,*‡ etc., and *Parade.*§ The public would be astounded by so much freshness.

Broadcasts. Went to Colette's to rest for an hour. Sometimes she's vague and very remote. Today she was lively and present. At lunch tomorrow, the president of the Republic will begin his speech on the telephone, addressing her. They've already photographed Colette on the telephone. This lunch is going to be a terrible ordeal. But I don't want people to think I'm sulking in Paris. For the same reason I'll go to Giraudoux's play *Pour Lucrèce*¶ tonight. Colette says: "The play can't be good. I feel it here," and she taps her solar plexus.

---

*Ballet by Boris Kochno after Molière, music by Auric, choreography by Bronislawa Nijinska; curtain, set, and costumes by Braque, created by Diaghilev's Ballets Russes in 1924.

†Ballet by Francis Poulenc, choreography by Bronislawa Nijinska; curtain, set, and costumes by Marie Laurencin; created by Diaghilev's Ballets Russes in 1924.

‡A farce by Cocteau, music by Darius Milhaud, costumes by Fauconnet, set by Raoul Dufy, created in 1920.

§Ballet by Cocteau, music by Erik Satie, choreography by Léonide Massine; curtain, set, and costumes by Pablo Picasso, created by Diaghilev's Ballets Russes in 1920.

¶A play in three acts by Giraudoux, staged by Jean-Louis Barrault, with sets by Cassandre, costumes by Cassandre and Dior. Written in 1942, the play was first performed in January 1953.

. . . .

NOVEMBER 6

Giraudoux's play. Like all his works for the theater, *Pour Lucrèce* is a ventriloquist's play. I was all the more struck by this last night because of his absence. It's always the same man, speaking through mannequins. What almost saves Giraudoux from this hateful "poetic" language our public so enjoys is that he has an active diction— that is his privilege: an active diction. But it is only his diction which is active. His clumsiness in the realm of action is incredible. Jouvet was able to cover it up somewhat (though actually very little). Last night the public was in church (what used to be called, in the parish of La Madeleine, "the mass of the lazy"). To which was added that love of the late lamented, of funeral rites, which Paris, which dares not look death in the face, prefers to anything else. Borniol, the chrysanthemums, the processions to the sacristy, the speeches over the graves. The *treat* of a Giraudoux dialogue whereby this little world gives itself a certain elevation, was deliciously combined with a salute to Suzanne,* an emotional glance at her tics and her dark glasses. I was careful never to show our judges that my perspectives are not theirs.

During the intermission Steve Passeur† approached, his plague journal in hand. "What do you think?" "Magnificent?" "That's all?"

The only miracle of the evening will doubtless remain a dead letter for our Giralducians. This was Yvonne de Bray. As an old procuress out of Goya,‡ she accompanied Edwige§ in silence. You wondered why this supernumerary was our greatest actress. I know my Yvonne. The performance of the two ladies (Madeleine and Edwige) terrified her. Her somnolent lioness's gaze followed

---

*Widow of Jean Giraudoux, born in Bellac in 1882, died in Paris in 1944.
†Dramatic author (1899–1966).
‡The role of Barbette was the last acted by Yvonne de Bray (1889–1954).
§Edwige Fevillère and Madeleine Renaud played the two heroines, Paola and Lucile.

the two wrestlers facing each other in the ring, astonished at their maneuvers. At the end of the last act, Madeleine dies; Edwige exits. At last the ring is empty. Yvonne is alone with a dead woman and five lines of text. What happened remains unforgettable for me. Like those old gamblers at Monte Carlo who slowly and cunningly apply themselves to raking in a pile of chips, she gathered up everything in a single gesture. Hervé Mille telephoned me the next day that he didn't believe such a tour de force was possible. And the funniest thing is that Yvonne isn't interested in her lines, thinks they're conventional and theatrical. It doesn't matter. After the triumphant combatants leave the stage, and without taking any trouble at all, she's the one who triumphs and who overwhelms them both.

Masterpiece of Claudel. Masterpiece of Anouilh. Masterpiece of Giraudoux. Masterpiece after masterpiece. The theater rescued. Admirable theme for our critics. Genius on their level. And they are comparably sublime. The silliness of *Christopher Columbus*. The vulgarity of *The Lark*. Giraudoux's embroidery. This way they can lay claim to *altitude*. It's over themselves that they're exulting, over their intelligence, their finesse, their greatness of soul. Poor devils. If they had any perspective, they would realize that soon no one will endure all this visibility, and the *invisible* will appear out of the shadows. Which doesn't keep Claudel from being Claudel, Giraudoux from being Giraudoux—but a masterpiece cannot be visible to criticism. It can only disturb it and shock its habits, suddenly and disagreeably waken it from its torpor. Hence we must dread the praise which kills and endure what all masterpieces have always endured: the hatred of our critics.

Yesterday the banquet of the Académie du disque with the Auriols at the Hôtel Rohan, rue Vieille-du-Temple. Curnonsky* had created the (remarkable) menu. I was embraced, cajoled, given

---

*"Prince des gastronomes" since 1927.

the best place at table (between the prefect of police and the president of the city council) . . . One charming thing. Colette's voice, sick as she was, and Auriol's response, by telephone.

Auric was furious because my absence from the voting and Maurice Yvain's* insistence cost him the prize for his waltz.† Yvain was getting his own back for Auric's hostility to his *Blanche-Neige* at the Opéra, which Georges called "dirty snow."‡

Nothing is stranger than to come up from the Cape and to plunge into this frog pond which intoxicates the Parisians and whose emptiness they do not even notice. Sauguet's glance: nothing of all this escapes him.

A "Parisian" day. Eleven in the morning: Conversation with Orson Welles *in English* for the BBC. Twelve-thirty: Banquet of the Académie du disque. Four o'clock: Favre Le Bret comes to beg me to resume my presidency of the Cannes festival. Six o'clock: Swiss Radio. (Tell my life story. Easy enough!) Seven-thirty: Pathé-Marconi, recording of the text serving as a preface for the long-playing record of Les Six. Eight o'clock—free! No. Three Germans from Hamburg are waiting for me at the studio door in the rue Magellan; they want an article on Paris. I escape to Milly and go to bed.

. . . .

NOVEMBER 7

(In the plane to Madrid.) We left Orly at 1:25. We're over Biarritz and will arrive at about five.

You may be surprised by my frankness. A dead man is speaking to you. When these lines are published—if they are—I will no longer be a target.

---

*Composer (1891–1965), chiefly of operettas and songs, creator of the music for the ballet *Blanche-Neige*, 1951.

†"Moulin Rouge," in the film of the same title by John Huston, 1953.

‡An allusion to Simenon's novel *La Neige était sale*, 1948.

Saw at the BBC, in a newspaper citing the "Hundred Men of the Century," my photograph with the following note: "Result of a snobbery which has still lost none of its power." Try to preserve to the end that equilibrium over the abyss—that patience toward an inevitable injustice which is the only true consecration.

Muses in your dark barns,
Who knew you would press down
on my brow a laurel crown
*sharper than any thorns?**

What can it matter if I say here what I think? I've always been a good team player. Later on, either I'm wrong and will harm no one but myself or I'm right and will have a certain ethical triumph. Amen. Besides, I'm taking these notes high in the air among ladies and gentlemen who are looking for the signs of glory in a pile of magazines.

Magazines. Paris-Match. Utrillo's daubs. Café style. Painting by accordion. Dance hall painting. These splendid masterpieces (the reporter declares) were copied from postcards. Title: "Utrillo— He and Picasso the World's Most Expensive Painters." Enough to lay the ghosts of Vermeer, El Greco, van Gogh, Renoir, and Cézanne.

Saw Peyrefitte at Nora's exhibition.† (I had forgotten, in yesterday's program, that gallery in the rue de l'Élysée where people dropped in and never looked at the canvases, some of which were exquisite.) I told him his book was a secret—subtract the gossip and it is a first-rate history, not a comic one. "Your hundred thousand readers are satisfied with the gossip."

---

*Second stanza of the poem "De tous les partis . . . " in *Clair-Obscur.*

†Nora Auric, née Nora Vilter, exhibited portraits of black children and Gypsies, as well as canvases inspired by underwater fishing.

. . . .

NOVEMBER 8

Madrid. Since I was supposed to come tomorrow, only Luis and Edgar were at the airport. At the Ritz, only Miguel Perez Ferrera and the ABC critics Sirerol and Utrillo. The film will be shown Tuesday night. Monday night there's a big charity ball. Alberto telephones. The Barcelona date still not set. Splendid weather. Dinner at Horcher's with Neville, who is to "introduce" me Tuesday night.

Lunch at Neville's with Mme Membrives* and Conchita. Conchita has one of those tiny actress's faces and an authority which makes Edgar melt—a pity the censorship sets up such obstacles to plays; it is so feared that these women dare not oppose it, and they would succeed if they did, for the censor no longer triumphs here. It is apologetic and a little shamefaced. Lola Membrives is, apparently, astonishing in *Les Parents terribles* (in Argentina). She dreams of playing the part in Madrid, but I advise against doing the single chamber-theater performance. *Les Parents terribles* is too effective with all kinds of audiences to be presented in such a peculiar fashion. I described Yvonne's tour de force in *Pour Lucrèce*. Conchita describes that of Mme Membrives, who, the other evening, came to recite a few lines of verse at the end of a flamenco evening and eclipsed all the dances in a single gesture, her great voice erasing all before it.

The Americans in Spain. The Spanish will absorb them, and burn them later.

After all I have said and written about Spain, O. says to Luis, "Rumor has it that Cocteau likes Spain."

---

*Lola Membrives, celebrated Argentinean actress who performed Lorca's plays in Buenos Aires and Madrid (1933–1935).

Read *Saint-Simon par lui-même*.* Perched on the golden dunghill of Versailles, the duke flashed his cockerel's eye everywhere. But if you ask him for no depth, you would still prefer him more cruel and more intense. True, Versailles must have been a real labyrinth, such a swamp that the duke dared not keep an exact record. Besides, vice was steeped in boredom (that mortal boredom which brewed so many plots). Inevitable that you feel it in what the duke does manage to tell. The page on the matter of precedence among the princesses and duchesses is typical. I kept thinking of Stanislas's poem in *L'Aigle à deux têtes* . . .

Philippe Erlanger, in *Monsieur, frère du roi*, is the first historian who actually shows this court in its barnyard aspect, the dung heap and the fowl pecking at it.

The day before yesterday, during his address, the president of the Republic, speaking of the poets who serve history, leaned toward me as if in a friendly salute. "Why is he nodding toward you?" the prefect of police asked me. I answered that as prefect of police, he surely knew. I suppose it was because of my text for the Versailles celebrations (?).

All the walls of the buildings in Madrid are clean. In Paris they are filthy. The air in Madrid (altitude eight hundred meters) must be very dry and pure. I don't feel the discomfort that distresses me in our cities. Summer sun in the autumn trees. Madrid is a city of trees. In a deforested Spain, trees take refuge in the cities. The opposite of Singapore, carved out of the jungle.

Yvonne. Membrives. Pastora Imperio. The authority of the gesture. Of the word. The young and their fear of "exaggerating." When I acted the part of the baron in *Le Baron fantôme*,† I was reproached for my grimacing, and I was told that if I continued

---

*François-Régis Bastide, *Saint-Simon par lui-même*, in the series *Écrivains de toujours* (Éditions du Seuil, Paris), 1953.

†A film by Serge de Poligny (1903–1983), dialogue by Cocteau, 1942.

in that fashion, the scene would have to be reshot. When the rushes were shown, everyone apologized, finding the figure extraordinary. But it would never have been extraordinary if I had obeyed them. And the mediocrity would have been attributed to me. This is why I reproach directors for their fear of exaggeration and relief—in short, their fear of personality—which impels them to extinguish any boldness or discoveries on the part of the young. Boldness and discoveries they regard as professional defects. When I was making *Les Parents terribles*, I told Yvonne to pay no attention to the chalk marks and the lights. If her hand fluttered in front of the lens, I couldn't care less. As a result (Jeannot told me) the television technicians were saying the other day, "That's how it should be done—and we don't dare do it."

. . . .

NOVEMBER 9

Dinner yesterday at Escobar's. I.e., from his little apartment, and through the doors and stairways of the Escorial, you pass mysteriously into a palace where the dinner took place.

Conchita astounded (as was I) to learn that a performance was being arranged of *Le Bel indifférent* (very quickly), for which there doesn't even exist a Spanish text. I gathered that everything depended on a photographic session with Unamuno. Unamuno, for political reasons, is kept out of the press. This would be a way of reintroducing him. Now, not only is the number I wrote for Piaf too slight to represent me in Spain, but they would also be quite willing to wreck it [so] as to do a favor for a press colleague. Very irritating business, the kind that always happens to me.

This morning, phone call from Dali, who arrived in Madrid last night. "Allo—*ici Ritz donc Palace*." He's staying at the Palace Hotel and is coming to lunch with us.

Five o'clock. Lunch with Dali, who arrives while I am being

interviewed—which permits a curious duet on our mutual loathing of fantasy, on Picasso's monsters that have turned so charming, on the martyrology of the magicians who will overcome the monsters, etc.

Dali's mustachios and his crystal cane. His mustachios are antennae. Longer than ever, like the mustachios of Velázquez's models. Dali speaks of Velázquez. "With a hand painted by Velázquez," he says, "it is impossible to determine whether it fills the space proper for a hand. Put it on the ground and you would take it for a pigeon, for any mysterious and enigmatic object." During the entire lunch he develops his theme of "Laugh, clown, laugh" through various works, out of which he wants to make a film. And Picasso—bring Picasso back to Spain. Let Picasso come to Dali's famous corrida with its submarine and its helicopter. Kidnap him, if need be, and bring him back, if Picasso will venture as far as Perpignan. When I said to the journalist that I wouldn't want to meet the man my legend has made of me, Dali quotes Voltaire, "Greet him, but don't shake his hand." "Myself," he says, "I cultivate the man of my legend from a distance, I keep him well watered. It is possible that some day you may want to meet the man of your legend." I add, "Maybe to ask him for charity." "Send him a telegram from time to time," Dali concludes.

After the journalist leaves, Dali indicates his satisfaction. "We made a fine confusion. Exactitude is dangerous. We are protected by mess." After lunch he said some quite accurate things about the impressionist and cubist painters who, without understanding it at all, preceded the discoveries concerning the dissociation of matter, the swarming multitude of solids...

Spanish hours. You wake up at noon. You dine at ten. We are going to see Neville's play at seven. Tomorrow *Orfeo* is on at eleven. I am brought a brochure by Carlos Fernandez Cuenca on *"Orphée" y el cine de Jean Cocteau*. I had never seen this before.

The better the means of corresponding, the farther countries are from one another. It's a sieve. Nothing remains.

Conchita, *charming* in Neville's *charming* play.

At ten, Dali gives us a sumptuous Spanish dinner. Dining room decorated with garlands. Table lit by candelabra with green candles which drip and bend like his watches. This huge table is loaded with fruits and seafood. Utrillo embraces and insults everyone. Dominguín and his sister. Poets. Painters. No one knows anyone else. People sniff each other out. There is something authentic in these contacts by waves—persons who believe they know us and our work know little more. One is better divined than known, through the wall of languages.

Sirerol. He has taken such pains with *Orfeo*. Spain rejects European films. He has rented the hall. He has fought battles. Tonight the showing is at the same time as the official banquets, so that he will not have newsreel coverage. He wants to organize a showing of the French version on Friday, with the newsreels and the embassy. But Friday night Antonio is dancing. The Barcelona date remains vague. All this (and the seats) unfolds in a real Mediterranean chaos. Alberto and Margarita Puig are arriving on the nine o'clock plane.

Dali talks a lot about phoenixology (human layerage). "Thanks to a bit of our skin, to a nail paring, we will be able," he says, "to be reborn exactly as we are, after our death."

It is likely we shall return to Paris before the Barcelona showing. I will ask Alberto to arrange matters. Nothing is more difficult for me than this friendship of countries outside the official mechanism which has nothing to do with me. The embassy still seems to be unaware that I am being received here better than its own representatives and that more warmth is generated around me than by propaganda visits.

. . . .

NOVEMBER 10

Projection of *Orphée* in a gigantic (and packed) hall. This mysterious story remained a dead letter for a motley, coughing public. It seems to me that our friends suffered as much as I did, for the places that lag in a film are generated by the public's incomprehension. Besides, the dubbing, which had amazed and even delighted me in the little hall, etiolated the work in the big one. I recognized the deadly uneasiness that greeted *La Belle et la Bête* at Cannes and *Orphée* at the Paris gala. The great German public is a film-club public. That is what misleads us. That is the source of the triumphs in Germany. The Madrid public, gorged on American films, turns out to be incapable of following a difficult plot. I am particularly sorry about this for Sirerol, who has taken such trouble and expended considerable sums.

No matter how much I am told that I have drawn the wrong conclusions, that the Madrid public is *like that*, that the work was accorded *the greatest respect*, I remain convinced of an irreparable flop. In Paris *Belle* and *Orphée* have struggled against the current and ultimately won. In Spain the case is different. And the insoluble question is that, on the one hand, the big Spanish public is too ignorant for such a film and, on the other, the censorship forbids showing, for instance, *Les Parents terribles*, which would be able to win them over.

After the film we went to have a drink with the Puigs, Dali, Dominguín, Neville, Conchita, Pastora Imperio, Escobar, the whole friendly crew whose warmth manages to erase that absurd anxiety that grips me when I feel a work is not "taking." The same hall gave me the warmest welcome before the film was shown, when I spoke a few words after Edgar Neville's introduction.

I have come to share the unfavorable opinion of my colleagues about dubbing. Between the person and the foreign voice he bor-

rows, there is formed a void, a death. Half the effectiveness collapses. I think I would have done better with French dialogue,
even poorly understood, than with a Spanish dialogue in which
the terms pass right and left of the target. In Germany and in
German, in Sweden and in Swedish, in America and England in
English, *Orphée* would not have had its opportunity.

Never again get involved with such phenomena, which make
me ill. As we came out, Édouard murmured to Francine, "I could
see him growing older before my eyes."

Noon. After an hour of moral gymnastics, I am myself again and
I have got rid of these repellant glooms. I must realize once and
for all that contacts have become increasingly difficult for me. I
am inhabited only by things people never think of. And I never
think of the things that inhabit them. They'll say, "Why try to
communicate?" For a few souls.

Analyze my weakness. A poet is an athlete and a child. It is the
child who is disappointed when the athlete takes the punishment.
There is also the fact that *Orphée* is a posthumous work, having
weighed anchor. Unbearable to relive the minutes which preceded
this phase. Still to be giving birth to a progeny which has already
taken to the high seas.

. . . .

NOVEMBER 12

All the reviews excellent and bearing no relation to what the
projection made me fear. There is always that handful of men who
think for the others in Spain. At eight-thirty I met at Dionisio's
what passes in Madrid for an elite. Priests and philosophers. Unfortunately, I couldn't stay as long as I wished. I was dragged off
to a stupid broadcast, with an audience! When I returned to our
friends, I had to leave again for a dinner which count de V. was
giving for us. In the afternoon I attended a rehearsal of *Le Bel*

indifférent being given at the Teatro de Camara with Unamuno's play.

Increasingly I realize that there is no flaw in the film (in the realm which matters to me). There is only the eternal divorce between the public that thinks in Spain and the public that doesn't.

Almost all the people invited last night knew the film in the French version (which will be shown on Friday evening).

Dali and Dontancredism. Don Tancred is the name of that white figure who sits on a table in the center of the ring and whom the bull doesn't touch because he remains motionless. Franco is a Don Tancred. He doesn't move. He has no opinion. He remains standing and motionless. The bull sniffs him, turns away, and disembowels Hitler and Mussolini.

I speak to Dali about the Dontancredism of the Commander in *Don Juan*. He is a Don Tancred *who moves*. "Your politicians in France," Dali says, "are Don Tancreds who move. There is a Dontancredism that moves and a Dontancredism that doesn't. And there is also a Don Tancred who collapses in a heap; that is the attitude of India toward the British."

It will be very hard for Dali to grow old. He loathes old age and death. He wants his hair and mustachios to be black as ink, and his back as straight as his transparent cane. He goes tense when he laughs, for fear of wrinkles.

This morning at the Prado. The masterpieces look like people you know, taking coffee at tables. You pass. You greet them. The *Madrileños* pass one another and palaver. It is like the Galleria in Milan, the Mail in Aix.

Visit to the ambassador. Always the same refrain: He deplores France's total incomprehension of the Spanish problem and actually says that the only ambassadors are the artists. He asks me to speak to the president of the Republic, the Socialist party being the first obstacle to understanding. They are not trying to find the source of the clandestine radio broadcasts from Bayonne; they are letting the refugees make propaganda against the regime. "Now," he says, "the right of asylum does not include that of open political warfare." I will have lunch tomorrow at the embassy. And tonight I'll go to the cocktail party given for me by François de Rose and his wife, Yvonne, diplomats here.

Leaving the embassy, I meet the Franco parade (for the Chilean ambassador)—of an incredible magnificence. The coaches of scarlet and gold, the footmen in white wigs, the horses plumed with yellow and red, the Moroccan guard in burnooses. All this with an orderliness, an elegance, a sumptuousness less anachronistic in Madrid than all the British pomp in London. The procession (which I will meet again at the Ritz) is wonderfully assimilated here. Nothing in Spain "harks back." Things *continue.* It is the privilege of a people destructive of everything except the great national image. Around that image they slaughter one another and burn the country down.

The ambassador tells me about the visit of a Dominican father who was giving lectures in Zaragoza. "The church in Spain," he said, "is concerned with problems solved everywhere else twenty years ago."

Dionisio Ridruejo and Cesar Gonzalez Ruano have brought me their books.

.   .   .   .

NOVEMBER 13

Roses' cocktail party. Inhuman and barbarous custom. Everyone standing. The hostess dead with fatigue. One person snatches you away from another to whom you are talking, etc. The director of the Institut français says, "You have worked the miracle of having become in a few days a guest of honor of Spain."

Dinner at Horcher's with Luis Miguel, Margarita, Escobar.

Since the journalist of *L'Information* has me saying things I did not say and others that I asked him not to say, I have written to the director and noted the matter at the embassy.

I ask Luis Miguel if he likes to eat his bull. He answers, "I'd like it better if I could eat the torero who shares my fight."

Apropos of Neville's son, victim of a morals charge at Torremolinos, Luis Miguel says, "If they kick Rafael out of Spain, I'll marry him and bring him back with honors."

This noon, lunch at the embassy. Yesterday morning, a quick stroll through the Prado. Once again I remark the disconcerting simplicity of genius. Velázquez and Goya seem to paint at top speed with an incredible "luck" in each touch. No matter how close one comes, inspects, analyzes, one fails to understand how what has been done was done. And the boldness. The bolero of the *Maja*: the brush dashes down a bit of yellow paste, and in it there remain streaks of other colors. Velázquez, the lace of the infanta: as if he had let the paint run out of its tube with the caprice of honey flowing over honey. Dali was speaking of eyes that sully the pictures and of certain museums which make paintings sick. He cites a museum in Switzerland where the Spanish pictures have "bad days." Besides, there's a certain modesty I feel about not looking at a masterpiece for a very long time. Nothing embarrasses me like those young couples, hand in hand, riveted to the banquette, eyes fixed on some masterpiece. I pass by quickly, as if voyeurs were arousing themselves by the spectacle of art stark naked. A great painter exhibits himself to such a degree by means of a canvas and a model that one dares not take up a stand in front of them. There would be a kind of indiscretion in doing so.

I have come to the point of wondering if it is not this mysterious sentiment of exhibitionism which has embarrassed, tormented, deceived me as to the public's response during the projection of *Orphée*. I must have taken my embarrassment for that of the public.

Lunch at the embassy was a success. There was only the French colony, and this is one of the first times that one of our embassies did not resent the personal success I managed to score abroad. The ambassador and his wife and their guests could not adequately express their gratitude and unreservedly acknowledged what they called a unique phenomenon: the friendship and the approval of the Spanish obtained in a few days.

Pietri (ambassador) had bought for almost nothing this countrified property, which will be enlarged and become the French Embassy.

But how tired I am! In this day and age, people talk standing up. No one dreams of sitting down. The chairs are ranged around the walls, and empty. I remembered those exhausting receptions in Egypt where I used to say to the king's sisters: "Sit down, so that I can sit down," and they would answer: "Impossible. We're afraid of spoiling our gowns." And in the past, those huge gowns, those frock coats, those swords . . . and a circle was formed—and everyone sat down!

. . . .

NOVEMBER 14

Spoke last night to the audience of the French version. Then joined Conchita at Antonio's performance . . . In the flamenco (unaccompanied), Antonio is a virtuoso. He must prefer the "ballet"— which recalls the worst moments of the Ballets Suedois. The Spain of *Carmen*, alas, without genius. Stupid sets and dreadful, multicolor lighting. The first dancer is a parody—she has nothing but the mechanism. Because of my little speech at the film, I missed the first dance (the one in Neville's film, in front of the Escorial). Apparently it was a triumph. But the rest is very, very weak. It's not the fault of Spain alone. This weakness prevails everywhere in the world, unfortunately.

Antonio. His feet think . . . Incomparable in the flamenco syntax.

But he seems thirsty for "art" and a kind of pseudoclassical dance. The least little Gypsy pleases me more.

Sirerol says: "In Spain, the film clubs are the death of great films. When a great film reaches us, it has already been projected everywhere and very badly in sixteen millimeter."

For me *Orphée* is a success. For Sirerol I am afraid it was a disaster. The public at large is too ignorant to follow the opinion of the press.

If I were subject to pride, I would be fulfilled by this trip. But I am not, and I feel only the melancholy of the misunderstanding which exists among peoples, realizing that the only link which brings them closer together is the mediocrity by which they all understand one another. Since in Spain the divorce is complete between those who think and those who do not, those who think are obliged, in order to live, to come down to the others' level. But even if they resist and doom themselves to solitude, fatigue leads those who think to indulge mediocrity. Poets like Dionisio telephone to take me to see the wretched painter who has done Antonio's sets, and in Ridruejo's apartment, the walls are covered with pictures that certainly do not correspond to the host's style. Same thing at the Puigs' in Barcelona. What would Picasso do in Spain? And even Dali seems to be a foreigner here. Here it is the people who are the poet in their manners and their veiled violence, but the active poem of Spain must not be confused with a taste for Spanish poets. The Spanish poets are alone, and alone the people who create their masterpieces by actions, elegance, rebellion, and conflagrations. What is missing is a king who would care for genius and impose it on the crowd. The crowd nowadays is a poor queen out of *Ruy Blas*, dimmed by the Church. The artists are Ruy Blas. All they have is deception or suicide, if the government discovers the nobility of their imposture.

I wonder why the young journalists who come to interview me take so much trouble over their notes, since they invent things I have not said and change the things I have. Ever since I've been in Madrid, articles come out every day attributing the most absurd and mediocre remarks to me, whereas I have gone to some pains to speak what it is not customary to say about Spain and to say it with some clarity and some exactitude. I have always had along someone capable of translating with exactitude. But inexactitude must be a rule of journalism. Which is incomprehensible, since I provide these people the opportunity to do an article out of the ordinary. Henceforth I myself shall write what I want to be said and have it translated by a friend, insisting that not a line be changed.

. . . .

NOVEMBER 15

Dinner last night with Pastora Imperio in the restaurant owned by Rafael, who is to fight tomorrow night in Seville. Pastora speaks French poorly, but she feels, she guesses. She tells me that everyone is talking about *Orphée*. She emphasizes this by one of her splendid Gypsy gestures, which seems to be crumpling paper or rubbing wood to make sparks fly out of it.

Pastora is taking one of her "psychic" friends to *Orphée* tomorrow. Pastora's father was a great "seer." This woman, so famous and so rich, is now penniless and living only on the charity of the Puigs, about whom she speaks with tears in her eyes . . . I keep thinking of Yvonne de Bray—Gypsy in her genre—and in so many respects resembling Pastora (the eyes).

I take advantage of a *less terrible* moment to make this note: I was lunching in a bistro with Escobar and one of his intimate friends. Suddenly, at dessert, I was gripped by a horrible pain in my stomach and kidneys. I turned so pale that Francine and Édouard were alarmed. I was taken to the Ritz, bent double. The doctors were there almost as soon as we were. I was given one shot after another, and a blood sample was taken. Then I was rushed to the Madrid clinic, where I was X-rayed. The diagnosis was specific. A kidneystone moving toward the bladder. I refused to stay in the clinic where suffering becomes a piece of furniture, a normal state. Back at the Ritz, I could only cry out and try to find a position that was not to be found. . . . It is midnight. In the last ten minutes, the pain has become endurable. Between two and eleven, it was at its peak. It seemed to me impossible to suffer more. Of course Escobar canceled the dinner. I regret this misfortune which deprives me of Gerardo Diego. This morning Carlos Fernandez Cuenca came to see me, and the Dutchman who wants me to make the film on Goya's *Disasters of War*.

Cuenca is the author of the book *"Orphée" y el cine de Jean Cocteau*. As for Ruano, people find his interview remarkable. Myself, I have great reservations, even about this superior example of journalism. It's better than the others, but no more than that.

I gave Cuenca the corrections I had made after reading the articles. He's the only one capable of setting things to rights.

Between three and four, I believed I was dying. Which would be nothing if it were not for those one leaves behind.

Shooting pain, but steadier than before, I have been injected with enormous doses of morphine and Pantopon, which make me nauseous.

X-rays. The radiologist says, "Your scoliosis is considerable, but your spinal column is that of a Hercules." Hence my resistance.

. . . .

NOVEMBER 16

According to the seven o'clock X-ray, the stone has passed. I return, calmer, to the hotel and talk to Don Luis and Alberto. I eat a little. And now the terrible pain starts again. I am writing this note after a shot of atropine.

. . . .

NOVEMBER 17

Ravaillac's phrase—"The day will be bitter." The day has been bitter. The attacks resumed after a short respite. At six I was taken to the doctor, who with a robot's cruelty gave me, without warning, two shots of calcium and salt serum. This was the thistle poultice on the wounds of Torquemada's victims. I was taken back to the hotel shrieking with pain. The doctor was no doubt right to do what he did, though, since it is ten o'clock now, and I am calming down. He thought he shouldn't warn me. But I detest surprises.

Alberto takes dinner with us in the room. He tells me he has received the *Revista* and, unsigned, from some faraway village, a fine translation of my "Homage to Góngora." He has begun inquiring who this person can be, since he may be the ideal translator for the Spanish poems of *Clair-Obscur*.

I have written to Dr. de la Peña to apologize for acting like an animal in public, for having "hissed at his masterpiece." If he had warned me of the shock, perhaps I would not have had the courage to take the risk. After the two injections, I cursed him and called him a monster. He made his escape.

. . . .

NOVEMBER 18

This morning I am sore all over, as if I had been beaten, but the pain is gone. Paris is fogged in. Planes are landing in Bordeaux. Dr. de la Peña asks us not to leave till Saturday. Jeannot and Alex have telephoned Francine that it would be absurd to risk such a trip.

Yesterday, before I left to see the doctor, Pastora Imperio came to my room, exactly as, so long ago in Algiers, the lovely Fatma came.* (Still very lovely.) Sitting beside the bed, she concentrates, knots a scarf and impregnates it with her fluid. Then she slides the scarf under my head.†

Everyone here is incredibly kind, discreet and helpful. Luis comes and goes as though through doors, despite his sick mother. She was the true queen of Spain, and her children are like pictures in the Escorial. She no longer shows herself. She remains at home because her reign is over.

Luis Escobar says that the doctor was right not to warn me of the shock. He risked a refusal, an evasion, and he knew that this was the only way to save me (he telephoned this morning to say as much).

Yesterday, for fifteen minutes, I really thought I was going mad. It must have been those fifteen minutes that have caused this fatigue—like that of a convalescence from a long illness.

Pastora Imperio was also a queen of Spain. But now she is poor and old. She no longer dances in the Seville procession. The crowd kneels and touches her gown to ask her to make a few gestures. These provoke delirium. Olivier and Jean-Pierre were present at this phenomenon at the feria before last. It must have been a strange spectacle, my leaving the Ritz bent double in a bathrobe, pale as a dead man and leaning on her, amid the terrified respect of the concierges and bellboys.

Yesterday Alberto's sister touched my chest and then clasped her hands to drive away the pain. Afterward, she washed her hands and arms up to the shoulders.

---

*On the trip Cocteau and Lucien Daudet made to Algiers in March 1912 and on their visit to Mme Fatma, see Cocteau's article "Vocalises de Bachir-Selim," in *La Revue des lettres modernes*, nos. 298-303, 1972.

†The spell against pain by the famous Gypsy dancer is the theme of Cocteau's "Homage to Pastora Imperio" in *Clair-Obscur*.

. . . .

NOVEMBER 19

My exhaustion is so profound that I cannot write. The whole guitar is untuned. The strings are slack. Even lying down exhausts me. Exhaustion exhausts me. I did not imagine so strong a counter-shock, especially since Dr. de la Peña doesn't want me to be moved. First I must eliminate the drugs he has injected into my veins.

Poor Francine has become a telephone operator. I was able to speak this morning (what they call morning, in Madrid—two o'clock) to Jeannot. Without Francine's help I am incapable of speaking on the telephone.

Luis Escobar brought a record of the Rodrigo *Concierto de Aranjuez* and a phonograph for me to listen to it on—it was actually of some help, and made me feel less exhausted.

(Orengo has a son.) I'm happy to publish poems at his Éditions du Rocher de Monaco, far from the Parisian publishers—to keep my distance from the *events* of the theater or film world, from all that feeds the press.

By some vehicle, plane or train, we must leave. I can no longer endure these articles where I am made to say what I have not said, these terrible photographs. Even though I barely glance at the papers that are brought, a glance always manages to pick up some mistake, some grimace. That nobility we dream of being surrounded by at my age has nothing to do with the real world, with politics and crimes. You can't help being mixed up in this sauce. Only Picasso keeps out of it, with a persistent and un-imaginable good luck. Protected by some taboo. The rest is ter-rifying. It's like a sort of plastic hatred that's bent on my destruction. When I'm in good health, I manage to live on the edges of that sauce. But sick, I sink into this grimacing shadow I loathe, blotting out everything I value, my love of exactitude and clarity.

. . . .

NOVEMBER 20

On the one hand, fate gives me nothing but incomprehension and injustice—on the other, two angels who allow me to endure them: Édouard and Francine. So I cannot complain.

Pastora Imperio says: "Anyone can put a flower in her hair and a fist on her hip. That's not what it's all about. Nowadays, those things are enough, even in Spain."

Alberto has realized how frivolous the journalists are—even in the *Revista* article. I had been careful not to open my mouth, to spare him pain.

While I was sleeping like a dead man, Francine arranged everything. Plane tomorrow morning at ten. We shall be in Nice at noon. Returning to Paris, after a stop at Santo Sospir.

I know no hotel more likable, more attentive, better run than the Ritz in Madrid.

Adieu Madrid.

"How do you feel tonight?" Luis asks me. "Like a fish in water." (Cannot even describe the state I am in.)

. . . .

NOVEMBER 21

In the plane, Madrid-Nice. What remains most vivid about this trip for me? A great attack of pain and certain intensities of friendship. An envelope of kindness, as just now, at the airport, where everyone put himself out to spare me fatigue. I was feeling quite dizzy, moreover, and it must have been obvious.

Orfeo reached only a few rare souls. Luis Escobar's, for example, whose friendship is no passing thing, or old Pastora's, who "divines" me. All the rest is a buzz of journalists who repeat what they imagine they have heard and serve me up in the same sauce as in

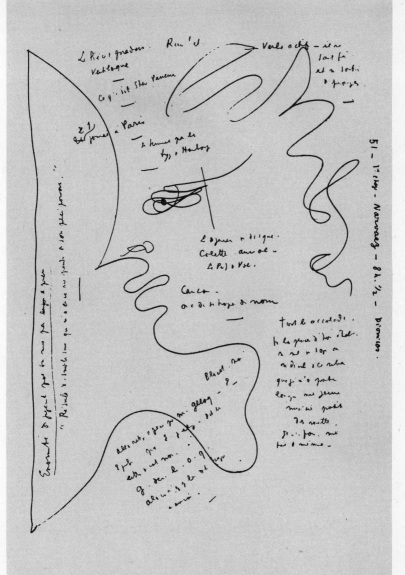

Paris. They imagine they are correcting the image Paris forms of me and providing the right one, whereas they provide the same one while accusing Paris of constraining me and praising Spain for liberating me from such constraint—which is false on both sides and frequently puts me in a disagreeable posture with regard to France, about which they don't mind at all making me seem to speak ill.

To sum up, what I am taking away is that memory of having suffered terrible pain, the Dali dinner, that charming Dr. de la Peña, who refuses to take any payment, the Velázquez infanta, Utrillo's bulldog eyes, the faces of Escobar and Puig, the smiles of the Ritz staff—the Ritz, which certain great Spanish ladies *never* leave, as if they had taken the veil there. And Pastora's sadness, a reigning queen who has lost everything.

We are approaching Nice, although in these huge fast planes you feel no more than a kind of motionless shudder, and not seeing the landscape go by, you don't realize that you are moving ahead. For almost an hour the man on the other side of Édouard has been giving him a flamenco lesson, singing and clapping softly. We didn't suspect, when we left Santo Sospir, that circumstances would be bringing us back so soon. Landing.

. . . . `. . . . .

NOVEMBER 22

I awaken at Santo Sospir as if I had not been in Madrid, drained of all my substance by a nightmare in which the friendships, *Orfeo*, the terrible pains all mingle. It seems to me that I'll never write again, that I'll never think again, that I'll know nothing but bore-dom—that monster I thought I had put to flight. Last night Orengo telephoned that he will come next Saturday and bring me the typescript of *Clair-Obscur*. My last burst of work was the "Homage to Velázquez" and the "Homage to Pastora Imperio." But I have anguished thoughts about my promises with regard to plays, films . . . I know that it is possible to regain lost ground, and that both body and soul have mysterious resources. But it seems as if this Madrid attack has put me against a wall where I was struggling to testify to my presence, and that I shall struggle no longer.

Dr. Ricoux stopped by to see me, and I have consented to have a booster shot. I don't want to drag Francine and Édouard down with me. The doctor has come from Florence. The young people in the schools there were rioting against the French, against all foreigners—posters were being pasted on the statues, in a city which foreigners have kept alive.

If a veil were rent . . . If the veil were rent . . . But which veil?

Being oneself is hateful. No longer being oneself is hateful. One wonders . . .

Reworked several times the homages to Velázquez and Pastora. My only possible work. I shall rework them some more, so that even translated, their constructions remain meaningful.

. . . .

NOVEMBER 23

Telephoned to Aubusson about sending *The Birth of Pegasus*.

Weather like April—cloudless sky, flat sea. Flowers blooming. But my soul is in November.

Spent yesterday stretched out in the studio. Not that I torture myself with dark thoughts, but that I no longer have the strength to put them to flight by reading or work. All day I was a prey to those viscous monsters which change into one another and engender still others.

My company: I imagine Pierre P. had big ideas, anticipating millions. He was thinking, "Films, plays . . ." My work rhythm disconcerts and fails to interest him. He cannot understand it, and says that Francine keeps me from undertaking such projects (favorite theme of his wife's).

On the other hand, Charles Orengo seems to understand my methods, because he is a publisher and because our interests coincide. Hence the company will greatly profit by taking root at Éditions du Rocher in Monaco—which would relieve Mme Bourgeois in Paris* and be under Édouard's and my surveillance here. (With the exceptional advantages of being in the principality.)

What interests me at the present moment has nothing to do with magazines or with big business. What interests me is putting my works in order, and I attach more importance to the publication of *Clair-Obscur*, even if the book meets with indifference, than to the boom-boom of a Technicolor film.

I am not saying that if a play comes to me I won't entertain it, but I will not force the lock. There is too much to do as it is, beginning with my *Bacchus* murdered by Marigny and whose successes in Germany prove its real merits.

.   .   .   .

NOVEMBER 24

Awoke with a pain in the left kidney. Terror. Ricoux stops by and thinks there is no danger. Consult Douglas for this scoliosis. Saint-Simon on the dauphin's. When I was young, we weren't cared for any better. The body badly sustained. Weaknesses—fatigue.

Reworked once more stanzas 1, 2, and 4 of the "Homage to Pastora Imperio."

Édouard's younger brother François arrived last night. He will stay with us two days so that he can be X-rayed and have blood tests after his otitis. Robert drove him to the radiologist's in Nice.

---

*Gisèle Bourgeois, Cocteau's secretary in Paris.

To know or not to know. After the last tests of the radiologist, where I *saw* my S-shaped spinal column, I keep thinking about it and dreading a physical collapse. I wonder by what bizarre phenomenon of equilibrium I manage to stand on my feet.

. . . .

NOVEMBER 25

A change in the weather. Fog.

François is charming. So timid he barely manages to answer yes or no. But his eyes express the rest. Yesterday Francine had taken him to Monte Carlo to buy him a suit, a shirt, warm shoes. He delighted the whole shop by his amazed expression on seeing himself in the mirror wearing a new suit.

Mario Brun spent the day at the villa, with his photographer. He has just been as sick as I was. This morning he publishes the article describing his visit here. Too bad he puts such bad French into my mouth. To his question, "Is it true you are presenting yourself as a candidate for the Académie française?" I answered that it was not true and that it was the press which had announced this news to me in Madrid.

I suppose that Mario was in a hurry to come, despite his physician, for fear that one of his colleagues might scoop him.

I still have the pile of notes on the Greek trip and on Proust waiting for me. The reluctance to deal with old notes, to dictate them . . . Yet there are things on Proust's work that have never been said.

All kinds of people send me remedies, recipes, tisanes . . .

A visit from Raymond and his photographer (same business as Mario). I had prepared notes for his article.

Photographed *Mother and Daughter* in color . . .

Answered about fifty letters.

. . . .

NOVEMBER 26

And here I am, stupidly spending the morning teaching geography, finding ways to keep François from mumbling—and then tying his tie for him and dressing him up in his new suit. All this mixed up with a poem which has come to me. The one that ends, "Simulating a life on the arms of dead soldiers." With a boy like François, I would become senile. I let him get away with everything. While I'm writing this, I hear him murmuring " . . . Boulogne a northern fishing port . . . ," getting only the words by rote and not trying for a second to understand them. Of this old-school method—learning by heart—nothing remains.

Pasquini dines with us. He tells me the details of the trial whose incredible verdict condemns his two clients to hard labor for life.

A filthy old tramp, quite rich, endlessly robbed and mistreated, whom even jails refuse because of his stench and the money he carries on his person, is assaulted with a club. The assailant gets seven years. The old man dies from the attack a few days afterward. Meanwhile, two fellows pick him up in their car, rob him, and leave him beside the road. The body is found five days later. The two fellows are accused of the murder, though from all evidence they were carrying no weapons and had no motive to kill. The jury quite coldly condemns them to hard labor. These men are of no interest, but the case is horrifying. The bourgeois jury inflicts this dreadful sentence on them much more for the social irregularity they represent than for a dubious crime. Pasquini is certain of their "innocence." A strange margin between the parents who torture their children and get off with a few months detention and these two petty thieves who are given a punishment worse than the death penalty.

"I've given Pasquini the poster for the 1954 Nice carnival. I did it yesterday on the request of the director of *Nice-Matin* and of *L'Espoir*. I think it's worth more than a front page. Pasquini wants it to be adopted as the second poster.

In 1953 ugliness inspires a kind of respect. Beauty seems insipid. The dilettant suspects works which seduce him. Ugliness reassures him. He thinks it will turn beautiful tomorrow and be worth a fortune.

Picasso has imposed monsters. But every beautiful work is a monster. This is what the dilettante is incapable of understanding.

Feeling much better since I've cut out alcohol. People cure you as quickly as they bury you. They telephone, tell me, "I didn't know you were ill, but I see that it's nothing." This is usually to ask me to do some favor.

Received the photographs of *Les Chevaliers* at Oldenburg, a big success. Funny costumes! Germany cannot rid itself of expressionism. But the postures, the faces have something sharp, lit from within. With a certain secret sexuality.

François back at Biot. His sister Émilienne came for lunch and returns with him. Francine has invited them to Paris for Christmas.

Finished the draft of the article about Paris which Hamburg commissioned.

Journalists are always astonished to see a Larousse on the bed where my papers are scattered about. They wouldn't do so badly to use one themselves from time to time.

Weather fine again.

Sacha Guitry's article about his film. He is amazed that there exists no play, no book about Louis XIV. Because he resembles Louis XIV (he says), he imagines himself to be a genius. Now, Louis XIV was a monument of stupidity. Saint-Simon and Chamfort attest to that. People placed bets at Versailles: "Is there a man in the world stupider than the king?"

Mario Brun telephones at nine o'clock. A Parisian paper has published a remark by Françoise Gilot: "I've had enough of living with a historical monument." Now, she certainly never said this, or said it differently from the way the journalist reports it. He tells me that the agencies are telegraphing from all over and that the photographers are swarming to Vallauris—where Picasso doesn't happen to be, moreover. I answered that I never meddle with my friends' affairs of the heart, that I regard the articles on Princess Margaret as a shame and a scandal, and that it would be more of the same to torment Françoise and Picasso.

Telephone call from Mme Béhaine.* I tell her that our newspapers want us all to be Miss Europe or Martine Carol. They think that the poetic curse is an outdated thing, that a certain darkness in which one works is a weakness, etc. In short, it is the same thing beginning all over again in another form.

N.b.: Those who may be reading these lines will no longer know who Martine Carol is.† More than a bad actress, she is a sign of the times. From cocktail party to cocktail party, she is our greatest star. She represents France at the court of England, the way Rachel or Sarah Bernhardt once did.

The business with my poster is out of Molière: Everyone is quarreling over it—a question of precedence. This one was supposed to have asked me for it, and not that one. Finally the newspaper declares the matter closed. Phony story. The real one is my absurd enthusiasm to do some work before it is officially asked of me.

Bernstein is dead.‡ Radio Monte-Carlo just called, and wants me to record a few words by telephone.

Henry Bernstein was an extremely nasty man, very funny when

---

*Mme Béhaine and her husband the writer René Béhaine (1880–1966), author of a cycle of novels, *Histoire d'une société*, lived in Villefranche-sur-Mer.

†Star of the fifties, Martine Carol (1922–1967) often appeared in mediocre films, though she was also used by René Clair (*Belles de nuit*, 1952), Max Ophüls (*Lola Montès*, 1955), and Roberto Rossellini (*Vanina Vanini*, 1961).

‡Henry Bernstein, born in Paris in 1876, died there in 1953.

he told stories and incredibly arrogant. He could not endure other people. A certain period, when the stage was divided between him and Bataille, left him with memories of triumphs which it irked him that his current plays no longer achieved. Guitry, Simone, Réjane* created a certain glory out of his dramatic *faits divers*. And in the long run he thought he was thinking. His confused style made this impossible. He obtained a show of strength only by actions which he believed were "human" and which were merely the development of a situation. His last plays were hateful and held the boards because of the actors whom he still kept under his thumb by a kind of prestige. And by the Théâtre des Ambassadeurs, which he took away from me in 1938, unable to bear the success of *Les Parents terribles*. He stirred up the Municipal Council, accused my play of being "a provocation of majors to debauchery," a phrase which had a certain currency, and we were forced to leave the theater by one maneuver of this kind after another, and we continued at the Bouffes.† Bernstein was a very large man and suffered from a trembling of the head which communicated itself to his voice and made him intolerable in anger and first class in anecdote. He besieged his artists and friends by telephone calls in the middle of the night, pouring out interminable grievances. His death shocked me. One could not think of him as dead. It was by an intensity of life that he played his part. The "literary" tendency of our contemporary theater devoured and killed him.

---

*The actor Lucien Guitry (1860–1925), father of Sacha; the actresses Simone (born 1877) and Réjane (1856–1920).

†"The affair of the Théâtre des Ambassadeurs" provided a topic for Parisian newspapers at the end of 1938. This theater (then the property of the city of Paris), where *Les Parents terribles* had been playing since November 14, was directed by Roger Capgras, whom Henry Bernstein was seeking to oust. The Municipal Council, considering the play immoral and outraged that author and director could consider offering free seats to school audiences, withdrew the theater concession from Capgras. Cocteau, attacked in the official municipal bulletin, replied in vigorous terms in an open letter to the press. In January 1939 *Les Parents terribles* was obliged to emigrate to the Théâtre des Bouffes-Parisiens.

. . . .

NOVEMBER 29

Incredible provincial salad tossed by Mario Brun because his editor in chief did not entrust him with the mission of asking me to do this poster. Such a simple thing provokes the kind of internecine disputes at *Nice-Matin* which bring me letters, visits, and telephone calls, all incomprehensible.

Last night Orengo brought me the finished copy of *Appogiatures*. Perfect, if the printer hadn't insisted on "Federico" instead of "Federigo" in the poem to Lorca, despite five sets of proofs.

The typed copy of *Clair-Obscur* is filled with absurd mistakes. And I was particularly careful in my manuscript to form each letter very clearly. This leads me to believe that this journal will be illegible after my death and that no one will decipher it. For I write very carelessly most of the time. The thought runs faster than the pen. (Gave Orengo the last poems: two homages to Velázquez—"Homage to Pastora Imperio," etc.)

Sun. I've caught up with my correspondence. Copied out the last poems. Sunday. Church is closed. Rest.

Example of the journalists' carelessness. I had told Mario Brun and Hécot: "I've done a drawing of Alexandre Dumas for Robert Gaillard's book, and I've sent Sartre a print which I used in making it, congratulating him on his triumph with *Kean* at the Théâtre Sarah Bernhardt. They print that I did this drawing to publicize the play. (No doubt because they loathe Robert Gaillard.)

Sent *Vogue* yesterday the text on *Les Monstres sacrés* for the page of photographs of Mounet-Sully and Sarah Bernhardt at home.

I loathe inexactitude and make every effort to be exact. Pagnol was traveling with Orengo yesterday. He told him, in Marseilles fashion, the story about Simenon on the brink of death and the doctor who said that he was fit as a fiddle. Through Marcel's narrative, this anecdote became a five-act drama, ending by a bronchial pneumonia which I caught because of a night spent at the bedside of Simenon, who believed himself at death's door.

There doesn't seem to be much noise made about Bernstein's death. Dreading the classic phone call from *France-Soir*, I had prepared this text in any event:

"Intolerable and charming Bernstein—wrested from this life to which he clung so tenaciously.

"He excelled in anecdote, and it was his desire that the situations in which he put his characters be grave psychological problems. He boasted of writing as a man talks, but alas, a man talks badly. Instead of cooking up his anecdote, he served it raw. In my youth the so-called "Boulevard Theater" ruled. The left had not yet moved to the right. The sacred monsters of the boards—Réjane, Simone, Lucien Guitry—raised the stakes of the Bernstein-Bataille duel very high, disputing the glory of the opening nights. Bernstein was the last testimony of an epoch when it sufficed for the characters of a play to be swept away in a storm. Moreover, this is the significant title of one of his works* in which the hero, fleeing from debt to debt, ran to his death behind a door against which Mme Simone collided and collapsed.

"*Samson*† brought the temple of the Bourse down on the man who cheated it of its triumph. *Le Voleur*‡ is accused in place of a young woman who steals in order to buy dresses that will please her husband. In *Le Secret*§ a wicked woman ruins marriages.

"In short, the style of the action triumphs over style. But, let me say again, Bernstein, vanquished by literature, possessed a great secret of the theater: the secret of action."

O'Neill dead. Telegraphed Oona (Mrs. Chaplin). He was sixty-five. Died in Boston.

La Rafale, 1905.
†1907.
‡1906.
§1913.

Poetry is the highest expression granted to man. It is natural that it should find no credence in a world interested only in gossip. Since I am not interested in gossip, it is to poetry that I dedicate myself.

Picasso. Secrets shouted at the top of his lungs. Never has there been such racket made around a *silence*. The journalists want to get hold of the Françoise drama. Ignoble custom which consists in forcing themselves into the wings of our theater. Picasso must have made his escape. He has told no one where he is. It is Françoise who will bear the brunt. I exult every single day over living outside the world. The inexact trifles printed about me remain indifferent to me.

Francine's father tells me that in his youth he attended a reception for Sarah Bernhardt in Brazil. The students had unhitched her carriage and dragged it from the theater to the hotel. At the hotel they lined the staircase, covered it with their jackets, saying: "Pizez là-dessus" which in Brazil meant, "Posez vos pieds là-dessus" [Put your feet here]. But Bernhardt had understood them to say, "Pissez là-dessus" [piss here], and was stupefied by this unexpected form of enthusiasm. The story still amuses the young who have grown old, and the young to whom the old tell it.

A good, long (and short) Sunday with dinner at ten (*à l'espagnole*). I redid four posters in another more festive style, two of which seem to me quite good—less beautiful than the first laughing profile but more in accord with a niçois style. I'll take them myself to the newspaper tomorrow morning, to avoid problems.

Wrote an open letter to the prefect of police, who wants it for his gazette. Dictated to Édouard the article on Paris for Hamburg. My writing was a chaos of illegible signs. Retouched and finished *Mother and Daughter in a Garden*, which must be sent to Marie Cuttoli so her workshops can execute the tapestry.

Orengo was right after all. It is Federico, and not Federigo, García Lorca.

Apparently the doctor has digested my chapter "On Distances," for he said to me, apropos of the apparatus which dissects microbes: "Not the microbes but the amoebas. The amoebas are *infinitely small*. But the microbes are *infinitely far away*" (gigantic). Which is what no one would say, what no one would understand. This basic difference between the small and the far away is what I develop in *Journal d'un inconnu*, and someday will be the source of some curious discoveries.

. . . .

DECEMBER 1

Weather in Paris as fine, apparently, as in Nice. We leave with Orengo tomorrow, taking the eleven o'clock plane.

I took the new poster, one more in accord with the spirit of his paper, to Bouqueret* yesterday.

Sadko.† I've been asked to write a prologue. But *Sadko* opens December 11. I'll be in Paris the third—hardly time. And if the notion of *Sadko* pleases me, the film will have to please me too. It would be amusing to say that the cinema permits the Russians to *show*, as *realistic* phenomena, what seems to belong to the realm of dreams.

. . . .

DECEMBER 5

Impossible to write in Paris. Too much to write. Too tired. Too many people. And my back is still giving me trouble.

Milly. Do the text for the film *Sadko*. Finish the open letter to

---

*Charles Bouqueret, editor in chief of *Nice-Matin*.
†*Sadko's Journey*, a film by Alexander Pushko, 1953, inspired by Rimsky-Korsakov's opera.

the prefect of police about speeding. The fifteen drawings for *Thomas l'imposteur* in Germany. Portrait of Radiguet and preface for *Devil in the Flesh* in Desch's edition. Have the Paris article typed for Hamburg.

Yesterday I took Peyrefitte to a photographer after a broadcast on Greece. The photographer wanted a shot of us together. That morning he had given his photographs to a girl of eighteen who had come with her mother the day before. When he asked the girl if her mother would like a set of proofs, she answered with a shrug, "What could a person of thirty-five understand about anything!"

This morning Colette seemed to have emerged from her cocoon, from her torpor. She wasn't even deaf any longer. She sparkled. Everything that had gone soft in her face was sharp and pointed. She told stories, she listened to them, she laughed.

I told her that Henri Mondor derived his apple cheeks and his smooth complexion from the fertilizer of his scatological stories and that long ago Misia's rosy freshness grew from the manure of her husbands: Natanson, Edwards, Sert. She immediately found several new examples of this theory.

And tomorrow I can find her back in the cloud which she helps form around her, out of a kind of discouraged fatigue, a fear of the world.

The Palais-Royal is a classified monument. No one can change or repair anything in it except the Beaux-Arts. Now the Beaux-Arts sends workmen, and it is we who have to pay them, as owners of the building. To *repair* one of the stone vases which ornament the balustrade of the top floor (where the Berls live),* will cost us 1,600,000 francs. Incredible.

Listened to the recording of Piaf in *Le Bel indifférent*. I don't

---

*The writer Emmanuel Berl (1892–1976) and his wife, the singer-composer Mireille.

know if I like the silences and the stage noises—but Piaf has incomparable moments. She ends with one of her songs. The end is good. In silence it would have been vague.

. . . .

DECEMBER 6

Last night, in a single session, I did the thirty illustrations for Desch's *Thomas*. I took my inspiration from the images in Gallimard's edition.* But I gave them a power and vitality which I lacked at the time.

Poking around upstairs, I have come across a host of extraordinary documents for the Beaux-Arts exhibit. They'll have to be sorted and collected. With distance, the merest photograph, the merest letter is astonishing. A prodigious one from Radiguet at fourteen.

I sketched the German preface for *Devil in the Flesh*.

I still have to correct the typescript for *Clair-Obscur* and answer the letters that have been waiting. (Done.)

. . . .

DECEMBER 7

Yesterday I did not stop working from nine in the morning till nine at night. Backache.

. . . .

DECEMBER 8

I went to see Françoise. She says: "I was turning into an old woman with Picasso, and he was growing younger and younger with me.

---

*Thomas l'imposteur, illustrated with forty drawings by the author. Paris, NRF, 1927.

But he thought I was heavier than I am; a breath of wind blew me into his life, and a breath of wind blew me out of it. I've decided to leave so that seven perfect years won't end by scenes and recriminations. My ticket is always one way, never round trip. One of the first times I went up the stairs to the studio in the rue des Grands-Augustins, Picasso showed me the dust in the corner of one of the steps and says, "You don't count any more for me than that dust there." I answered, "The difference is that I'm the kind of dust that doesn't like being swept out—the kind that will leave when it wants to." Picasso doesn't like an old box of matches to leave his house. He keeps everything. That's why my leaving must have been unendurable for him."

I told Françoise: "And your calm was that of a witness. Picasso, caught up in his whirlwind, must have felt *seen*, observed by a motionless eye. After our last lunch at Vallauris, he kept losing the thread of what he was saying because he felt your eyes on him. He can't endure anyone 'getting their hooks into him.' He fears any kind of commitment and puts up with the most mediocre people for that very reason—he suspects anyone else—any other kind."

"Really," Françoise told me, "at the end he loathed me." And I answered: "No. He adored you, but he was furious with himself for adoring you. *He was cheating on himself* with you. He is a tender man who believes that tenderness is a bourgeois virtue and that strength requires monstrousness."

Yesterday on the radio, Bérimont* asked me, "What use is poetry?" Answer: "If I could tell you, I would be a plant that could read horticultural treatises. Poetry is *indispensable*, but I don't know for what."

Letter from Bernstein's daughter in answer to a cruel article by Mauriac (more against Anouilh, actually, than against Bernstein).

---

*The poet Luc Bérimont (1915–1983), producer of a radio series devoted to poetry.

Very dignified answer, *preceded by* Mauriac's answer to this answer. Great cunning in the form of great nobility.

Our spiritual enemies will be those who represent officially what we defend in secret.

That dead weight which accumulates until it topples everything. Something even the very young feel.

Yesterday at Véfour, Brandel* says, "I have just bought the rights to *Orphée* and *La Belle et la bête* for American television." "From whom?" "From Paulvé." We shall doubtless learn that Paulvé has sold them for nothing. I didn't even ask Brandel for the figure, since he is in on the deal.

Françoise tells this story: "When I came to Picasso, I must have wanted to recover the style of my own father. My father adored trees, and he was especially fond of one in our garden. He said it was the most beautiful tree in the world. And he loathed cats. One day he saw a cat sitting in his tree. He tried to drive it off with the garden hose, but the cat stayed. Nothing would make it come down. So then my father got an ax and a saw and cut down his tree."

Dreadful days. And the requests, the appointments pile up. I'm going to have to do the drawings for the film† with a very complicated system of tracings over glass. And rehearse *La Machine infernale*, and have massages, and follow diets. And the procession at the door. Paris does not allow sickness. You have to be either well or dead.

I hear Georges Auric's waltz from *Le Moulin rouge* being whistled wherever I go—workmen, shopkeepers, people on bicycles . . .

---

*Joseph Brandel, film producer, husband of Simone Berriau, director of the Théâtre Antoine.

†*Une mélodie, quatre peintres*, a German documentary color film by Herbert Seggelke, images by Georges Meunier and Norbert Schmitt, music by Bach. The four painters are E. W. May (Germany), Gino Severini (Italy), Hans Erni (Switzerland), Jean Cocteau (France).

Saw the Russian film *Glinka* (Gregori Alexandrov) this morning. Overwhelmed by it from beginning to end. Glinka—Pushkin—Liszt—what actors they find! And what a national treasure!

The director of the Cinéma Marbeuf wants to revive all my films and devote the theater to me for several weeks.

Francine has convinced Orengo not to do my *Oeuvres complètes* at Rocher de Monaco but with Plon. He must not make himself liable to the reproach of getting hold of me and taking all my works for his own firm.

G., who is organizing a troupe to perform outside Paris, wants to put on *Bacchus*. But since Jeannot is to revive the play at the Bouffes, it seems a bad idea to give a difficult play to second-order actors.

Agathe Mella* has asked me for something more: to record all of *Portraits-Souvenir*.

I was forgetting that the Club du livre wants to publish *La Difficulté d'être* and *Journal d'un inconnu* together, and the Club du meilleur livre, *Le Potomak* and *La Fin du Potomak*.

Too much to write. Impossible to write.

Paris: no respect for what you do, only for that vague aura that surrounds what you do.

Not one of the people you meet has the same opinion about a play, a film, an actor. In general, everyone finds everything "impossible."

. . . .

DECEMBER 13

Milly. Weather beginning to assume that special atmosphere which comes around Christmas. Annam wild with joy when we arrive. He sulks when we leave. And he's bored. He never leaves my

---

*In 1947 Agathe Mella had adapted *Les Enfants terribles* for radio, with original music by Henri Sauguet.

heels, and indoors he collapses with a sigh. Already he wants to be in another room.

Radiguet would be over fifty. Jeannot has just turned forty. This terrible thread is spun out, through us. Last night, eight o'clock, at the snack bar of the Studio Billancourt, we went to give him a hug. Then the broadcast of the trial of Father Christmas. (If we burn Father Christmas as a monster of heresy, we must burn as heretics all the children who believe in him or pretend to believe in him, out of an indestructible craving for mystery, for surprise, for legend.) In the dark we can no longer find the rue du Recteur-Poincaré. Joined Jeannot and the others (Yvonne, Francine, Lulu) at the Studio Francoeur to see *Le Guérisseur* (Ciampi). The film is neither stupid nor boring, and Jeannot is remarkable. We all dine at midnight at Francine's, who must have stopped in at her house between Billancourt and Francoeur. I know her fairy-tale style. Formidable supper-dinner, with a birthday cake.

At this dinner-supper, I notice again that incredible divergence in Parisian opinions. It is true that I go rarely to plays and films. Virtually not at all. When I do go (especially to the theater), it is a treat, and I feel just what I felt on Sundays at the Châtelet in my childhood. I don't even recognize the actors. The whole spectacle profits from this great benevolent overture. I only escape it if the play encroaches on my prerogatives. But even then I am taken in by the footlights, by the curtain. And I am ashamed to judge. I try to listen only to the witnesses for the defense and not participate in that posture of my fellow jurors. The other night, during *Kean*, I was remembering Brasseur's start in my *Roméo* (1924!). How young he was. He played Romeo's page to Marcel Herrand's Romeo. And I played Mercutio, and Maurice Sachs was my page! Memories magnified the play for me, and other memories, those of this theater* where I came to hear *L'Aiglon*, Bernhardt and de

---

*Théâtre Sarah-Bernhardt.

Max in *La Sorcière* or *Andromaque*. People I meet say: "Isn't it awful—
I was too bored to stay. I left before the third act." And my
opinion, on Sartre's splendid writing, for example, quite fails to
convince them. I am treated as a provincial. People are no longer
simple enough to enjoy a story—not cultivated enough to recognize the style of the storyteller.

Orengo dines with us. As I write this, the sexton rings all his
bells he's so proud of. Annam loathes bells. He takes a stand on
his four thick red paws and howls.

Dali in Rome: "Cocteau is the opposite of Malenkov. Malenkov
is an eraser. A big eraser. Cocteau is a pencil—the world's sharpest
pencil."

. . . .

DECEMBER 14

Marie Cuttoli says the new tapestry is very fine. But difficult. It
will take ten months to execute. We'll see it in October.

Yesterday Orengo came to spend the day, and I made arrangements for my affairs to be transferred to Plon. Some things are
still too vague.

Among the dedications in the books at Milly, I find this one
from Gérard Prévôt (*Contemporary Architecture*): "To Jean Cocteau,
who prefers friendship to fame and can be sure of both." For friendship, I agree. For fame, I have handed out armfuls and harvested
a fingernail's worth. Unless you call fame the racket raised around
my person, and which has nothing to do with my work.

. . . .

DECEMBER 18

Infernal life. Impossible to write. How do Parisians manage? I don't
understand it. This silence a poet must have, must *be*, jammed into

this merry-go-round. I've spent three days at Erni's* with the projectors and the tracing glass and the chalks and the terrible camera which records the work, the improvisation which, once projected, will last all of what—six minutes? And the doctors— and the masseurs—and the shots. And at night, a hurried snack and a dash to the rue Pigalle, where we're rehearsing *La Machine*. Jean Marais, who is shooting *Monte-Cristo* during the day, arrives as exhausted as I am. The actress playing Jocasta disconcerts me. She seems to me incapable of finding the theatrical style which the play requires and which so mysteriously provokes *naturalness*. A *natural* actress is not enough. She has to sculpt a character and give it breath. Besides, I'm rehearsing in a room. The set isn't there, not even indications for the exits around which the action gathers.

This morning, since nine, the little hole of the Palais-Royal where I live is a chaos of people coming in, hanging on, one on top of the next, forming a crust in which I would be stuck without prodigies of balance which exhaust me. And Paris wonders why I live in Seine-et-Oise and the Riviera. Because Paris keeps you from living. The shadow of a brush here brushes the shadow of a carriage. The secret, dark work, the only work that counts, can only be done by cheating. Since I am incapable of compelling myself to cheat, I try to play dead.

. . . .

DECEMBER 19

Berl comes to see me and talks about Maurice Sachs. I say: "Sachs was occupied by me the way France was occupied by Germany.

---

*The painter Hans Erni, born in Lucerne in 1909.

When I retreated, he wanted to make people believe that it was
he who had driven me out."

Last night, Louise Conte remarkable in her sketch of the role
of the Sphinx. I'm going to listen to the radio version of *La Machine*.
If Germaine Montero suits me, I'll try to get her for Jocasta.

A very moving letter from Michel Perrin's mother because I
intervened to save her son.

Dinner last night at La Régence with Julien Green and Robert
de Saint-Jean. Green was stupefied by the public's hostile attitude
on his opening night. "I used to think," he said, "that people loved
me—that everyone would love me."

Letter from the minister of the interior asking me to accept for
the second time the presidency of the Cannes festival. What do
these ministers do for me? I answered that I don't know if my
health will permit me to respond to this "honor."

Letter from the president of the Société des auteurs, to say that
the society is making me a Christmas present of 33,000 francs. I
answered that this "small sum" hung on my tree will allow me
to decorate others.

Avalanche of letters and visits. Madeleine does much more for
me, by her kindness and her clear-sightedness, than any secretary.

Green tells me: "Why answer letters? I never do." Perhaps. But
it produces an atmosphere of hauteur and distance which doesn't
suit me.

Most of what are called "the great French writers" are journalists
of a higher journalism. Malraux, Montherlant, Camus—even Sartre—
are journalists.

Genet says, "It's good to see Sartre because he embraces and
reflects the person he's talking to."

. . . .

DECEMBER 20

Milly. Sunday with Coco Chanel, Marie-Louise* and Déon. Chat-
tered from one till ten at night without saying one nasty thing
about anyone. Coco amazingly revivified by reopening her house.
Francine and Édouard joined us for dinner: Francine came from
the workers' village created near Saint-Quentin by Mlle Deutsche
de la Meurthe,† where she had given away six hundred Christmas
presents.

Wrote the text for Georges Hugnet's book on Dada and surrealism.

Wrote the new text on Apollinaire for Marcel Adéma.‡

What I was saying about the atmosphere generated by a person
substituting for his work counts for our friends too. They don't
read our books. We can tell them everything that's printed there
as if it were brand new.

Did the big horse head in pastels for Alec.

Back into the whirlwind.

. . . .

CHRISTMAS · 1953

Milly. Last night Christmas party at Francine's. Émilienne and
François gorged on films, Comédie-Française, dumb with astonishment at the tree, the candles on the table, the floor covered
with presents. The bicycles had been hidden behind the curtains
of one of the windows. They took them to their rooms.

---

*Marie-Louise Bousquet, widow of Jacques Bousquet, represented *Harper's Bazaar*
in Paris. Her salon on the place du Palais-Bourbon was frequented by writers and artists.

†The Weisweiller and Deutsche de la Meurthe families are related.

‡Marcel Adéma was the director of the periodical *Le Flâneur des deux rives*.

We reached Milly after the little family party. It was one in the morning. Until six, we talked with Édouard about the Orengo-Plon deal, which gives me certain fears, though I take a very different attitude with people who put me on my guard. In this defensiveness, there is something authentic: it would be strange if I left my publishers for a house which owes its increase in capital to me and which keeps repeating, "you're in your own house here," without my seeing what that could mean. The projects remain just that, and nothing is decided, neither for clearing up my affairs nor for *Clair-Obscur* nor for the *Oeuvres complètes*. Such things, I will be told, cannot be worked out in five minutes. But Gallimard or Grasset would already have given me proofs.

It is to be feared that Orengo counts on Alec and Francine Weisweiller to share the expenses of a volume for which any other firm would already have signed the contract and paid an advance. I must let Orengo and Plon know this. Alec's present (and future) effort is due only to his desire to do me a favor and stabilize my work. It is only natural that everything should be made easy for me in return. Otherwise I'll go back to my usual publishers, and the beautiful dream of Plon will collapse. They were going to set up an office for me—no such thing. They were going to assign several young people to the problems of the *Oeuvres complètes*. I have not yet made contact with them. Etc. Talk, talk, talk. Nothing decided.

The Édouard-Monaco system permits Orengo to have extra rooms without paying much for them. It is possible that I am mistaken. But I am rarely mistaken when it is in my heart and not in my head that I have doubts. I have decided to speak to Orengo on Sunday about the delay in the book of poems. And then Francine will speak to Bourdel and put the finishing touches to the question. It is important that he understand that Alec and

Gérard Worms* are not making a "profitable investment" but are helping a dusty old firm set itself up with the sole goal of sparing me the vagueness of the Watiers and the banks. It would be odd if I served as an excuse to save a firm without deriving any benefits from it.

. . . .

DECEMBER 26

Francine gives me a Degas drawing (a dancer), and I have given her the manuscript of *Léone* (in the Japanese album).

Sunshine. I slept like a log, and I am still warned in my sleep if I am sleeping beyond the time I usually wake up. I know it when I dream too much—extra dreams. *The play is much too long.* An author's sentiment wakens me.

Wrote the text preface for the *Oeuvres complètes* (a few lines).

Tomorrow Herbert and Franck† are bringing an actress whom Ledoux‡ has recommended. She's from Lausanne. If she's inadequate, what can we do? The tour problem: a great actress's role played by a cheaper actress than the star around whom the tour is organized. Montero wanted to seem obliging yet insisted on conditions which the Herberts couldn't manage. I had heard Montero in the radio version: she played the part the way I read it, and without having heard me read it. She has the stomach for it, and the face. A big loss.

The other morning I recorded for the radio. On the floor below, Gabin was recording texts by Jean-Jacques Gautier. I went in during the break. We talked about Versailles. Jean-Jacques Gautier said the most compromising things about the elections. As I was leaving,

---

*Brother of Francine Weisweiller. He was president and director of Les Éditions du Rocher.

†Pierre Franck, administrator of the Georges Herbert Theatrical Tours.

‡The actor Fernand Ledoux.

someone showed me a tape on which had been recorded everything we said.

Since Madrid I have not really found myself again. I'm drifting. Very unpleasant.

. . . .

DECEMBER 28

Francine ill. Bronchitis. She'll stay at Milly until her fever drops.

Yesterday Herbert brought me the actress—Marguerite Cavadaski—from Lausanne. Jeannot was there. She read the part which her physique suits perfectly. (Somewhere between Elvire Popesco and Valentine Tessier, but young). I hire her. She returns to Lausanne to learn the part during the holidays and will come to rehearse next Monday. I'll get everything else ready.

Orengo for lunch. I have asked him to clear up everything that seems vague to me. Besides, it is not his fault if things are drifting. Work in the rue Garancière (Plon) is overwhelming him, and Bourdel rewards him meagerly for it, no doubt on that strange principle that he's working for love, that he's *in the house*, and that it is more necessary to reward others—that is, the countless employees who form a dead weight.

Read the letters of Mallarmé. Much more interesting to me than any novel. Except, alas, for many letters where manners reach the point of servility.

I've given Orengo the letter for Parisot to add to the poems.

Jeannot's incomprehensible character. He comes in unexpectedly, trips over Annam, the dog, asleep. Annam wakes up with a start and makes a gesture of biting. Jeannot kicks him and shouts, "Everything in this house hates me, even the dog." He refuses to stay to dinner: "I don't want to be waited on by *your* servants." Etc. He's got this into his head because of his mother and the quarrels she strews everywhere. These ghosts create a painful

327

distance between us, and it is impossible to bridge the chasm. It would be so simple to realize that this distance consists of foolishness, of ridiculous clumsiness. Jeannot adores me but never believes a word I say. I never manage to convince him. This is one of my greatest heartaches. Curiously enough, in his letters this distance disappears. There, nothing but his tenderness speaks.

Back in Paris. Saw the sets. Little to do over. Painted the shields. I'll rehearse the Sphinx scenes tonight.

Received the proofs of the Bruckmann monograph. Good general impression.

Works by Jean Cocteau

POETRY

POÉSIE, 1916–1923 (Le Cap de Bonne-Espérance.—Ode à Picasso.—Poésies.—Vocabu-
  laire.—Plain-Chant.—Discours du grand sommeil)
ESCALES, with André Lhote
LA ROSE DE FRANÇOIS
CRI ÉCRIT
PRIÈRE MUTILÉE
L'ANGE HEURTEBISE
OPÉRA, ŒUVRES POÉTIQUES, 1925–1927
MORCEAUX CHOISIS, POÈMES
MYTHOLOGIE, with Giorgio De Chirico
ÉNIGME
POÈMES ÉCRITS EN ALLEMAND
POÈMES (Léone.—Allégories.—La Crucifixion.—Neiges.—Un Ami dort)
LA NAPPE DU CATALAN, with Georges Hugnet
LE CHIFFRE SEPT
DENTELLE D'ÉTERNITÉ
APPOGIATURES
CLAIR-OBSCUR

POÈMES, 1916–1955
PARAPROSODIES
CÉRÉMONIAL ESPAGNOL DU PHÉNIX
LA PARTIE D'ÉCHECS
LE REQUIEM
FAIRE-PART

POETRY OF THE NOVEL

LE POTOMAK
LE GRAND ÉCART
THOMAS L'IMPOSTEUR
LE LIVRE BLANC
LES ENFANTS TERRIBLES
LA FIN DU POTOMAK
DEUX TRAVESTIS

CRITICAL POETRY

LE RAPPEL À L'ORDRE (Le Coq et l'Arlequin.—Carte blanche.—Visites à Barrès.—Le
   Secret professionnel.—D'un ordre considéré comme une anarchie.—Autour de Thomas
   l'imposteur.—Picasso)
LETTRE À JACQUES MARITAIN
UNE ENTREVUE SUR LA CRITIQUE
OPIUM, Journal d'une désintoxication
ESSAI DE CRITIQUE INDIRECTE (Le Mystère laïc.—Des beaux-arts considérés comme
   un assassinat)
PORTRAITS-SOUVENIR
MON PREMIÉR VOYAGE. Tour du monde en 80 jours
LE GRECO
LA BELLE ET LA BÊTE, Journal d'un film
LE FOYER DES ARTISTES
LA DIFFICULTÉ D'ÊTRE
LETTRE AUX AMÉRICAINS
REINES DE FRANCE

DUFY
MAALESH, Journal d'une tourneè de théâtre
MODIGLIANI
JEAN MARAIS
GIDE VIVANT
JOURNAL D'UN INCONNU
DÉMARCHE D'UN POÈTE
DISCOURS DE RÉCEPTION À L'ACADÉMIE FRANÇAISE
COLETTE
LE DISCOURS D'OXFORD
ENTRETIENS SUR LE MUSÉE DE DRESDE, with Louis Aragon
LA CORRIDA DU PREMIER MAI
POÉSIE CRITIQUE I and II
PICASSO, 1916–1961, illustrated by Picasso
LE CORDON OMBILICAL
LA COMTESSE DE NOAILLES, OUI ET NON
PORTRAIT-SOUVENIR. Interview with Roger Stéphane
ENTRETIENS AVEC ANDRÉ FRAIGNEAU
JEAN COCTEAU PAR JEAN COCTEAU. Interview with William Fifield
POÉSIE DE JOURNALISME, 1935–1938

POETRY OF THE THEATER

LE GENDARME INCOMPRIS, with Raymond Radiguet
PAUL ET VIRGINIE, with Raymond Radiguet
THÉÂTRE I: Antigone.—Les Mariés de la tour Eiffel.—Les Chevaliers de la Table Ronde.—
Les Parents terribles
THÉÂTRE II: Les Monstres sacrés.—La Machine à écrire.—Renaud et Armide.—L'Aigle
à deux têtes
ORPHÉE
ŒDIPE ROI—ROMÉO ET JULIETTE
LA VOIX HUMAINE
LA MACHINE INFERNALE
THÉÂTRE DE POCHE
NOUVEAU THÉÂTRE DE POCHE
BACCHUS
L'IMPROMPTU DU PALAIS-ROYAL

GRAPHIC POETRY

DESSINS
LE MYSTÈRE DE JEAN L'OISELEUR
MAISON DE SANTÉ
25 DESSINS D'UN DORMEUR
SOIXANTE DESSINS POUR LES ENFANTS TERRIBLES
DESSINS EN MARGE DU TEXTE DES CHEVALIERS DE LA TABLE RONDE
DRÔLE DE MÉNAGE
LA CHAPELLE SAINT-PIERRE, VILLEFRANCHE-SUR-MER
LA SALLE DES MARIAGES, HOTEL DE VILLE DE MENTON
LA CHAPELLE SAINT-PIERRE
GONDOLE DES MORTS
SAINT-BLAISE-DES-SIMPLES

BOOKS ILLUSTRATED BY COCTEAU

LE POTOMAK
LE SECRET PROFESSIONNEL
LE GRAND ÉCART
THOMAS L'IMPOSTEUR
LE LIVRE BLANC
OPIUM
LA MACHINE INFERNALE
PORTRAITS-SOUVENIR
RENAUD ET ARMIDE
ORPHÉE
PORTRAIT DE MOUNET-SULLY
LÉONE
DEUX TRAVESTIS
LES ENFANTS TERRIBLES
LE LIVRE BLANC
ANTHOLOGIE POÉTIQUE
LA NAPPE DU CATALAN
OPÉRA
DÉMARCHE D'UN POÈTE
CARTE BLANCHE
LE GRAND ÉCART—LA VOIX HUMAINE

WORKS BY JEAN COCTEAU

LA CORRIDA DU PREMIER MAI
THÉÂTRE I ET II
LE SANG D'UN POÈTE
NOUVEAU THÉÂTRE DE POCHE
LE CORDON OMBILICAL
QUERELLE DE BREST, by Jean Genet
LA COURSE DES ROIS, by Thierry Maulnier
LE BAL DU COMTE D'ORGEL, by Raymond Radiguet
SOUS LE MANTEAU DE FEU, by Geneviève Laporte
DOUZE POÈMES, by Paul Valéry
JEAN COCTEAU TOURNE SON DERNIER FILM, by Roger Pillaudin
MONTAGNES MARINES, by André Verdet
TAUREAUX, by Jean-Marie Magnan

CINEMATOGRAPHIC POETRY

LE SANG D'UN POÈTE
LE BARON FANTÔME, dialogue for the film by Serge de Poligny
L'ÉTERNEL RETOUR, with Jean Delannoy
LES DAMES DU BOIS DE BOULOGNE, dialogue for the film by Bresson
LA BELLE ET LA BÊTE
RUY BLAS, with Pierre Billon
L'AIGLE À DEUX TÊTES
LES PARENTS TERRIBLES
LA VOIX HUMAINE, with Roberto Rosselini
LES NOCES DE SABLE, commentary for the film by André Zwobada
ORPHÉE
LES ENFANTS TERRIBLES, with Jean-Pierre Melville
LE ROSSIGNOL DE L'EMPEREUR DE CHINE, commentary for the film by Jiri Trnka
LA VILLA SANTO SOSPIR
LE TESTAMENT D'ORPHÉE
LA PRINCESSE DE CLÈVES, dialogue for the film by Jean Delannoy
DU CINÉMATOGRAPHE
ENTRETIENS SUR LE CINÉMATOGRAPHE

WORKS WITH MUSICIANS

PARADE, ballet (Éric Satie)

HUIT POÈMES (Georges Auric)

CHANSONS BASQUES (Louis Durey)

LE PRINTEMPS AU FOND DE LA MER (Louis Durey)

COCARDES (Francis Poulenc)

LE BŒUF SUR LE TOIT (Darius Milhaud)

TROIS POÈMES (Darius Milhaud)

DEUX POÈMES (Jean Wiéner)

LES MARIÉS DE LA TOUR EIFFEL (Groupe des Six)

SIX POÉSIES (Arthur Honegger)

LE TRAIN BLEU, ballet (Darius Milhaud)

SIX POÈMES (Maxime Jacob)

ŒDIPUS REX (Igor Stravinski)

LE PAUVRE MATELOT (Darius Milhaud)

ANTIGONE (Arthur Honegger)

CANTATE (Igor Markevich)

CHANSONS DE MARINS (Henri Sauguet)

LES TAMBOURS QUI PARLENT (Florent Schmitt)

LE JEUNE HOMME ET LA MORT, ballet (Johann Sebastian Bach—Ottorino Respighi)

PHÈDRE, ballet (Georges Auric)

LA DAME À LA LICORNE, ballet (Jacques Chailley)

LA VOIX HUMAINE (Francis Poulenc)

LE POÈTE ET SA MUSE, ballet (Gian-Carlo Menotti)

LA DAME DE MONTE-CARLO (Francis Poulenc)

PATMOS (Yves Claoué)

ŒDIPE ROI (Maurice Thiriet)

Index